The Carriage Trimmers' Manual and Guide Book

Forward by Merri Ferrell

The Astragal Press
Mendham, NJ

Published by
The Astragal Press
5 Cold Hill Road, Suite 12
PO Box 239
Mendham, NJ 07945-0239
©2007 by Astragal Press

This is a reprint of the original edition published by
W. N. FitzGerald in 1881
In the Office of the Librarian at Washington, D.C.

International Standard Book Number 978-1-931626-23-1
Library of Congress Control Number 2007925454

Cover Design by: Donald Kahn
Manufactured in the United States of America

Forward

Merri Ferrell

Dedicated to the memory of Gladys Marsh Whitehead

Carriage manufacturers assimilated a variety of materials into a complex but unified finished product. Regardless of type, a carriage was "a combination of many different parts, widely separated in the crude state, but intimately blended into one finished whole."[1] Carriages were composite objects and required numerous, separate skills for fabrication. These skills responded equally to structural and decorative requisites. The body maker created the style of the carriage and was a skilled woodworker. His work determined the vehicular type, the overall appearance, and the proportions of the carriage. The smith was responsible for metalwork that included mechanical parts of the vehicle such as springs, axles, and the fifth wheel on which the front axle pivoted. Using wood, iron and steel, the wheelwright constructed wheels which were the means of conveyance, and had to be in proportion with the style and anticipated function of the vehicle. Painters applied protective coatings for structural components while enhancing aesthetic appeal through the application of color, color combinations, and, if appropriate, striping and other decorative elements.

Trimming (the overarching term for upholstery, tops and fittings) was the branch of carriage manufacture that most directly addressed the comfort of the passenger. The carriage trimmer was charged "to adapt his work to the comfort and convenience of the carriage-user."[2]

It is necessary to interpose between those occupying the carriage such material or appliances as shall counteract the effects of motion, lessen the vibration, and supplant the body in the most agreeable manner; so that the occupant, by the act of reclining or sitting, may feel no discomfort from the pressure of the body against those parts supporting it.[3]

i

Trimmers had to be apprised of the guidelines of fashion, the popularity of certain colors and the suitability of styles particular to vehicular types. Seats for public carriages were covered with durable fabrics with little or no squabbing whereas the interiors of more formal vehicles could be trimmed in silk satin with squabbing as elaborate as drawing room furniture. Both the quilted satin that cushioned passengers in formal carriages and the leather folding top of a humble buggy were products of the trimmer's art. It was in the formal, enclosed vehicles (whose patrons demanded no small degree of luxury) that the trimmer displayed the highest degree of skill. Enclosed carriages served as conveyances and mobile shelters. The exact fit of the doors, the thick beveled-glass windows, calling card cases, vanities, shades, shutters, and sumptuous linings provided a commodious, intimate interior. The somber exterior of the enclosed carriage was an expression of restrained taste and refinement. By contrast, the interior extended the private domain of the passenger, which formed a barrier of comfort, privacy and exclusivity between the occupant and the public.

Trimming required considerable skill. *The Art and Craft of Coach Building* suggested that "a trimmer must quilt like an upholsterer, stitch like a harness-maker and sew like a tailor, and it is just as necessary that he should have good taste and a knowledge of design, proportion and color."[4] The trimmer was responsible for fabricating the interiors of carriages—cutting, stitching, and installing dashes, wings, curtains, folding and extension tops, aprons, and other functional and decorative elements of the carriage. The materials he used, one industry adviser declared, were "more numerous than those employed in any other branch."[5]

The carriage industry supported a broad base of trade literature as a means to improve skills among its workers and to disseminate information to a burgeoning workforce. Although most of the trade periodicals for the carriage trade included monthly columns on trimming, *The Carriage Trimmers Manual* was the most comprehensive addition to trade literature on the subject. Its author, William N. FitzGerald (1830-1904), was a veteran of the industry. Born in 1830 in Newark, New Jersey, he apprenticed as a teenager with Myron H. Clark and later, P.M Crandal, both of Canandaigua, New York, where he learned the trade of body making. In 1850, he worked for John Drake of Newark, New Jersey and later a succession of firms that included Stephen Tooker of Rahway, New

Jersey, James M. Quinby & Co. of Newark and Miner & Stevens of New York City. In 1855, he published the *Harness Makers' Manual.*

During the Civil War, he served with the Seventh Regiment, New Jersey Volunteers as a 1st Lieutenant of B Company. Ill health forced him to withdraw for two years, but in 1865, he was employed by one of the many permutations of the famous house of Brewster, then Brewster, Parker & Baldwin of New York and later Lawrence, Bradley & Pardee of New Haven, Connecticut.. His fragile health, which vexed him most of his life, forced him into the less strenuous publishing profession. During this period, trade journals proliferated, especially for the carriage and related industries. Fitzgerald started working at the *Shoe and Leather Reporter*, located in New York City and in 1867 he took control of the *Harness and Carriage Journal*, which he subsequently purchased in 1875. He sold the journal in 1880 (although he retained editorial control until 1882) and then became the editor and proprietor of the *Coach, Harness and Saddlery Journal* where he stayed until 1887. He became the editor and editorial writer for that publication until 1892 when he assumed the editorship of *The Hub* following the death of George W. W. Houghton. In 1901, he became the editor of the journal *Harness* and well as a regular contributor to numerous other trade publications.

The Carriage Trimmers' Manual: Guide Book and Illustrated Technical Dictionary was edited and published by FitzGerald in 1881. The manual covers all topics germane to trimming, including instructions on selecting materials, tufting, installing fittings and an illustrated list of indispensable tools. For curators and carriage collectors, this book is an invaluable resource that provides descriptive text and illustrations of the numerous details and articles comprising a carriage interior. Furthermore, the book describes the complexity of materials and range of skills required for this branch of the trade. For conservators, restorers and dealers in antique furniture (especially upholstered 19th century furniture), *The Carriage Trimmer's Manual* is an indispensable guideline and practical, instructive manual for the upholstery trade in general. Tool collectors will benefit from the descriptions and illustrations of trimmers' tools such as stuffing sticks, round knives and shears. Not unlike the thrill of opening the door of a Brougham to discover a world of upholstered damask, coach lace, mirrored vanities and pleated headlining, the reader of *The Carriage Trimmers' Manual* will be introduced to a fascinating document of a heretofore forgotten trade.

[1] *The Hub* 22, 2 (1880): 70.

[2] John Philipson, *The Art and Craft of Coachbuilding* (London: George Bell and Son, 1897), 152.

[3] Farr and Thrupp, *Coach Trimming*, 1.

[4] Philipson, *Art and Craft of Coachbuilding*, 151.

[5] Ibid. 155.

Carriage Trimming Nomenclature

(Sources for terms and definitions: *Harness and Carriage Journal* 14.24 (1871); William Farr & George A. Thrupp *Coach Trimming* London: Chapman and Hall, Limited, 188; William N. Fitzgerald *The Carriage Trimmers' Manual and Guidebook*, New York: NP, 1881; and John Philipson *The Art and Craft of Coachbuilding*, London: George Bell and Sons, 1897.)

Apron: A piece of leather, enameled cloth or other impervious material used in partially enclosed vehicles such as Victorias to cover the lap of the passenger as protection from rain or snow.

Blind: A movable frame, with or without slats.

Body Linings: Cloth, leather and other material used to trim carriages.

Brocatel: A coarse or figure fabric, commonly made of silk or cotton, used for lining carriages.

Buckram: A coarse, stiff linen used as a lining and reinforcement to trimming.

Burlap: A coarse linen fabric.

Check String: Cord extended from the inside of a vehicle to the driver suspended on check string pulleys.

Chinz: Cotton cloth with a glazed surface used for carriage slip linings.

Corduroy: A thick ribbed or corded fabric used for trimming carriages, especially sporting and informal vehicles such as game wagons, traps and runabouts.

Coteline/Cotelean: A woven silk fabric used for interior trimming of fine, enclosed carriages.

Damask: Linen woven in imitation of silk damask, used for slip linings and head linings.

Damasse: Imitation damask, woven of mixed materials.

Ear Cushion: Small cushion hung from back corner, used as a head rest. Also called a "squab."

Enamel Cloth: Cotton or linen covered with a preparation of linseed oil, lampblack and turpentine, used for aprons, curtains, folding heads, on "cheap work." Also called "American Cloth."

Enamel Leather: Hides covered with several coats of a preparation of linseed oil, lampblack and turpentine, baked in a hot oven. Skin is stretched on a frame and put through a grainer.

Fall: An apron attached to the front edge of a seat or cushions.

False Lining: A lining for coaches made of a thin fabric to protect finer materials; also called slip lining.

Fringe: An ornamental border with loose or twisted thread pendants. Types used in trimming include bullion, festoon and carpet.

Glass Frame: Wooden frame supporting the glass in the movable windows of a carriage.

Glass Frame Lifter: A strip of lace, usually backed by a piece of leather or other sturdy material, attached on the glass frame; to lift the glass door or panel. Also called a glass string.

Glass String Slide: A section of ivory, bone, wood or other smooth substance installed in the door or panel to reduce wear of the glass string.

Head: A carriage top.

Head Lining: The lining of a carriage top.

Lace: A woven close web with a loop surface, plain or ornamental, used to cover seams, edges, or to bind cushions.

Lining: The inside trimming of carriages.

Lining Nails: Small iron nails that have an extra cap plated or japanned over the head.

Oil Cloth: Heavy cloth covered with thick coats of paint and printed with ornamental devices.

Oil Skin: Fine linen saturated with oil, used as an extra cover for dickey seats.

Patent Leather: Leather covered with coats of oil, lampblack and turpentine, with a smooth surface.

Plush: A fabric with a long velvet nap on one side, popular for trimming sleighs.

Rep: A silk or cotton fabric having a surface that looks as if it were made of small cords used for trimming sleighs and open vehicles such as buggies.

Rug: A coarse material made of woolen cloth having a long nap. Used to cover the floors of carriages.

Sash Holder: A lace or leather strip fastened to the bottom of the window frame, the loose end being finished off with a piece of fringe or other ornament, and hanging out in such a manner as to be of easy access; used for raising the window, also called a glass frame lifter or glass slide.

Satin: A glossing silk cloth of a thick close texture and overshot with wool. Used for trimming finer grades of carriages such as coaches, an coupes.

Scrims: A thin loose woven linen goods, better known as canvas, used for gluing against insides of panels to give them increased strength and stiffness.

Seaming Lace: A narrow lace having two selvages instead of one, as of "pasting lace," used to form welts in seams.

Seat Fall: The curtain of cloth or leather fastened to the front edge of the seat, and falling down to the bottom of the body as an ornament and finish to that part of the body.

Seat Roll: A cord covered with leather or lace, and tacked to the front edge of the seat frame to keep the cushion from slipping off the seat.

Seat Straps: Leather straps attached to the seat bottom and passing over the cushion to secure the seat.

Slides: Fixture of ivory, bone or metal attached to the top edge of the door lining upon which the lace or cord moved, which is used to lift the window in the doors; flat bolts having a notch in the end used to keep carriage windows in their places.

Slings/Neck Cushion: Pads hung in the corner of traveling coaches, used as a headrest.

Speaking Tube: A rubber tube passing from the inside of a coach to the driver' seat, the use of it enables passengers to converse with the driver. The ends are finished with a mouth-piece covered with a tassel.

Squab: Quilted or stuffed linings of backs or sides.

Stay Web: A twilled web which will not stretch.

Tassel: An ornament used on the ends of curtain strings, window holds, speaking tubes, etc.

Trimmer: A person who practices the trade of carriage trimming.

Trimming: The upholstering of carriages with materials such as leather, fabric etc.

Tuft: A knob of silk or worsted used in trimming to prevent the tie cords from drawing through and as an ornament.

Valance: Front strips of leather to the heads of tops; the loose fall attached to the inside of a dash (sometimes called a seat fall).

Velveteen: A kind of cloth made of cotton imitation of velvet, now used to a considerable extent for trimming light carriages and sleighs.

Warp: The threads that extend lengthwise of a woven fabric.

Web Lace: A strong hempen lace woven in such a manner as to be difficult to stretch, used for stays to the inside of culash tops.

Welt: A cord covered with cloth or leather, used as an ornament, and for the purpose of strengthening seams or borders. It is also used in place of seaming lace.

Wing: An iron frame covered with leather or canvas, and placed in position to protect the passengers from the dust or mod when the carriage is in motion. Wood is sometimes used in place of iron and leather.

FOUR-IN-HAND DRAG.

THE

ƑARRIAGE ƬRIMMERS'

MANUAL AND GUIDE BOOK

AND

ILLUSTRATED TECHNICAL DICTIONARY,

𝔄 𝔓ractical 𝔗reatise for the 𝔠arriage 𝔗rimmer.

———

By WM. N. FITZ-GERALD.

Author of "The Harness Makers' Illustrated Manual," "Harness Makers' Atlas," etc.

———

CONTAINING

INFORMATION ON LEATHER, CLOTHS, LACES, HAIR, MOSS, ETC
TABLES OF MATERIALS USED IN TRIMMING CARRIAGES,
TARIFFS OF REPAIRS, DIRECTIONS FOR SETTING AND
TRIMMING TOPS, MAKING CUSHIONS AND OTHER
PARTS OF TRIMMINGS, ETC., ETC.

CARRIAGE TRIMMERS' TOOLS,

DESCRIPTION AND PRICES.

ƦECIPES FOR MAKING PⱯSTE, BLACKS, STAIⱢS,

AND LEATHER VARNISHES.

NOTES ON STYLES OF TRIMMING AND MOUNTINGS.
HINTS ON THE CARE OF CARRIAGES.

———

FULLY ILLUSTRATED.

———

𝔑ew 𝔜ork.

1881.

AMERICAN TROTTING SULKY.

CONTENTS.

CHAPTER III.

TECHNICS OF TRIMMING.

CHAPTER IV.

SETTING TOPS.

8   CONTENTS.

CHAPTER V.

COVERING DASHES.

CHAPTER VI.

SEAT FALLS AND BACKS.

CHAPTER VII.

STUFFING CUSHIONS—COVERING GLASS FRAMES AND BOWS.

CHAPTER VIII.

DETAILED DIRECTIONS FOR TRIMMING A TOP BUGGY.

CHAPTER IX.

DETAILED DIRECTIONS FOR TRIMMING AN EXTENSION TOP.

CONTENTS.

CHAPTER X.

MISCELLANY—BRIC-A-BRAC.

CHAPTER XI.

HAMMER CLOTH SEAT.

CHAPTER XII.

WHIP SOCKETS.

CHAPTER XIII.

COACH AND CARRIAGE LAMPS.

CHAPTER XIV.

TRIMMER'S TOOLS.

10

CHAPTER XV.

REPAIRING CARRIAGES.

CHAPTER XVI.

RECIPES.

CHAPTER XVII.

CARE OF CARRIAGES.

CHAPTER XVIII.

TRIMMERS' TECHNICAL DICTIONARY.

RUSSIAN TROTTING WAGON.

PLATES.

PREFACE.

With the exception of a single German work of about fifty pages, the author knows of no distinctive guide book for carriage trimmers. The trade publications of the day contain valuable information, and serve to illustrate the progress made in this branch of the carriage business, but, instead of filling the want, they have made a condensed guide book a necessity. In the effort to supply this want, the author of the "Carriage Trimmers' Illustrated Manual and Guide Book" has aimed to avoid treating on special methods of construction or peculiar styles, knowing that the one is but an individual method, and fickle fashion dooms the other to obscurity after a short time ; but with a view to preserving an historical record they are freely illustrated as representatives of the present styles.

In preparing this work the author has called to his aid some of the best talent in the trade, and he is also indebted to a number of carriage manufacturers for valuable assistance. With the aid of these he has prepared a Manual to which the employer and employed can refer on all subjects of a specific character.

Materials, such as cloths, leather, laces, stuffing, etc., are treated in detail. The tables of kinds and quantities of material used in trimming carriages—some fifty in number—will be found reliable and useful in making up estimates of cost. The tables of repairs will also aid in estimating cost of retrimming or repairing old work.

The practical matter supplies valuable information on setting tops, putting up each specific part of the work, fitting up the trimming shop, etc., and a list of tools, together with illustrative description and prices. Under the caption of Bric-a-Brac is given a variety of illustrations and miscellaneous information of great value.

The illustrated Technical Dictionary is the first work of the kind ever published. In it, as far as possible, cant terms of local significance have been ignored. Trade names already well established, or likely to become so, owing to their connection with manufacturers' lists, are given. Various articles used are, as far as possible, illustrated, thus, by illustration and description, establishing the name and character of each specific article, and rendering the names uniform throughout the trade.

Carriage trimmers, as a class, are less given to making public their methods of working, or looking elsewhere for information, than any other, while employees, as a rule, are less informed on this branch of their business. Should the publication of this work lead to more liberal research on the one hand, and a better knowledge of the business on the other, the author will feel that his labor has not been in vain.

INTRODUCTION.

Carriage trimming, as a branch of business, has not received the attention it should, from those who are working to improve pleasure vehicles. This is owing, in part, to the fact that it is an art, as well as a mechanical branch, and, more than any other, has a personality imparted to it by the artistic taste of the workman, which personality cannot be portrayed or described.

Some of the most elegantly trimmed vehicles of the present time are those which, at the first glance, are pronounced plain; but the luxurious and symmetrical appearance at once reveals their true character. A fine drawing misleads, and often brings loss to the trimmer, for, when worked up, it is found to produce a much different result from that anticipated. Ornamental devices of all kinds are given to the trade, but the plain cushion, or squab, is by far more elegant when in the vehicle than its more pretentious rivals.

One difficulty, often overlooked until it is too late to remedy it, is the conformation of all the parts to be trimmed; harmony is at all times an essential element, and a pattern that would look well in a body, with shallow, narrow seat and low back, would be entirely unsuited to another body, even though precisely of the same outlines, if of greater proportions. A body the lines of which are straight, or nearly so, should not be trimmed in the same pattern as one in which every line is a full curve.

The comfort of the occupant is also another consideration. A flat, back squab would look well in some of the intricate patterns, and, if the occupant of the vehicle was one who stooped when standing or sitting, the squab would prove a comfortable one; but, if the occupant should prove to be one who sat upright, the flat squab would be no support except at the shoulders, and a full squab would be necessary. If such full squab were made up to the same pattern as the flat one, comfort might be secured, but it would be at the sacrifice of appearance. The French trimmers are admitted to be the most artistic of any, and the cheapest French carriages are often very attractive, because of the harmony of materials, colors and outlines.

A trimmer needs to be an artist; he must be an expert in colors, so that the style of trimming selected may produce the best results. Such an one would select laces and all interior mountings that would harmonize with the material used, and the pattern selected. He would be governed by the form of the body and the colors used in painting, and by a harmonious combination and artistic construction he would secure the desired result.

Defects in trimming reveal themselves more readily

than those in any other department; putty gives the painter a level surface, even if it be fictitious, but a cushion or squab that is askew, or not evenly tufted, stands forth in all its defects; if the leather on a top, dash, or wing, is badly drawn on, wrinkles tell the story of carelessness or want of skill; a cushion unevenly stuffed is sure to bring complaints from the user; bad stitching stares the buyer in the face, and all efforts to correct the evils after they are created result in failures. Then, too, everybody who examines a carriage seems to look upon the trimming as the one object upon which it is perfectly legitimate to exercise his skill as a handler; the cloth is rubbed, seams tested, cushions pounded, tufts pulled, tops raised and lowered, dashes, laces, etc., handled as though no damage could be done to them, and if, after passing through this ordeal a score of times, the trimming looks a little the worse for wear, the blame is always put upon the trimmer. This fact, alone, serves to illustrate the importance of having the work well done.

"Touch not with unclean hands," should be the motto of every trimmer; in no other branch are cleanliness and order more essential. A trimmer that does not keep everything snug and clean around him brands his trade-mark "slovenliness" upon the work he does, and is withal an expensive workman. A careless clip of the scissors in a piece of cloth or silk, or a slip of the knife in patent or enameled leather may cause a loss equal to the wages paid; dirty fingers make indelible marks on cloths and silks; everything used by the trimmer is clean—even the paste pot can be handled without damage to anything else if it is well kept.

In arranging benches they should be high enough for the workmen to work by them standing, and high stools provided for seats. Each table should be not less than six feet long and four feet wide. A swing rack for holding boxes of tacks, thread, etc., should be provided, and so suspended that it can be easily and quickly moved out of the way. A trunk, for tools, may be set on the bench, or supported on a slide shelf under it. The necessary hooks for holding the work and making threads should be so arranged as to be out of the way at all times. A separate cutting table should always be in the shop, even if not more than one man worked thereon, under which leaves could be arranged for holding stock of all kinds; also a small cutting board, four feet long, two feet wide, and two inches through; boxes for all scraps worth keeping, cloth, leather, etc., should be provided.

A neat, tidy work-room indicates a careful, tasty and economical workman—one who can be trusted—while to the employer it speaks of economy and success. None but those who have given careful attention to the waste in the trimming shop realize how great it is, and the importance of reducing it to the lowest possible point —a result that can be reached only by system in buying, cutting and working stock.

THE

CARRIAGE TRIMMERS'

MANUAL AND GUIDE BOOK,

AND

ILLUSTRATED TECHNICAL DICTIONARY.

CHAPTER I.

CARRIAGE TRIMMERS' MATERIALS.

CARRIAGE CLOTHS.

SELECTION—CLEAN STOCK VS. SHODDY—WEIGHTING—DOMES-
TICS, ENGLISH AND GERMAN CLOTHS—UNRELIABILITY OF
COLORS — INDIGO AND WOOD DYES, WOOL AND PIECE
DYED—LUSTROUS AND DULL SURFACES—PIECE LENGTHS,
WIDTHS, WEIGHTS AND PRICES.

The selection of carriage cloths is one of the most
difficult operations connected with the purchase of
material for carriage trimming. The quality of most
other articles can be ascertained, on examination, by a
person who has given the subject a few months' study,
but with cloths few men become sufficiently expert to
enable them at all times to select just such a grade as
they are in want of, or to duplicate a previous purchase.
The buyer should possess a thorough knowledge of

all the peculiarities of material, and manufacture so as
to be able to determine whether the article is all wool
or part cotton; clean stock or shoddy; if wool and
shoddy, what the proportions of each; if all wool, what
the quality; whether the weight is real, or is the result
of foreign or inferior material, worked in for the purpose of "weighting." All these points may be learned,
but this will require years of study, close observation
and continued practice; but even with this knowledge
there is much that must be left to the honesty of the
manufacturer. It is therefore equally important that
the names and brands of manufacturers, who have
earned a reputation for making reliable goods, be
known—a knowledge that too few possess.

It is impossible to lay down any rule or set of rules
by which a buyer can be governed, in place of the
knowledge obtained by practice; but there are certain
leading points and characteristics which, if understood,
will materially aid in acquiring the necessary knowledge, and make it possible for the buyer to act under-
standingly. To point out these will be the object of
this chapter.

The cloths used are domestics, that is, the products
of American looms, English, French and German. Domestics are much used in the lower grades, but they
are unreliable, it being almost impossible to secure any
number of pieces of uniform color or quality; they wear
well, and in some instances have a fine finish; the finer
grades are not weighted, but until our cloth manufacturers secure greater uniformity, domestics will not be-

come popular, no matter what good qualities they may possess.

French cloths are not used to any extent, and as there are but few in our market adapted to carriage makers' use, no material benefit can accrue from describing them.

English cloths are more used than any other, as the range in quality and price is such as to suit them to all classes of work. The lowest grade is describ d as part wool and part cotton; cotton, however, predominates, and the little good wool that is used is no more than is absolutely necessary to hold the flock together while spinning. Some of these low grades are weighted by the working in of flock on the back during the operation of weaving, giving the cloth the appearance of being much better than it really is. This weighting with flock is one of the great evils of English cloth, and so common has the custom become that it is almost impossible to find, even among the finest cloths, any that are made entirely of clear stock. Another fault with English cloths is the unreliability of colors—the drabs, blacks and common browns being the only colors that are reliable. The best of English greens yet introduced will gradually change to a greenish blue, while the common grades will fade and streak to such an extent that after six months' use it is extremely difficult to determine what was their original shade.

The finest and most reliable cloths in our markets are of German manufacture, the Wülfing being the most reliable; until this brand was introduced there were no greens or maroons in the market that would not fade ; these cloths are all wool and of pure stock ; they do not run as low in weight as other brands; they are remarkably uniform in shade and quality ; none of this brand are ever weighted ; the different grades, in all cases, are regulated by the quantity and grade of wool used. Their purity of color is due to the use of indigo, which is the basis of all fast colors. Domestic and English cloths are, in most cases, colored with wood colors, logwood, etc.

Another important factor in determining the durability and purity of colors is the manner of dyeing ; the two processes are technically known as wool dye and piece dye ; by the first the wool is dyed before it is spun or woven ; by the latter the cloth is dyed after it is woven. The first process gives the best result, but is the most expensive ; heavy, firm cloths that are piece dyed do not take the color uniformly throughout ; the surface will appear equally as pure as that of cloth that is wool dyed, but below the nap the color is less dense, and, as soon as the nap wears off, the difference in tint is distinguishable; an expert may be able to determine the manner of dyeing, but an ordinary buyer must rely upon the statement of the seller or the brand of the manufacturer.

Carriage cloths are finished with and without lustrous surface—the result of pressing ; hot pressed cloths have a lustrous surface, and buyers are often governed in their purchase by the surface appearance, a high luster being looked upon as a quality to be commended. A fine surface is necessary, but this does not imply a lustrous surface. All hot-pressed cloths must be sponged and cold-pressed or they will spot, and just here is one of the marked good features of the German cloths; they possess a remarkably fine surface—it is mellow and soft, but not lustrous, these cloths in all cases being cold pressed.

Carriage cloths are made up fifty-six inches wide, and put up in pieces of about thirty-two yards each. English cloths weigh from nine to ten ounces to the yard in piece dye, and fifteen to twenty ounces per yard in wool dye. Wülfing cloth weighs from thirteen to twenty-one ounces to the yard; domestics, pure stock, twelve to twenty ounces, weighted, thirteen to twenty-four, and English, ten to twenty-four. At the present time (1880) the prices of English cloth range from $1 25 to $5 per yard. Domestic cloths, $1 to $5 per yard, and German $3 25 to $6 per yard.

PATENT AND ENAMELED LEATHER.

HIDES USED — TANNAGE — METHODS OF SPLITTING — MACHINE STRETCHING — HAND AND MACHINE BUFFING — GRADING, MEASURING, CUTTING, ETC.

The hides used by manufacturers of patent and enameled leather are selected from the best home slaughtered stock; the qualities sought after are broad spread, fine grain, freedom from blemishes of every kind and from injuries by the knife. For many years the Philadelphia Hide Association was the only source from which reliable hides could be procured. A growing demand, however, stimulated others, who adopted the Philadelphia rule for selection, and now the hide associations of New York, Boston and Chicago also furnish the grade desired.

The choice hides are those taken from young fatted beef cattle, grade and Durham steers being the best. The long, lank Texas steers, or others of that build, do not furnish good hides, they being coarse-grained and ill-shaped. The prices paid for green selected hides, suitable for patent leather, are about four cents a pound above the general market rates for green hides.

The best leather is tanned with young oak bark. Hemlock bark and chemicals are used to a limited extent by those manufacturers who aim to furnish leather below the regular market rates, but the stock produced is of an inferior character. Leather tanned with hemlock bark is red and hard; that tanned with chemicals has a good color, but it is harsh, coarse and defective in strength.

All hides used for patent and enameled leather are split; this operation is performed in two ways: in one the hide passes between a knife and a large roller, which gauges the thickness; it is fed through by another roller, around which it is wholly or partially wrapped. By the other method it is split with a belt knife; by this the hide is forced against an endless knife, which operates much in the same manner as the belt saw, excepting that the blade is in a horizontal position. The latter method is considered the best, as the hide is not subjected to so great an amount of strain as with the former, and, when properly controlled, the splits are more uniform in thickness.

The splits are made into various kinds of leather, all of which are specified. Enameled top leather is made exclusively from the grain or outside split; other kinds of leather are also made of the grain split, but they are all japanned upon the split side, while enameled is japanned on the grain.

In preparing the leather for the japan it is necessary to stretch the hide and allow it to dry, in order to remove all wrinkles and irregularities. This operation is performed by stretching, by means of cords, on large frames, or by setting out on power frames, care being taken to stretch no more than is absolutely necessary in order to remove the wrinkles, etc. Another method is to stretch by machinery; this operation is performed by throwing the hide over a horizontal movable bar, and securely tacking the edges to fixed plank on the lower edge of the frame ; the upper or movable bar is then forced up by powerful jack screws until the leather is drawn as tight as a drum-head ; by this operation six to eight feet is added to the measurement of what would otherwise be a 60-foot hide, but the leather is damaged in quality and unfit for such work as requires its being shaped while making up. The leather is weakened and made more porous by the fibers being drawn apart. The gain effected is not a permanent one, as the leather shrinks back to its original size on exposure, and, as leather of the best quality will shrink more or less, it can readily be seen that the extra shrinkage which occurs with machine-stretched leather increases the difficulty of preventing tops being drawn out of shape by the leather shrinking when exposed to dry air or the sun. This kind of leather should never be used on carriage tops.

Buffing is another necessary operation ; this consists of removing the thin crust from the surface of the grain. When taken off by hand the workman, with a knife made for that purpose, removes at each stroke a thin shaving about six inches long and an inch or two wide. This operation requires skill and care, and the shavings removed are valueless, but the grain is unimpaired. Another method is to remove this crust by machinery; this is simply taking off a thin split by means of a machine, and with it a great portion of the grain fiber, working an irreparable damage to the appearance and wear of the leather.

Splitting is a rapid operation, and as the buffing thus removed is in demand for hat linings and various other purposes, it is more profitable to use the machine than to follow the better plan of hand buffing. When japanned and well boarded it is difficult for a non-expert to select the machine from the hand-buffed stock when new, though its true character is soon revealed when put to use. But no buyer need be deceived, for when offered stock at prices far below those quoted by reputable houses, it is safe to assume that there is some defect in quality.

It can readily be seen that machine-stretched and machine-buffed leather can be produced at much lower figures than hand-stretched and hand-buffed stock.

All kinds of japanned leather are sold by measurement, the price being based upon each square foot of surface. The measuring is done by a frame divided off by cords into squares, each representing one square foot. If the hide were perfectly straight on its edges, correct measuring would be an easy matter; but so many feet in every hide are represented by the flanks and irregular edges that it requires much practice to be able to credit and debit the various irregularities accurately. The buyer is virtually at the mercy of the seller, and with this, as with hand-stretched and buffed leathers, the buyer should demand the maker's brand as a guarantee of quality and measurement.

In grading, Nos. 1, 2, etc., as a rule, represent quality and spread, but the conditions are such as to bar any set rule. A No. 1 enamel hide may measure not more than 50 feet, while a No. 2 may measure 75 feet or upward; but the general rule is to classify hides of 55 feet and upward as No. 1, providing they have a fine fiber, and are free from material defects. A blemished hide, no matter how fine the quality, is marked No. 2. Defects of a minor character, however, on the flanks are not necessarily of so serious a nature as to condemn the hide, but a slight hole or other blemish on the body marks down the quality.

A careful buyer will be governed in a great measure by the character of the leather. A No. 2 hide, when the marking down was due to a cut, or other similar injury, can often be worked without waste, and when cut, every piece can strictly be marked as No. 1.

The grade known as "landau" is from large, heavy hides, of even texture and fine grain ; the process of manufacture, however, does not differ from that employed in making other enamel leather. This class of top leather is used for heavy tops, such as landaus, cabriolets, doctors' phaetons, etc.

Railing and trimming leather are smooth finished, and are alike in every respect, except that railing is generally the lightest ; but as trimming is furnished in different weights, the distinction is not arbitrary. Dash leather is also smooth finished, heavy and light, grain and split ; all kinds are, however, tanned alike, but the manufacturer selects such hides as, in his opinion, will make the best leather of each kind. The best binding or railing leather is made of cow hides, they being finer grained and generally lighter than others.

Enameled hides of seventy feet and upward command the best prices, owing to the scarcity of large hides in the market ; but it is not always to the trimmer's advantage to buy them. Many of the best carriage builders prefer small hides of like thickness as the heavy ones, for all kinds of heavy tops, when they can be used.

The shape of the hide is an important feature ; the nearer it approachs the square the better it is, but the shape is an arbitrary feature, over which the tanner has no control ; buyers must take what they find in the market.

Patent and enameled leather are sold by the square foot instead of by weight. To correctly determine the number of feet in a hide requires skill and experience on the part of the operator. Were the edges of the hide all straight, the operation would be a simple one; but, as it is, all the leather in the tabs and such other portions of the hide as project beyond the outlines of the frame, must be accounted for. To do this by moving the frame would greatly increase the labor of measuring. The operator, therefore, resorts to a system of debting and crediting; thus, all such parts as extend beyond the frame, as well as the fractional parts in all squares, are credited, while the unfilled fractional parts in the squares are debited. The measuring is done by a large frame, eight feet long and four feet wide, having three cross pieces, which divide it lengthwise in four sections; each of these sections is divided into four equal parts by means of cords or wires. The frame is divided lengthwise into eight parts by means of cords or wires; each one of the small squares formed by the cross lines represents three square inches; four squares, one square foot. In measuring, the hide is doubled in the middle and the frame laid on; the squares are counted and the proper estimates made of debit and credit, and the whole doubled, which gives the measurement of the full hide. In some places a frame sufficiently large to cover the whole hide is used, but the principle is just the same as with the smaller frame. Fig. 1, page 38, shows a hide with frame in position.

A hide of leather is composed of a mass of fine fibers interwoven, but running in a general direction parallel with its length. Through the center portion these fibers are nearly straight, except at the hip, where there is a knotty mass, but as the flanks are approached the fibers lose their direct course ; at the shoulder they curl and knot up in spots ; at the flanks they curve, become coarse, and, in a measure, lose their individuality ; on the belly they are nearly straight, but they are coarse and not well knit together. These fibers cannot be stretched—the most that can be done is to straighten them. A microscopical examination of a piece of machine-stretched leather shows every fiber drawn out straight, while a piece of the same leather, not subjected to the stretching machine, shows the fibers to be slightly waved and curly. By stretching, these curls are taken out and the fiber assumes a thread-like appearance; these threads will break off short without any material increase in the length if sufficient additional strain is applied. Owing to the fact that the increase in the length of the hide is due to straightening out of the curls, etc., in the fiber, it necessarily follows that the backs and other portions where the fibers are the straightest will stretch the least, while the flanks, etc., will stretch the most. It is important, therefore, that the trimmer recognizes these peculiarities, and cuts his leather with a view to utilizing the advantages to be gained, but how to do this is the debated question.

Some trimmers claim that the fiber must run lengthwise, that is, from the back to the front bow of the top; others, that it must run crosswise. The first are governed in their views by a desire to take advantage of

the non-elasticity of the fiber, assuming that if it runs
lengthwise it will aid materially to prevent the bows
sagging apart.   The other class, while recognizing the
importance of obtaining the support derived from the
fiber when running lengthwise, claim that the creasing
of the leather between the bows is a consideration
that must not be overlooked, and that the only way to
reduce the injury from this cause to the minimum
amount is to make up the top, with the fiber of the
leather running crosswise on all tops that are made to
fall.   It is not necessary to depend upon the leather to
prevent the bows being thrown out of position, as other
means more effectual can be employed.   While the
creasing between the bows must be left entirely to the
chances of use, it follows that the latter fault should be
the first to be controlled ; this can be done by properly
cutting the leather, but, to do this, the cutter must not
expect to cut a perfect top from one hide, unless it be
a very large one, in which case there will be a great
deal of waste.

Fig. 2, page 38, shows a hide laid out for one top for
a buggy.   The trimmer who aims to cover the greatest
possible surface with a single hide has a good guide in
fig. 2, which represents the relative proportions of
patterns and a hide measuring sixty to sixty-two
feet.   The line A, through the center, represents the
fold in the hide and forms a dividing line for the various pieces, excepting for the roof piece, which, as a
general thing, is a little longer than one-half the width
of the hide.   B B are the side quarters, C the roof

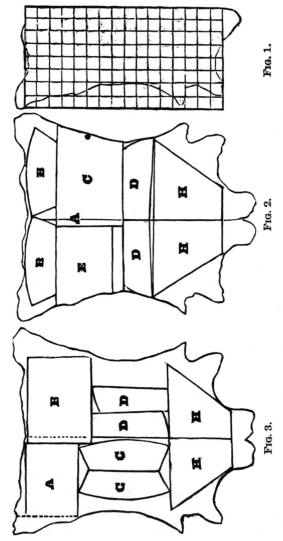

FIG. 1.

FIG. 2.

FIG. 3.

HIDES WITH TOP PATTERNS LAID ON AND MEASURING FRAME.

piece, D D the back quarters, E the back curtain, and H H the side curtains. If economy in outlay only is to be considered the plan for cutting, as shown, will give the best results, but if durability is to be a factor in determining cost, then it is the most expensive. Every trimmer, or other person accustomed to using or working leather, knows that there is a marked difference in the density and firmness of the hide in different parts. As has been shown, the fiber of the flanks, shoulders and belly is coarse and loose, and the central parts firm and compact. Now, if side quarters are cut, as shown on the diagram, the back ends are cut from a firm part of the hide, and the front ends from a coarse, soft part ; the difference is plain to the eye while new, and becomes more and more apparent as the top is used. The back quarters are open to the same objection, and the additional one of being cut across the grain ; nearly one-half of each side curtain is cut from the shoulders—the softest and least desirable parts of the hide ; a good top cannot be made of leather cut in this way.

The true plan is to cut each piece from a portion of the hide best adapted to it. The side quarters may be cut with the fibers running crosswise, as in the diagram, but from the middle of the hide ; the roof piece and back curtains from the back ends ; the back quarters from the center of the hide, running parallel with its length ; the side curtains, if for an open top, from the front end, but as far back as possible to avoid the soft shoulders. If the side quarters are to be close, as in a doctor's phaeton, or other close top carriage, they should be cut with the fiber running as nearly as possible on a line with the fold of the leather quarter when the top is down. All roll-up curtains, whether quarter or back, should be cut with the fiber running crosswise, so that when the curtains are rolled and unrolled there will be no creases to disfigure them. To cut in this way necessitates the use of more than one hide, but not one extra inch of leather is used, while the pieces left are all of such a size as to make them of value for other purposes.

Fig. 3, page 38, shows a hide laid out with a view to using the best of the leather, and allowing the grain to run in the proper direction to secure the best results. If the shape of the hide is good it will require one with a spread of about five feet more to cut all the pieces for one top than if cut as shown by fig. 2.

HARNESS LEATHER.

WEIGHTS MOST AVAILABLE — CUTTING — FINISHING — OAK
TANNED VS. HEMLOCK — LONG, WEIGHT AND TRIMMED
STOCK—BACKS.

The carriage trimmer is not called upon to use much harness leather, but what he uses is for straps that are in exposed positions, and, in most cases, bear a heavy strain. It is important, therefore, that the quality be good, and that the trimmer work it up to the best advantage. The amount used on an ordinary carriage is so small that price should not be allowed to interfere with its selection, and, when a greater quantity is needed, it is for thoroughbraces or hanging straps for Cee springs. The best of oak-tanned stock only should be employed.

For general use, select trimmed sides weighing from fourteen to sixteen pounds ; for thoroughbraces, pole straps, etc., eighteen to twenty-pound sides are preferable. It is poor policy, however, to cut from one edge only, as this compels using the best first, and necessitates the use of thin, soft stock where it should not be applied, or the throwing away of much of the belly and flank pieces. A better way is to cut the side in two, lengthwise, at a point eighteen to twenty inches from the back ; this gives three edges to cut from, each of which tends toward a different characteristic of the leather. Approaching the belly and flanks, it becomes thinner and softer as each succeeding strap is cut off, while cutting upward from the lower edge the leather grows firmer and stronger ; the back is left for the longest and best straps. Cutting a side this way makes it possible for the trimmer to use up every portion of it.

With most straps it is important that the best finish be secured ; if care is taken in this respect the finished straps will look smooth and silky on the grain, and the edges will be smooth, black and true. If the strap is to be finished in the best manner, cut to the desired width and put the leather in water and allow it to remain until it is moistened through ; some decide as to this by leaving the strap in the water until the grease begins to show itself on the grain of the leather ; then hang up the straps, and, when they become surface-dry,

lay them on a board and coat both sides with warm
tallow, and lay away stretched upon a board until the
water has dried out. During the drying the grease
fills up the pores of the leather, penetrating to the
very center. When dry, remove the surplus grease
with a rag and rub the strap with a slicker; this will
set the fiber firmly together, and give a smooth, fine
grain. Trim the edges smooth, and black with iron
and acid black; afterward color with hatters' black, and
rub with a silk cloth. Edges finished this way will appear as fine as the grain and will not rough up.

Few buyers of carriage materials are well versed in
harness leather, and the result is, the poorest finished
part of the carriage is the strapping. The finest leather
is made of cow or steer hides, tanned with oak bark
and curried with tallow and neatsfoot oil; but it requires the skill of an expert to determine the quality.
Oak-tanned leather is of a light buff color, and pliable,
but the art of bleaching is so well understood that hemlock leather is made to resemble the darker grades of
oak stock. This bleaching can be detected by cutting
the leather and examining the edge. If the side has
been bleached the flesh and grain sides will show a
thin light colored strip at each surface, while the interior will be red. Some of the grades of hemlock
leather are very fine, and, when the quality of the hide
and the currying are first class, the leather will be all
that can be desired as to quality, but the color operates
against its use on fine carriages.

Harness leather is known in the trade as long harness, weight, trimmed, and backs. Long harness is that in which the hides are tanned and curried without being trimmed. Weight stock is much the same as long stock, though in some localities the shanks, etc., are shortened and trimmed ; both of these grades are sold by actual weight at time of delivery. Trimmed harness is that in which the legs and thinner portion of the bellies are trimmed off before being curried. This is sold at its rough weight, with an additional charge of $1 to $1 50 for finishing. With this the buyer has no guarantee of weight, as each side is weighed, and the weight is cut on the grain at a convenient place. The bellies are trimmed, and the shanks cut off after the side has been branded. The buyer pays for all the wastage, and oftentimes something extra, as there is no way of ascertaining whether the rough brand is correct or not. This is one of the least desirable kinds of stock to buy. Backs are strips eighteen to twenty-two inches wide, measuring from the back bone line ; these are sold at an advanced price at their actual weight, the price asked being such as will cover the original cost of the side before being trimmed, and the cost of currying. These contain the best portion of the side, and carriage makers who are desirous of having their strapping of the best quality find them to be cheaper than trimmed or weight stock.

The carriage maker is not called upon to use much fair or russet leather, yet there are times when it must be used. The best of this stock is made of large spread cow hides, as these produce a finer grained and

softer leather than steer or other hides. One freak of
fashion is to bleach the leather quite light, then color
it with a yellowish brown stain, so as to produce what
is known as cuir color. When this color is used but
little stain is necessary for the edges of the straps, and
trimmers will find it to their advantage to purchase the
stain from the manufacturer of the leather. The ordinary brown and yellow stains are easily made, recipes
for which will be found in another chapter.

MOROCCO.

The best moroccos are made of large goatskins,
tanned in sumac. Those prepared for carriage trimmings are finished without oil or grease; the grain
has a very fine finish; the "grained" surface being
produced by passing the skins under a grooved roller;
the color is imparted by means of a dye, applied with
a brush. The French produce a very fine quality of
moroccos, which, though higher-priced than others,
are generally preferred for fine work. A very good
grade is also imported from Germany. American morocco is used to a considerable extent. Sheepskins are
also finished up as moroccos, but are entirely unsuited
to carriage trimming. A great deal of very fine trimming leather, which closely resembles morocco, is made
from the grain split of fine cow hides; these are
tanned in the best manner, colored all desirable shades,
finely grained and given a dull finish; this leather is
far superior to sheepskin or low grades of morocco; it

is sold by the square foot. Goatskins and sheepskins are sold by count.

COACH LACES.

THEIR LONG-CONTINUED USE—PAST AND PRESENT STYLES— AMOUNT USED—CLASSIFICATION—COLORS AND SHADES— WORSTED AND SILK LACES—REP AND CUT—WIDTH—LENGTH OF PIECES—TUFTS, TASSELS, GIMP, NAILS, CORDS, ETC.—HOW LACES ARE WOVEN —MACHINE VS. HAND-MADE.

Laces perform an important part in carriage trimming being of a class of articles that is both ornamental and useful ; they were introduced almost simultaneously with upholstering of carriages, and, though fashion has occasionally decreed their banishment, they have never gone entirely out of use since their first introduction.   At times they are made in a variety of colors and of elaborate designs ; then, again, they reach the minimum of plainness.   At the present time the favorite style is a plain rep face, with a scroll or leaf ornament, cut or plain.

Pasting and seaming laces are the trimmers' main reliance, wherever a seam is to be corded, or a raw edge covered up ; without these, strips of cloth or leather must be used.   They answer fairly well for seaming, but are a total failure as a substitute for pasting lace.   Heavy carriages are seldom trimmed without laces, though there is a great difference in the amount used by workmen, even on the same classes of work.   Fashion, however, as a rule, regulates the amount as well as the style.

Coach laces are of three kinds, known respectively as

broad lace, seaming lace, and pasting lace. Broad lace is used for cushion fronts, broad ornamental borders, arm rests, lifters, etc. ; seaming lace, as a covering for cord and joining seams ; pasting lace, as a finishing edge and border. Not many years ago all these laces were made with a silk face ; now, fine laces seldom have any silk in them except a few threads which form the selvage. When silks were used for the face, the various figures were made of different colors and shades, in order to bring out the pattern and to give the desired effect, but the colors faded, and the beauty of the lace was marred. Now, all fine laces have a worsted face, the finest being of one color throughout. The figure, which is woven with a higher loop than the body, is afterward cut, giving it the appearance of velvet, and making a strong contrast with the close rep ground ; so strong is this that few persons would be willing to admit that the velvet figure was of the same shade as the rep. The effect of this plush or velvet ornament is very fine ; it gives the lace a rich appearance, without the tawdriness so noticeable in old style silk laces, and, as the entire face is of one material and color, if it fades, all parts fade alike.

Laces are rep or cut. The rep laces have a plain corded face ; the cut laces are those in which the ornamental figure is cut, to give it the appearance of velvet. Some of the lower grade laces have a silk stripe or "lay" near the edges, and occasionally finer laces have a silk stripe the full width of the figure, which shows a silk rep ground next to the rep figure. The latter, however, are generally made to order, as fashion, at the present time, favors the worsteds.

Broad laces are woven to the uniform width of $2\frac{1}{2}$ inches; all other widths are special, and are made to order only. Seaming and pasting laces are made to match the broad laces in color and pattern. These are all made of one width, the pasting being about seven-eighths of an inch wide, and the seaming one and one-eighth inches wide. These are plain rep, or cut to match the broad lace. One popular pattern has every third cord or row of loops cut; this gives it a very rich appearance.

A piece of broad lace, when made for the trade, contains forty yards. Seaming and pasting laces have fifty yards to the piece. These lengths, however, are not arbitrary. At the present time, greens of various shades are the standard colors; next to these are the fashionable shades of browns, clarets, and blues.

Many leading carriage manufacturers design their own patterns, and hold exclusive control over them until such time as they see fit to make a change.

As the tastes of people improve, the necessity of harmony in all the interior decorations becomes more and more important, and to secure this many builders order laces, tufts, tassels, etc., in sets, thus securing a uniform shade throughout. This is a matter that requires the closet care. Very few carriage makers are sufficiently well acquainted with colors to be able to select silks and worsteds that will harmonize, and it is always best to leave the matching to lace makers, merely giving them a sample of the cloth or silk used in trimming, and the shade of broad lace desired.

Tassels are made to match the laces ; holder tassels are all made two and one-half inches wide, flat, with netted heads and heavy bullion fringe; they are made up in a number of grades, length and weight being the gauges of quality. Curtain tassels are made in two patterns—the plain round tassel with lace head and bullion fringe, and the French tassel—the " pompon "— a tassel made over a form with a pear-shaped body ; the material is cut, which gives it the appearance of a plush ball. Small tassels, known as trigger tassels, used on the trigger cord of spring curtain rollers, etc., are made in the "pompon" pattern and acorn pattern. The latter has an acorn-shaped wooden form, covered with plain silk and a plush top and bottom. Speaking-tube tassels are made wlth a net head, and bullion fringe around the mouth-piece of the speaking tube.

In addition to the tassels there are other articles that belong to the same class of ornaments, such as guard strings, small cord loops about six inches long, having wooden, conical-shaped frogs, covered with net ornaments. Speaking tubes, tubes covered with silk, in imitation of cord. Frogs made of wood, covered with silk in netting and other devices. Curtain braids or gimps. Curtain cords. Gimp nails with silk heads. Worsted ball tufts, tufts having the appearance of plush, with small uncut loops of strong contrasting colors, and plain cord tufts.

All the cords, tassels, etc., are made of silk, and as

they are to be used in connection with worsted laces, broadcloth, leather, satin, etc., it is important that they match in color.

Not many years ago all the coach laces were hand-made, and the finer grades were necessarily very high-priced. Now machinery has been so perfected that the finest qualities of coach lace are made at less cost to manufacture than the commonest grades of hand-made. So far as the material used and the process of weaving is concerned, there is no variance in the machine and hand-made laces; the only difference is that machinery, with automatic action of shuttles, treadles, needles, etc., driven by steam, takes the place of the human machine, who works with both feet on the treadles, and one hand working the shuttles, the other the needles and beam. The loom is the Jacquard, with some modifications, but the original principle exists as it did when first introduced. To those not familiar with the weaving of coach lace the operation is one of interest. With hand looms the operator must be skill-ful, as upon the proper working of the treadles depends the correctness of the figure, while the handling of the shuttle and needles, and beating up, require care, in order to secure an even face and a firm body. With power looms very little skill is required, except in "mounting the loom." To do this a man must be thoroughly acquainted with the business. When the loom is mounted it has a ground warp of Scotch linen thread, a slack ground warp of cotton thread, the worsted or silk which forms the face, and runs parallel with the warp, and the filling, which is of cotton or linen thread. The loops are formed by needles thrown in across the lace, under such threads as form the face. These needles are single for plain rep and double, on such laces as have a raised figure, the upper needle holding the figure threads. On hand looms these needles are drawn and placed by the weaver, the number used being much greater than with the power loom. With the latter the needles are worked by an automatic nippers, which at the proper time catches the needle, draws it out, carries it forward, places it between the threads, drops it, and returns to its original position in time to perform the same operation with the next needle.

Broad lace is woven in a single strip; seaming and pasting are woven together or single. The cutting, where there is a raised figure, when by hand, is done by leaving a number of needles in position on the lace, and trimming off the loops close to the needles with a razor or other keen-edged tool. When the cutting is done by machinery, the lace passes over and in close contact with the blades of a swiftly-revolving cylinder of knife blades which cuts off the top of the loop, and at the same time under a revolving brush, which removes all cuttings and loosens up the plush.

Machine-woven lace is quoted at about thirty per cent. lower figures than hand-made; the entire difference is due to the saving in the labor of weaving and cutting, as a like amount of stock is used in each. Some carriage manufacturers use hand-made solely, but the warmest friends of the hand-made do not claim for it any special merit over machine lace. Very little lace is imported, but all that comes from abroad is hand-made. Owing to the fine quality of American laces, large quantities are annually exported to England, France and Germany.

THREADS AND SILKS.

LINEN THREAD—NUMBERS AND SIZES—SILK—SKEIN THREAD.

Good thread is an absolute necessity, whether the carriage to be trimmed is first-class, or of a lower grade. Silk only is used for sewing cloth., etc., on fine work, but for general uses flax thread is equally durable and much more economical. Cotton thread is used, but it has no qualities to recommend it. Good linen thread possesses great strength; is free from knots and other irregularities; it has a firm, but not hard twist; if twisted too hard it will not take wax well; if too soft it untwists while using and breaks. Uniformity in numbers is also desirable, particularly when the thread is to be used for fair stitching.

The numbers of ball thread best adapted to carriage trimmers' use, are Nos. 10, 3 and 12. These numbers are furnished in half bleached, blue and yellow. Nos. 5, 6 and 19 are each a trifle finer than No. 12, and of like size, but of different colors : No. 5, black ; No. 6, white ; No. 19, yellow. No. 10 is the coarsest thread, and is only desirable for stitching heavy harness leather straps ; No. 3, the next size, is a good size for general work, though most trimmers prefer the next finer grade,

No. 12, for all joining seams and for stitching light
harness leather straps. Nos. 5, 6 and 19 are used in
place of No. 12, when special colors are preferred. For
machine stitching the two sizes most in use are 3-cord
No 16 gray, and 6-cord No. 35 black. These work
well for upper and lower threads, and are suitable for
under threads, when C and D silk are used for the
upper. A little heavier thread is needed when E silk
is used in the needle. Skein threads are numbered the
same as ball threads, but, owing to their close twist
and extra smooth finish, the corresponding numbers
appear to be one size finer.

CURLED HAIR, MOSS, ETC.

QUALITIES OF HAIR—MARKET PRICE—PROCESS OF MANUFAC-
TURE—PICKING—BLACK MOSS—HOW CURED—"EXCELSIOR"
—" ROWEN."

The carriage trimmer has at his command several
materials for stuffing cushions and other parts of the
upholstering, the prices of which range from the fractional part of a cent to sixty, or even eighty, cents a
pound, so that the matter of selection is one that need
not cause any trouble as to price. Pure curled hair is
the best article known ; it is light, clean, elastic and
durable. The best is made from horses' manes and
tails; a second grade being made of the long hair on
the ends of cattle tails. Lower grades are made of a
greater or lesser percentage of short hair twisted up
with the long, the lowest grade in the market hav-

ing no more long hair in it than is absolutely necessary to hold the short hair while being twisted. A
very large proportion of all the hair in the market is
hog's hair, mixed and twisted with long hair.

The highest priced hair in the market is the white,
it being preferred because of fancied purity and cleanliness, but it is in no way superior to long black hair,
though selling at from five to ten cents more per pound.

The process of manufacture of all kinds of curled
hair is essentially the same. It is first cleansed, then
twisted into cords about three-eighths of an inch in diameter, the hair being heated and moistened by steam
while being twisted. These cords are then twisted into
rope, passing through boiling water while being worked,
after which the rope is placed in a hot oven to dry;
this sets the curl, and gives the desired elasticity. The
condition of the hair while being twisted, the amount
of twist given, and the drying, all to a greater or less
extent determine its quality. Hard rope, all other
conditions being equal, is the best; as soon as the rope
is dry it is fit for the market.

Picking, that is, untwisting the rope and separating
the hair, is the next process, and it is one that has
much to do with the value of the hair when ready for
use. Hand-picking alone gives good results, as in this
way only can the hair be separated without breaking
or otherwise injuring it. A great deal of the picked
hair in the market is machine-picked; it is a trifle
cheaper to buy hair picked in this way, but its impaired
quality more than counterbalances the amount of money

saved. The best plan is to buy the hair rope and pick as wanted—that is, if the work to be done is to be first-class.

Pure mane and tail curled hair always commands a good price. All low grades are mixtures, which are inferior to some of the cheaper materials used.

Black moss is next in value to curled hair ; the finest being superior to the third rate hair, and equal to much that is sold as second rate. This moss is found in all the forests in the extreme Southern States, but it is the most plentiful in the Florida forests, where it grows more rapidly, is finer and more uniform than elsewhere. The green moss is gathered and placed for decomposition into large tanks, which will hold fifteen to twenty tons each. The moss is occasionally saturated with water and allowed to heat; this decomposes the outer or woody portion, and leaves the black thread-like fiber. As soon as the separation of the wood and fiber is complete the moss is placed in the sun to dry; when dry it is run through the picker, which crushes and removes the wood and all foreign substances ; the moss thus cleansed is then baled and sent to market. The trimmer should always pick it thoroughly before using it; if it has been well prepared it makes a clean and durable stuffing, one that is cheaper and far more desirable than much of the curled hair in the market.

The other articles, "excelsior"—wood shavings—and "rowen," short fine grass, have but little to recommend them except cheapness. The quality is a secondary consideration, but if there is any advantage in either it is with the "rowen," as it will not pack quite so hard as the "excelsior."

TRIMMERS' PASTE.

WHEAT AND RYE FLOUR PASTES—HOW TO COOK—PREPARED
PASTE FOR SUMMER USE.

Trimmers' paste requires to be smooth, elastic, free from moisture as possible, and possessed of great adhesive qualities. If too moist it will soil the cloth or silk to which it is applied, and if not well cooked it will mold and rot; its adhesive qualities are dependent upon the materials of which it is made, and the manner of mixing and cooking. The materials used are wheat and rye flour. The paste of commerce is made of a very low grade of wheat flour, cooked by steam; it is not a good article for trimmers, as it contains too much surplus moisture.

To make wheat paste select a low grade, but sweet wheat flour, and stir it into cold water until thoroughly dissolved; then place the kettle over a quick fire and stir it until it boils; it should be allowed to cook five or six minutes after it is brought to a boil, and be well stirred while boiling and until it is cool; if made in this way it will contain no surplus moisture and will be smooth and free from lumps.

For rye paste select good fine rye flour, place the necessary amount of water into a kettle over a quick fire, and when the water boils pour in the flour slowly, stirring it thoroughly; continue to add flour until the desired thickness is obtained; then allow it to boil about five minutes, after which remove it from the fire and continue to stir until boiling ceases, then cover and allow it to stand until it is cold. Rye flour paste made in this way is the smoothest, most adhesive and elastic paste in use. It is particularly valuable for pasting cloth on wood or leather.

The dry paste that gathers on the kettle should not be thrown away; if it is soaked in cold water until it becomes soft, and again heated up to boiling heat, it is stronger and more elastic than when first made. Wheat or rye paste can be preserved from mold, etc., by adding a little carbolic acid or essential oil. The addition of a little dissolved gum arabic adds materially to the adhesive qualities of flour paste. Paste for summer use that will keep a long time is made of rye paste, prepared as above; when cold, pour it on a smooth board and set it in the sun to dry; when dry it can be broken up and kept for use. To prepare it for use, place a small quantity in a kettle and cover with cold water; allow it to remain until soaked soft, then pour off the surplus water, place the kettle over a quick fire, and stir it until it boils.

Another plan is to cook the paste, pour it on a cloth, lay it in a clean, warm place for ten or twelve hours, roll up the cloth and lay aside for use. Paste treated in this way will keep sweet for a week or more even in the hottest weather.

CHAPTER II.

TABLES OF TRIMMING MATERIALS.

CHEAP MATERIALS NOT A REQUISITE FOR MEDIUM GRADES OF
WORK—WASTAGE IN CUTTING STOCK—TRIMMING CHEAP
WORK—PROFITS—LITTLE THINGS TO BE LOOKED AFTER—
LEAVE LOW-PRICED WORK TO LARGE MANUFACTURERS—
THE WORK THAT IS THE MOST SALABLE—VALUE OF THE
TRIMMING TABLES.

The numerous tables of materials for trimming given
in this work are such as are used in trimming medium
and fine grades. The number of low-priced carriages
built yearly in this country is very great, but the business is confined to a comparatively small number of
manufacturers. These firms conduct their business
with such thorough system that outside of their respective factories their tables of materials would be
valueless, except as a comparison. In numbers the
manufacturers of medium and fine grades constitute
the great majority. A few of these carry on the business on an extensive scale, but the greater number are
small manufacturers, and to these, as well as to journeymen, these tables cannot fail proving of great value.

Trimming is an important and expensive branch of
the carriage business, and manufacturers are compelled
to exercise the utmost prudence in order to keep

down the cost while keeping up the character of the work, and in no department are the chances of wastage greater than in the trimming shop.

A carriage may be trimmed cheaply, but yet made to look and wear well, but to do this the materials must all be cut economically, and the labor performed in the most systematic manner. The common error is to suppose that cheap material is the first essential requisite, no thought being taken that the time wasted in trying to make the work with poor material will more than counterbalance in cost the difference between the good and the poor article. This is particularly the case with patent and enameled leather. A good, clean, plump hide can be cut without wasting more than two per cent., while an inferior hide will waste ten to fifteen per cent. The margin in price between a No. 1 and a No. 2 hide will not exceed $2\frac{1}{2}$ cents a foot, or $1 20 on a 60-foot hide; the loss in cutting, of a single top-quarter for a buggy top, would equal in value the amount saved in price, while the time wasted in laying on patterns, so as to work out the worst blemishes, will amount to a like sum, and when the whole is cut up, some of the pieces are not fit for use. With No. 1 stock, on the other, there is no time lost in cutting, no waste other than occasioned by cutting to shapes, and when cut, every piece is good; so well is the fact recognized that good leather is the cheapest, that the large manufacturers of carriages who cut from five to ten thousand hides a year, are the most careful buyers, demanding a uniform spread of hides, and strictly No. 1 in quality. With cloths there is no such difference, but strength is a necessity, and the loaded shoddies that have no strength are the most unprofitable kinds.

In trimming low-priced carriages the tops should be of uniform size. In setting the bows use a frame, giving all the same pitch and spread. Use one gauge for locating top props, and when putting on the leather secure the bows firmly in position, using but one measurement in all cases; if possible, round the bows by machinery, so that the covers may be stitched by machine and drawn on; if care is taken the top props can be made without loss of time in measuring each top.

Cover the tops with good leather quarters and back stays, rubber cloth roof, and flock curtains; line the cushion tops, but do not use a false top, and stitch as much as possible with a machine. The cheapest material for stuffing is "excelsior," but builders, who have given the matter attention, find it profitable to use moss.

All laces and extra fittings must be omitted, and everything used must be purchased in large quantities, and direct from manufacturers. The difference between the wholesale and retail prices will aggregate full ten per cent. on the entire cost of an ordinary carriage.

There are so many little things to look after in the trimming shop that it will not do to slight anything. A few pennies here and there aggregate a considerable sum when the whole are added together. A few cents saved on top props looks like a trifle, but three or four dollars are easily realized by just such little savings.

A man carrying on a small shop working a dozen hands cannot compete with the one in a large factory working two or three hundred hands. A profit of $5 to $10 on a cheap buggy pays the man who turns out ten to fifteen thousand a year, but the one who turns out a hundred a year cannot get along with any such profit. There is no reason, therefore, why manufacturers who do not count their products by the thousands should aim to compete with those who do. There is always a good demand for stylish medium work, and strictly first-class easily finds buyers at high prices.

A careful study of the following tables will serve to materially assist the manufacturer of carriages in making up his estimates.

These tables have been prepared from original sources by men who have made the matter of estimates a careful study; they cover every class of carriage made by American manufacturers, excepting those that may be called sporting vehicles—such as track sulkies, skeleton wagons and four-in-hand drags. The former are trimmed so little that a table of materials is unnecessary, while the latter are built by one or two firms only.

In the line of buggies care has been taken to select representative vehicles, such as the one-man, no-top; medium road wagon, with top; the Britton and Goddard, two heavier styles; the doctor's phaeton, etc. Park vehicles—such as village carts, T-carts, driving phaetons, cabriolets and Victorias are the representatives of another class, which are given complete. Extension and half-top phaeton and rockaways, curtain, half curtain and paneled are also given in such numbers as to meet the demands of builders in all parts of the country. Heavier vehicles—such as coupes, broughams, landaus—curtain and glass front—are given in sufficient numbers to cover the field in them.

The illustrations are all drawn to a scale of one-half inch to the foot, and represent the most fashionable vehicles in their respective classes.

Trimmers should bear in mind that the materials given in these tables represent the amount required; the quality is in no sense arbitrary for cheap vehicles. Moss or other material may be substituted for curled hair; enameled duck for certain portions of the patent leather. Broad lace may be omitted, and plain tufts or buttons used in place of finer articles, and so on through the entire list, but yards, pounds and numbers represent the exact quantities used. These cannot be deviated from except when the quality of the work is reduced.

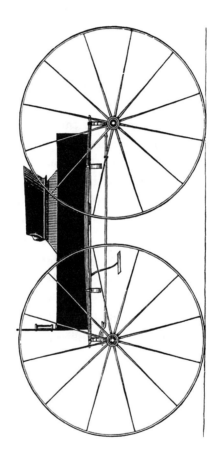

ONE-MAN ROAD WAGON.

TABLE NO. 1.

Material for Trimming Road Wagon (1 Man).

WIDTH ON SEAT, 21 INCHES.

3 feet Soft Splits.	18 Buttons.
$4\frac{1}{2}$ " Grain Dash.	18 Tufts.
$1\frac{1}{8}$ yards Body Cloth.	1 oz. Tacks.
1 " Cotton.	$\frac{1}{8}$ ℔. Cord and Twine.
$\frac{1}{3}$ " Enameled Cloth.	$\frac{1}{2}$ oz. Thread.
$1\frac{3}{4}$ " Rubber.	1 pair Shaft Tips.
$1\frac{1}{4}$ " Carpet.	$1\frac{1}{2}$ ℔s. Paste.
4 ℔s. Curled Hair.	1 Whip Socket.
$\frac{1}{2}$ " Wadding.	12 Safety Straps.

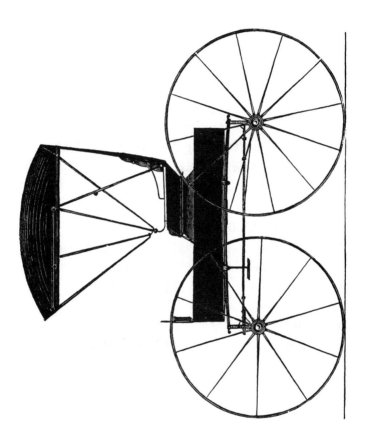

SIDE-BAR TOP WAGON.

TABLE NO. 2.

Material for Trimming Top Side-Bar Wagon.

WIDTH ON SEAT, 30 INCHES; SPREAD OF TOP, 3 FEET 6 INCHES; 3 BOWS.

65 feet Top Leather.

6 " Soft Splits.

7 " Railing.

8 " Grain Dash.

1½ yards Body Cloth.

3⅝ " Head Lining.

⅞ " ·Enam. Cloth.

2 " Rubber.

1⅝ " Velvet Carpet.

2¼ " Buckram.

8½ ℔s. Curled Hair.

½ " Wadding.

78 Buttons.

72 Nails.

31 Screws.

24 Knobs.

2 papers Tacks.

¼ ℔. Cord and Twine.

1 oz. Thread.

3 Bows.

1 set Joints and Props.

12 Rivets and Nuts.

1 Whip Socket and Fasteners.

1 set Slat Irons.

½ ℔. Paste.

4 Buckles and Billets.

1 Back.

2½ yards Webbing.

5 " Carpet Fringe or Binding.

1 Back Light.

13-feet Risers.

20 Straps.

4½ yards Muslin.

¾ " Patent Cloth.

4 Carpet Loops.

2 Steel Back Straps.

6½ inches Rubber for Prop Blocks.

4 Prop Washers.

1 pair Lamps.

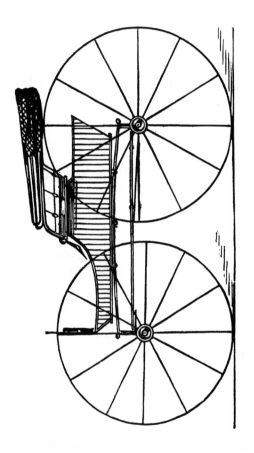

WHITECHAPEL BUGGY.

TABLE NO. 3.

Material for Trimming Whitechapel Buggy.

WIDTH ON SEAT, 30 INCHES; SPREAD OF TOP, 42 INCHES;
3 BOWS.

60 feet Top Leather.	1 ℔. Tacks.
2 " Jap. Trimming.	$\frac{1}{4}$ " Cord and Twine.
7 " Hard Splits.	$\frac{1}{2}$ oz. Thread.
8 " Railing.	3 Bows.
6 " Grain Dash.	4 Joints and Props.
2$\frac{1}{2}$ yards Body Cloth.	4 Rivets and Nuts.
3$\frac{1}{8}$ " Head Lining.	1 set Slat Irons.
3 " Cotton.	4 ℔s. Paste.
2$\frac{1}{2}$ " Burlaps.	4 Buckles and Billets.
1 " Cambric.	1 Back.
1$\frac{1}{8}$ " Enameled Cloth.	3 yards Webbing.
2 " Rubber.	8 Pressed Loops.
1$\frac{1}{4}$ " Velvet Carpet.	1 Back Light.
1$\frac{1}{4}$ " Buckram.	$\frac{1}{2}$ sheet Straw Board.
5 ℔s. Curled Hair.	$\frac{1}{4}$ ℔. Risers.
5 " Pig's Hair.	1 pair Safety Straps.
3 " Moss.	1 " Curtain "
1$\frac{1}{2}$ " Wadding.	1 " Shaft "
4$\frac{1}{2}$ doz. Buttons.	6$\frac{1}{2}$ inches Rubber for **Prop**
$\frac{1}{2}$ gross Nails.	Blocks.
$\frac{1}{4}$ " Screws.	1 Name Plate.
24 Knobs.	1 Whip Socket.

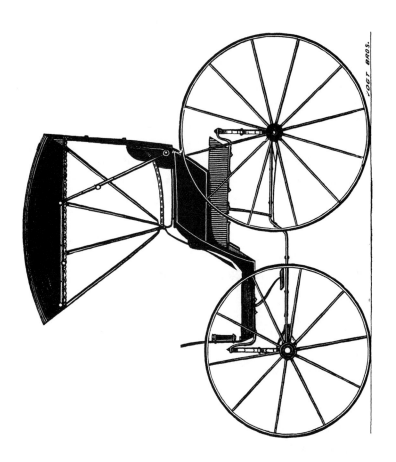

BRITTON BUGGY.

TABLE NO. 4.

Material for Trimming "Britton" Buggy.

WIDTH ON SEAT, 39 INCHES; SPREAD OF TOP, 48 INCHES;
4 BOWS.

75 feet Top Leather.	5 feet Molding, $\frac{3}{8}$ inch.
18 " Railing.	$\frac{1}{2}$ oz. Silk.
17 " Grain Dash.	4 Bows.
2½ yards Body Cloth.	4 each Joints and Props.
4¾ " Head Lining.	4 " Rivets and Nuts.
5½ " Cotton.	1 set Slat Irons.
6 " Burlaps.	5 ℔s. Paste.
1½ " Enameled Cloth.	6 each Buckles and Billets.
1 " Oil Carpet.	8 Covered Buckles.
27 inches Velvet Carpet.	1 pair Back Stays.
2 yards Buckram.	5½ yards Webbing.
4½ " Muslin.	10 Cushion Springs.
2½ ℔s. Harness Leather.	12 Loops.
7 " Curled Hair.	1 Back Light.
2 " Pig Hair.	¼ ℔. Risers.
60 Buttons, covered.	4 Apron Straps.
24 Nails.	Whip Socket and Clips.
54 Screws, assorted.	Rubber Apron.
34 Knobs.	4 Apron Hooks.
4 papers of Tacks.	4 Knob Holes.
10 spools Cord and Twine.	1 spool Machine Silk.
1 " Thread.	

GODDARD BUGGY.

TABLE NO. 5.

Material for Trimming "Goddard" Buggy.

WIDTH ON SEAT, 38 INCHES; SPREAD OF TOP, 45 INCHES;
4 BOWS.

65 feet Top Leather.	1½ lbs. Tacks.
2 " Jap. Trimming.	½ lb. Cord and Twine.
6 " Hard Splits.	½ oz. Silk.
13 " Railing.	4 Bows.
8 " Grain Dash.	4 Joints and Props.
2¾ yards Body Cloth.	4 Rivets, 8 Nuts.
4¼ " Head Lining.	1 set Slat Irons.
5 " Cotton.	4 quarts Paste.
4 " Burlaps.	4 Buckles and Billets.
2¼ " Cambric.	3 yards Webbing.
2⅛ " Rubber.	8 Springs (Pillow).
⅝ " Oil Carpet.	18 " (Cushion).
¾ " Melton Carpet.	6 Pressed Loops.
1 pair Coiled Springs for Top.	1 Back Light.
	1 Whip Socket.
10 ℔s. Curled Hair.	¼ ℔s. Risers.
48 Tufts.	1 pair Check Straps.
20 Buttons.	1 " Safety "
1 gross Nails.	1 " Shaft "
60 Screws.	1 " Roll-Up "
30 Knobs.	4 Dash Hooks.

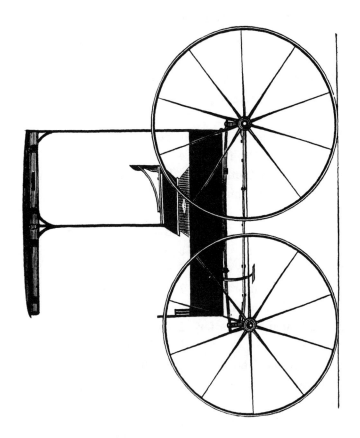

JENNY LIND.

TABLE NO. 6.

Material for Trimming "Jenny Lind."

WIDTH OF SEAT, 30 INCHES.

80 feet Enam. Top Leather.

7 " Railing Leather.

12 " Grain Dash "

5 " Soft " "

¾ ℔. Harness "

½ " Bridle "

2¼ yards Body Cloth.

5½ " Head Lining Cloth.

2¾ yards Russia Sheeting.

2⅛ " Buckram.

2 " Muslin, heavy.

2¾ " " light.

1 " Enam. Duck.

2 " Gum Cloth, 22 oz.

1⅔ yards Wilton Carpet.

3 ℔s. best White Hair.

2½ " " Gray "

1 " Cotton Wadding.

½ " Seaming Cord.

3 " Paste.

41 Covered Buttons.

21 Japanned "

36 " Knobs.

14 Harness Buckles, ⅝ in.

2 Covered " ¾ "

3 Curtain Frames.

1 Whip Socket and Fastener.

⅓ spool Machine Silk.

1 oz. Black Thread.

1 " Harness Thread.

3 papers Tacks.

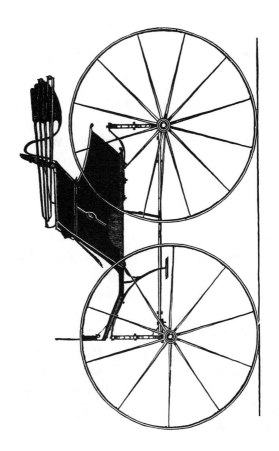

COAL-BOX BUGGY.

TABLE NO. 7.

Material for Trimming Coal-Box Buggy, with Top.

WIDTH ON SEAT, 26 INCHES; SPREAD OF TOP, 42 TO 44 INCHES; 3 BOWS.

69 feet Top Leather.	26 Knobs.
6 " Jap. Trimming.	2 papers Tacks.
4 " Hard Splits.	$\frac{1}{2}$ ℔. Cord and Twine.
3 " Soft "	$\frac{1}{8}$ " Thread.
14 " Railing.	1-16 ℔. Silk.
5 " Grain Dash.	3 Bows.
2 yards Body Cloth.	4 Joints and Props.
$4\frac{1}{4}$ " Head Lining.	4 Rivets and 8 Nuts.
$3\frac{1}{2}$ " Cotton.	1 pair Lamps.
2 " Drills.	1 set Slat Irons.
1 " Cambric.	4 ℔s. Paste.
$\frac{7}{8}$ " Enameled Cloth.	6 Buckles and 6 Billets.
$2\frac{1}{8}$ " Rubber.	4 yards Webbing.
$1\frac{1}{4}$ " Oil Carpet.	6 Pressed Loops.
$1\frac{1}{2}$ " Velvet Carpet.	1 Back Light, rounded.
$1\frac{1}{4}$ " Buckram.	$\frac{1}{4}$-℔. Risers.
8 ℔s. Curled Hair.	1 pair Cushion Straps.
1 " Wadding.	1 " Roll Up "
$1\frac{1}{4}$ gross Buttons.	1 " Apron "
1 " Nails.	1 set Shaft "
$\frac{1}{2}$ " Screws.	

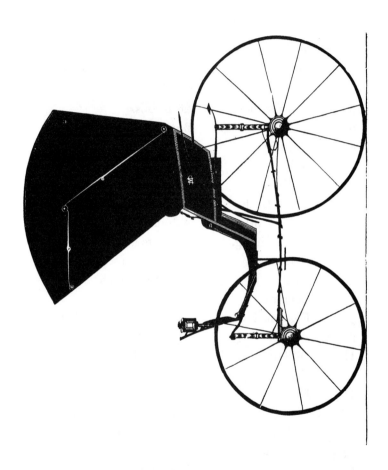

DOCTOR'S PHAETON.

TABLE NO. 8.

Material for Trimming Doctor's Phaeton with Side Lights.

WIDTH ON SEAT, 38 INCHES; SPREAD OF TOP, 48 INCHES; 4 BOWS.

70 feet Top Leather.	5 feet Molding, $\frac{3}{8}$ inch.
3 " Jap. Trimming.	$\frac{1}{2}$ oz. Silk.
11 " Hard Splits.	4 Bows.
$6\frac{1}{2}$ " Soft "	4 each Joints and Props.
$12\frac{1}{2}$ " Railing.	4 " Rivets and Nuts.
$7\frac{1}{2}$ " Grain Dash.	1 Rein Hook.
6 Goatskins, or $2\frac{1}{2}$ yards	$\frac{1}{2}$ yard Elastic.
Body Cloth.	1 set Slat Irons
$4\frac{3}{4}$ yards Head Lining.	5 ℔s. Paste.
$5\frac{1}{2}$ " Cotton.	6 each Buckles and Billets.
6 " Burlaps.	4 Silver Buckles or Dash
1 " Cambric.	Hooks.
$\frac{3}{4}$ " Enam. Duck.	1 pair Back Stays.
$2\frac{1}{2}$ " Rubber.	6 yards Webbing.
$\frac{3}{4}$ " Oil Carpet.	10 Cushion Springs.
$\frac{3}{4}$ " Velvet Carpet.	12 Pressed Loops.
$1\frac{1}{2}$ " Buckram.	1 Back Light.
1 Escutcheon Plate.	2 Side "
$\frac{1}{2}$ yard Canton Flannel.	2 " " Moldings.
16 ℔s. Curled Hair.	$\frac{1}{4}$ ℔. Risers.
$1\frac{1}{2}$ " Wadding.	4 Apron Straps.
90 Buttons, covered.	2 Check "
24 Nails, "	2 Safety "
54 Screws, assorted.	1 set Shaft Straps.
6 Knobs.	1 " Dash "
2 ℔s. Tacks.	1 " Back Curtain Straps.
$\frac{1}{2}$ " Cord and Twine.	1 pair Silk Frogs.
$\frac{1}{8}$ " Thread.	1 Whip Socket.

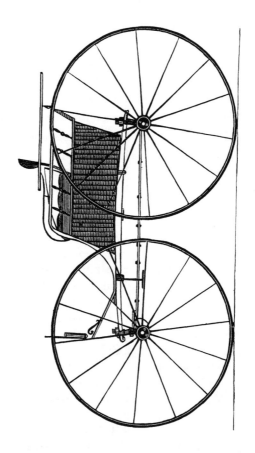

NO-TOP SURRY.

TABLE NO. 9.

Material for Trimming No-Top Surry.

WIDTH OF SEAT, 31 INCHES.

10 feet Grain Dash Leather.

1½ feet Valance Leather.

¾ ℔s. Bridle "

2 yards Body Cloth.

½ " Enameled Drill.

½ " " Muslin.

⅜ " " Duck.

⅞ " Wilton Carpet.

⅛ " Kersey.

½ " Muslin.

2 ℔s. best White Hair.

3 " " Gray "

1 lb Cotton Wadding.

1½ " Paste.

½ " Seaming Cord

24 Tufts.

24 Japanned Buttons.

2 Covered Buckles, ⅝ in.

3 papers Tacks.

1 hank Black Thread.

1 Whip Socket and Fastener.

½ oz. Harness Thread.

2 Covered Buckles.

1½ yards Webbing.

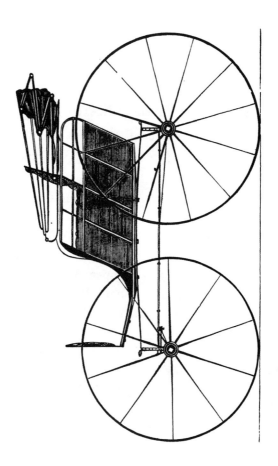

TOP SURRY.

TABLE NO. 10.

Material for Trimming Top Surry.

WIDTH OF SEAT (BETWEEN PILLARS), 31 INCHES; SPREAD
OF TOP, 43 INCHES; 3 BOWS.

65 feet Enameled Top Leather.

10 feet Grain Dash Leather.

7½ feet Soft Leather.

7 " Railing "

¾ ℔s. Harness "

½ " Bridle "

4 " best White Hair.

2½ " Gray Hair.

1 " Cotton Wadding.

½ " Seaming Cord.

3 " Paste.

10 Covered Roller Buckles, ⅝·inch.

18 Tufts.

18 Japanned Buttons.

36 Japanned Knobs.

22 Cloth Nails.

2 Metallic Top Stays.

1 Curtain Frame

2 Covered Roller Buckles, ¾ inch.

3 Bows.

1 Whip Socket and Fastener.

4 Top Props.

3 papers Tacks.

⅓ spool Machine Silk.

1 oz. Black Thread.

1 " Harness Thread.

1¾ yards Body Cloth.

4¼ " Head Lin'g Cloth.

2¾ " Russia Sheeting.

2 " Muslin, Heavy.

2¾ " " Light.

1 " Enameled Duck.

1⅝ " Wilton Carpet.

2 " Gum Cloth, 22 oz.

2⅛ " Buckram.

7 Eng. Diaper Web.

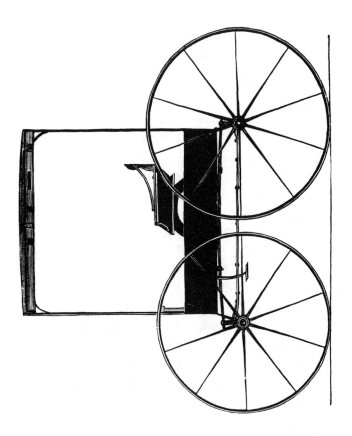

STANDING-TOP WAGON.

TABLE NO. 11.

Material for Trimming Standing Top, Two-Passenger Wagon.

WIDTH ON SEAT, 35 INCHES; 4 POSTS.

45 feet Top Leather.	1 dozen Screws.
2 " Jap. Trimming.	2 " Knobs.
9 " Hard Splits.	1 ℔. Tacks.
4 " Soft "	$\frac{1}{2}$ " Cord and Twine.
3 " Railing.	$\frac{1}{4}$ oz. Thread.
6 " Grain Dash.	$\frac{1}{4}$ " Silk.
$3\frac{1}{4}$ yards Body Cloth.	1 pair Shaft Tips.
$2\frac{1}{2}$ " Head Lining.	1 Whip Socket.
3 " Cotton.	4 lbs. Paste.
3 " Burlaps.	4 each Buckles and Billets.
$1\frac{1}{4}$ " Cambric.	1 pair Cross Straps.
1 " Enam. Cloth.	4 Silver Buckles.
2 " Rubber.	1 Silver Center Piece.
$\frac{3}{4}$ " Oil Carpet.	6 Springs.
$\frac{7}{8}$ " Velvet Carpet.	8 Pressed Loops.
1 " Buckram.	1 Back Light.
5 ℔s. Curled Hair.	1 sheet Straw Board.
7 " Pig "	$\frac{1}{4}$ ℔. Risers.
2 " Wadding.	1 pair Check Straps.
24 Tufts.	1 " Safety "
24 Buttons.	1 " Shaft "
$\frac{1}{2}$ gross Nails.	3 " Curtain "

PONY PHAETON—CANOPY TOP

TABLE NO. 12.

Material for Trimming Pony Phaeton.

WIDTH ON SEAT, 33 INCHES.

4 feet Jap. Trimming.
Leather.
35 ft. Colored Leather or
3 Goatskins, or 2 yds.
Body Cloth.
4½ feet Hard Splits.
21 " Soft Splits, or
Grain Dash.
6 feet Railing.
1 yard Cotton.
1 " Cambric.
3 " Enam. Cloth.
2¼ " Rubber.
½ " Oil Carpet.
⅝ " Velvet Carpet.
½ " Buckram.
4 ℔s. Curled Hair.
8 " Pig "
¼ " Wadding.
94 Buttons.

1 gross Nails.
24 Screws.
2 Knobs.
1 paper Tacks.
¼ ℔. Cord and Twine.
1 oz. Thread.
⅛ " Silk.
3 ℔s. Paste.
2 Buckles and Billets.
1 set Cross Straps.
4 Silver Buckles.
1 Center Piece.
1 sheet Straw Board.
¼ ℔. Risers.
1 pair Apron Straps.
1 " Check "
1 " Safety "
1 " Cushion "
1 " Dash "
1 Whip Socket.

Add Canopy Top if desired.

LADIES' PHAETON, WITH TOP.

TABLE NO. 13.

Material for Trimming Ladies' Phaeton With Top.

WIDTH ON SEAT, 36 INCHES; SPREAD OF TOP, 44 INCHES;
4 BOWS.

65 feet Top Leather.	5 papers Tacks.
3 " Jap. Trimming.	$\frac{1}{4}$ ℔. Cord and Twine.
6 " Hard Splits.	2 oz. Thread.
8 " Soft Splits.	4 Bows.
10 " Railing.	4 each Joints, Props and
3 " Grain Dash.	Rivets.
$2\frac{1}{2}$ yards Body Cloth.	8 Nuts.
4 " Head Lining.	1 Slat Iron.
$3\frac{1}{2}$ " Cotton.	$3\frac{1}{2}$ ℔s. Paste.
2 " Burlaps.	4 Buckles and Billets.
1 " Cambric.	4 yards Webbing.
$\frac{7}{8}$ " Enam. Cloth.	6 Cushion Springs.
$2\frac{1}{8}$ " Rubber.	4 Pressed Loops.
$\frac{5}{8}$ " Oil Carpet.	1 Back Light.
$\frac{3}{4}$ " Velvet Carpet.	1 sheet Straw Board.
$1\frac{1}{2}$ " Buckram.	$\frac{1}{4}$ ℔. Risers.
6 ℔s. Curled Hair.	1 pair Check Straps.
10 " Pig "	1 " Safety "
$\frac{3}{4}$ " Wadding.	1 " Curtain "
$6\frac{1}{2}$ dozen Buttons.	1 " Apron "
$1\frac{1}{2}$ gross Nails.	3 " Dash "
2 dozen Screws.	2 " Shaft "
$2\frac{1}{2}$ " Knobs.	1 Whip Socket.

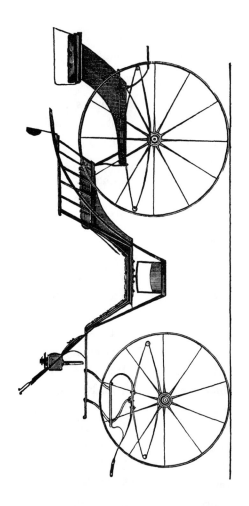

LADIES' PHAETON, WITH RUMBLE.

TABLE NO. 14.

Material for Trimming Ladies' Phaeton With Rumble.

WIDTH ON SEAT, 34 INCHES.

8 feet Jap. Trimming.

32 " Colored, or 2 yds. Body Cloth.

5 feet Hard Splits.

15 " Soft "

4 " Railing.

1 yard Cotton.

$\frac{1}{2}$ " Burlaps.

$\frac{3}{4}$ " Cambric.

$1\frac{1}{4}$ " Enameled Cloth.

2 " Rubber.

$\frac{1}{2}$ " Moleskin.

$\frac{7}{8}$ " Oil Carpet.

$1\frac{1}{4}$ " Velvet Carpet.

$\frac{1}{2}$ " Buckram.

5 lbs. Curled Hair.

6 " Pig "

$\frac{1}{2}$ " Wadding.

$\frac{1}{2}$ gross Buttons.

$\frac{1}{4}$ lb. Nails.

2 dozen Screws.

2 Knobs.

$\frac{1}{2}$ lb. Tacks.

$\frac{1}{4}$ " Cord and Twine.

$\frac{1}{2}$ oz. Thread.

3 lbs. Paste.

1 pair Cross Straps.

4 Silver Buckles.

1 Center Piece.

1 sheet Straw Board.

$\frac{1}{4}$ lb. Risers.

1 pair Safety Straps.

1 " Shaft "

1 " Curtain "

1 " Apron "

1 " Dash "

1 Whip Socket.

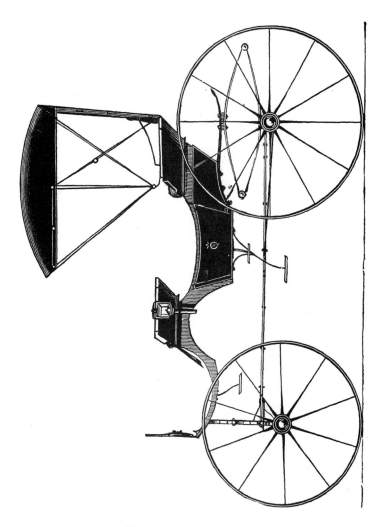

HALF-TOP PHAETON.

TABLE NO. 15.

Material for Trimming Phaeton, Half-Top, Four Passenger.

WIDTH ON BACK SEAT, 35 INCHES; SPREAD OF TOP, 46 INCHES; 4 BOWS.

73 feet Top Leather.	36 Knobs.
6 " Jap. Trimming.	1½ ℔. Tacks.
48 " Colored.	½ " Cord and Twine.
12 " Hard Splits.	¼ oz. Thread.
44 " Soft Splits, or	½ " Silk.
Grain Dash.	4 Bows.
9 feet Railing.	4 each Joints, Props and
4⅝ yards Body Cloth.	and Rivets.
4 " Head Lining.	8 Nuts.
2½ " Cotton.	1 set Slat Irons.
3 " Burlaps.	4½ ℔s. Paste.
1½ " Cambric.	4 each Buckles and Billets.
1¼ " Enameled Cloth.	4 yards Webbing.
2⅛ " Rubber.	8 Cushion Springs.
2¼ " Oil Carpet.	4 Pressed Loops.
2½ " Velvet Carpet.	1 Back Light.
2 " Buckram.	1 sheet Straw Board.
8 ℔s. Curled Hair.	1 ℔. Risers.
10 " Pig Hair.	2 Check Straps.
1½ " Moss.	2 Safety "
1¼ " Wadding.	2 Roll Up "
10 doz. Buttons.	2 Apron "
1 gross Nails.	3 Dash "
¼ " Screws.	1 Whip Socket.

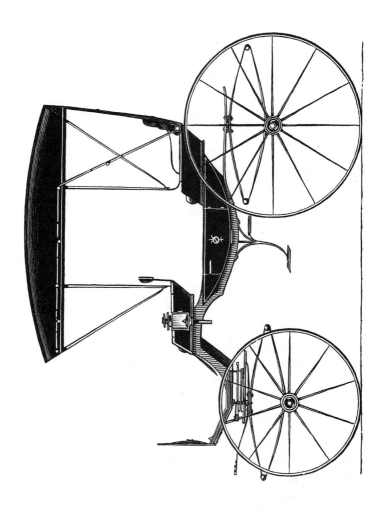

EXTENSION-TOP FOUR-PASSENGER PHAETON.

TABLE NO. 16.

Material for Trimming Phaeton, Extension Top, Four Passenger, with Fenders.

WIDTH ON SEAT, 39 INCHES; SPREAD OF TOP, 65 INCHES;
5 BOWS.

128 feet Top Leather.	$\frac{3}{4}$ lb. Cord and Twine.
55 " Colored Leather,	1 oz. Thread.
or $3\frac{3}{4}$ yds. Body Cloth.	$\frac{1}{8}$ " Silk.
5 feet Hard Splits.	5 Bows.
30 " Soft "	6 each Joints and Props.
6 " Railing.	6 Rivets.
6 yards Head Lining.	10 Nuts.
4 " Cotton.	1 set Slat Irons.
4 " Burlaps.	5 lbs. Paste.
$2\frac{1}{4}$ " Cambric.	6 Buckles and Billets.
$1\frac{1}{4}$ " Enameled Cloth.	1 pair Cross Straps.
$2\frac{1}{8}$ " Rubber.	4 Silver Buckles.
$1\frac{1}{4}$ " Oil Carpet.	1 Back.
$1\frac{1}{2}$ " Velvet Carpet.	5 yards Webbing.
2 " Buckram.	8 Cushion Springs.
10 lbs. Curled Hair.	6 Pressed Loops.
6 " Pig "	1 Back Light.
84 Tufts.	$\frac{1}{4}$ lb. Risers.
$1\frac{1}{2}$ lbs. Wadding.	1 Pair Curtain Straps.
42 Buttons.	1 " Shaft "
2 gross Nails.	1 " Apron "
6 dozen Screws.	1 " Evener "
3 " Knobs.	1 " Roll Up "
$1\frac{1}{2}$ lbs. Tacks.	1 Whip Socket.

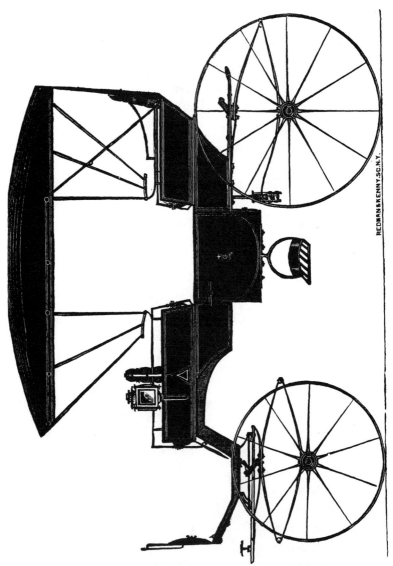

EXTENSION-TOP SIX-PASSENGER PHAETON.

TABLE NO. 17.

Material for Trimming Phaeton, Extension Top, Six Passenger.

WIDTH ON BACK SEAT, 39 INCHES; SPREAD OF TOP, 72 INCHES; 6 BOWS.

185 feet Top Leather.

4 " Jap. Trimming.

69 " Colored Leather, or 7¾ yds. Body Cloth.

12 feet Hard Splits.

4 " Soft "

38 " Railing.

8 " Grain Dash.

10¾ yards Head Lining.

11 " Cotton & Drills.

5 " Burlaps.

2¼ " Cambric.

1½ " Enam. Cloth.

2½ " Rubber.

2 " Oil Carpet.

2 " Wilton Carpet.

1½ " Buckram.

1 pair Outside Handles.

1 " Inside Handles.

1 Pull Handle.

20 ℔s. Curled Hair.

12 " Pig "

3 " Moss.

2¼ " Wadding.

170 Buttons.

2 ℔s. Nails.

¾ gross Screws.

54 Knobs.

2½ papers Tacks.

1 lb. Cord and Twine.

¼ " Thread.

6 Bows.

8 each Joints, Props and Rivets.

12 Nuts.

1 set Slat Irons.

7½ ℔s. Paste.

6 each Buckles and Billets.

1 set Cross Straps.

4 Silver Buckles.

6½ yards Webbing.

10 Cushion Springs.

6 Pressed Loops.

½ lb. Risers.

1 Back Light.

2 Evener Straps.

2 Roll-up "

2 Apron "

3 Dash "

1 Whip Socket.

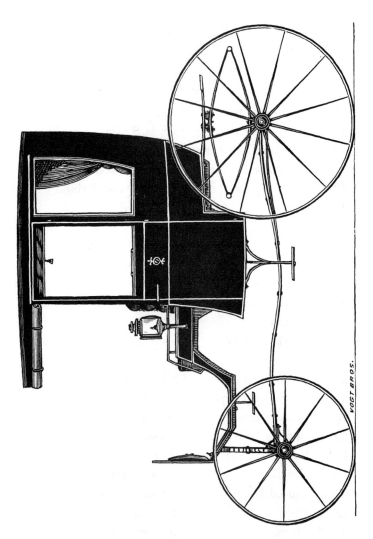

FOUR-PASSENGER ROCKAWAY.

TABLE NO. 18.

Material for Trimming Rockaway, Partition Front, Close Quarter, Four Passenger.

WIDTH ON BACK SEAT, 41 INCHES.

13 feet Top Leather.	1½ ℔s. Cord and Twine.
33 " Jap. Trimming.	¼ " Thread.
10 " Hard Splits.	9 Tassels.
3 " Soft Splits.	4 Spring Barrels.
9 " Railing Leather.	2 Rods.
10 " Grain Dash.	3 feet Molding.
6½ yards Body Cloth.	½ oz. Silk.
2½ " Head Lining.	6 Glass Lights.
7 " Cotton.	1 pair Silver Frogs.
4 " Burlaps.	8 yards Curtain Cord.
3 " Cambric.	2 " Large Silk Cord.
2 " Enameled Cloth.	6 ℔s. Paste.
2½ " Rubber.	6 Buckles and Billets.
16 " Broad Lace.	2 Silver Buckles.
50 " Narrow Lace.	4 Bone Slides.
2 " Oil Carpet.	4 yards Webbing.
2 " Wilton Carpet.	8 Cushion Springs.
2 " Buckram.	1 Back Light.
1¼ " Frame Cloth.	4 Side Lights.
14 ℔s. Curled Hair.	2 sheets Straw Board.
8 " Pig Hair.	½ ℔. Risers.
1 " Moss.	1 pair Evener Straps.
5 " Wadding.	1 " Dash Straps.
3 gross Buttons & Tufts.	1 Card Case.
1 " Nails.	1 pair Pull Handles.
½ " Screws.	1 " Spring Backs.
1 " Knobs.	1 " Frogs.
3 ℔s. Tacks.	1 Whip Socket.

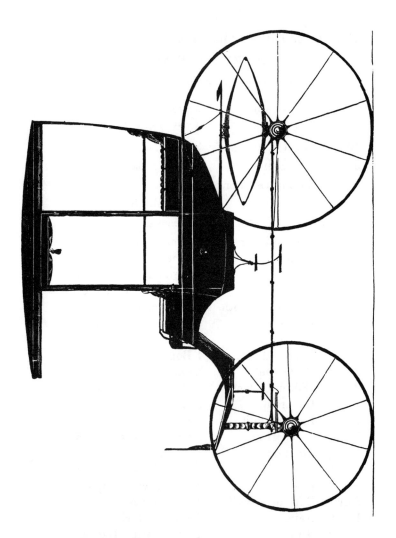

CURTAIN-QUARTER LOW-DOOR ROCKAWAY.

TABLE NO. 19.

Material for Trimming Rockaway, Low Door, Curtain, Four Passenger.

WIDTH ON SEAT, 39 INCHES.

65 feet Top Leather.	1¼ lbs. Wadding.
2½ " Jap. Trimming.	154 Buttons.
12 " Hard Splits.	½ gross Nails.
6 " Soft Splits.	¼ " Screws.
5 " Railing Leather.	50 Knobs.
3⅜ yards Body Cloth.	1 ℔. Tacks.
6¼ " Head Lining.	½ " Cord and Twine.
4 " Cotton.	1 oz. Thread.
2 " Burlaps.	3 ℔s. Paste.
1½ " Cambric.	8 Hooks and Rings.
1½ " Enameled Cloth.	1 Back Light.
2 " Rubber.	½ sheet Straw Board.
1½ " Oil Carpet.	⅛ ℔. Risers.
1½ " Velvet Carpet.	2 Check Straps.
1 " Buckram.	2 Curtain Straps.
1 pair Door Handles.	2 Safety Straps.
6 ℔s. Curled Hair.	2 Apron Straps.
8 " Pig Hair.	2 Cushion Straps.
3 " Moss.	1 Whip Socket.

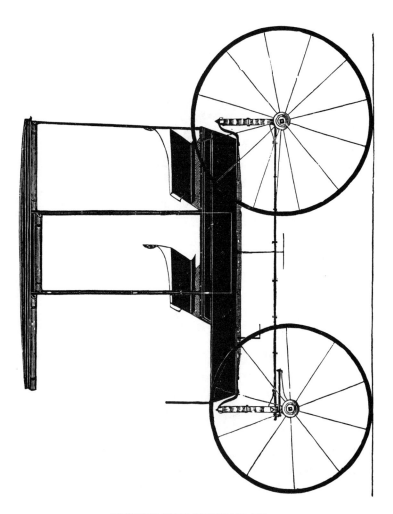

SQUARE-BOX ROCKAWAY.

TABLE NO. 20.

Material for Trimming Rockaway, Curtain, Square Box, Four Passenger.

WIDTH ON BACK SEAT, 40 INCHES.

48 feet Top Leather.	½ gross Nails.
4 " Jap. Trimming.	2 dozen Screws.
12½ " Hard Splits.	44 Knobs.
2½ " Soft Splits.	1½ lbs. Tacks.
5 " Railing.	¾ lb. Cord and Twine.
14½ " Grain Dash.	1 oz. Thread.
5½ yards Body Cloth.	2 Tassel Holders.
½ " Black Cloth.	2 Spring Barrels.
4½ " Head Lining.	1⅝ yards Silk.
6 " Cotton.	2 Glass Lights.
1 " Burlaps.	5 lbs. Paste.
2½ " Cambric.	1 set Cross Straps.
1 " Enameled Cloth.	2 Back.
2¼ " Rubber.	2 Bone Slides.
2 " Broad Lace.	8 Springs.
40 " Narrow Lace.	1 Back Light.
1½ " Oil Carpet.	1 sheet Straw Board.
1½ " Velvet Carpet.	¼ lb. Risers.
2½ " Buckram.	2 pairs Check Straps.
6 lbs. Curled Hair.	2 " Safety Straps.
13 " Pig Hair.	2 " Shaft Straps.
10 " Moss.	8 " Curtain Straps.
1¼ " Wadding.	1 Whip Socket.
112 Buttons.	

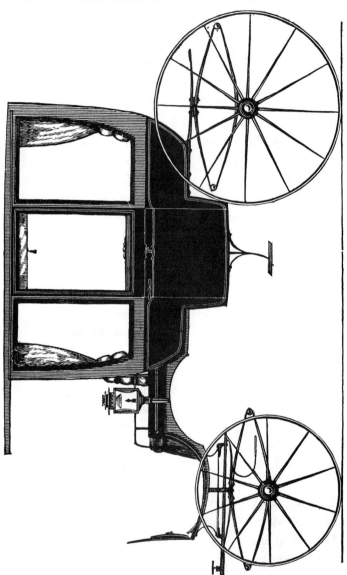

SIX-PASSENGER ROCKAWAY.

TABLE NO. 21.

Material for Trimming Rockaway, Partition Front, Six Passenger.

WIDTH ON BACK SEAT, 42 INCHES.

28 feet Top Leather.
30 " Jap. Trimming.
10 " Hard Splits.
4 " Soft Splits.
11 " Railing.
10 " Grain Dash.
7½ yards Body Cloth.
4½ " Head Lining.
8½ " Cotton.
4 " Burlaps.
4 " Cambric.
3 " Enameled Cloth.
3 " Rubber.
18 " Broad Lace.
55 " Narrow Lace.
2½ " Oil Carpet.
2½ " Wilton Carpet.
2 " Buckram.
1 Card Case.
1 pair Door Handles.
1 " Pull Handles.
1 " Frogs.
20 lbs. Curled Hair.
1¼ yards Black Cloth.
20 lbs. Moss.
4 " Wadding.

2½ gross Buttons.
1 " Nails.
1 " Screws.
¼ " Knobs.
3½ lbs. Tacks.
2¼ " Cord and Twine.
¼ " Thread.
9 Tassels.
4 Spring Barrels.
3 feet Molding.
6 yards Silk..
1 pair Frogs.
9 Glass Lights.
6 lbs. Paste.
2 Buckles and Billets.
2 Silver Buckles.
4 Bone Slides.
5 yards Webbing.
10 Cushion Springs.
39 yards Silk Cord.
1½ sheets Straw Board.
1 ℔. Risers.
1 pair Apron Srtaps.
1 " Evener Straps.
2 " Curtain Straps.
1 Whip Socket.

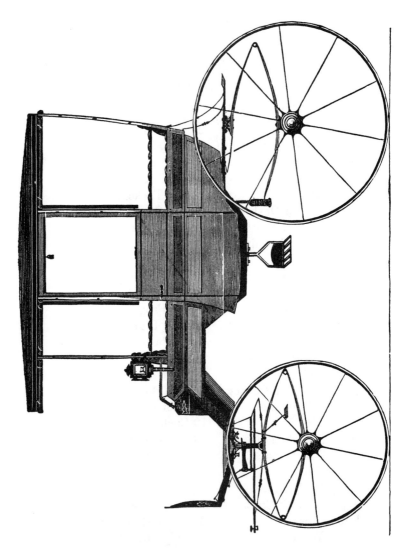

SIX-SEAT ROCKAWAY.

TABLE NO. 22.

Material for Trimming Six-Seat Curtain-Quarter Rockaway, with Squabs

WIDTH ON BACK SEAT, 46 INCHES.

12 yards Body Cloth.
3½ " Head Lining Cloth.
4½ yards Curtain Silk.
1⅓ " Black Cloth (frames).
26 yards Broad Lace.
50 " Seaming Lace.
50 " Pasting Lace.
2¼ " Wilton Carpet.
2½ " Oil Carpet.
2 " Enam. Duck.
6 " Curtain Cord.
2½ " Cotton Duck (roof).
6 yards Buckram.
5 " Muslin (heavy).
5 " " (light).
5 " Russia Sheeting.
1¾ " Cloth (lining apron).
15 ℔s. extra White Hair.
13 " pure Gray Hair.
4 " Cotton Wadding.
¾ " Tufting Twine.
6 " Paste.
1 " Seaming Cord.
4 " Harness Leather.
¾ " Bridle Leather.

56 feet Enam. Top Leather.
60 feet Trimming Leather.
6 " Valance Leather.
12 " Dash Leather.
1¾ " Skirting Leather.
2 " Railing Leather.
1 " Kip Leather.
9 Holder Tassels.
5 Curtain Tassels.
5 Trigger Tassels.
208 Tufts.
36 Covered Pins.
6 papers Tacks.
½ spool Machine Silk.
1 Whip Socket and Fastener.
7 Pillow Springs.
6 Pressed Loops.
2 Pole Strap Buckles (1⅜ in).
47 Japanned Knobs.
78 " Buttons.
5 Spring Rollers (curtains).
5 Lace Plates.
1 oz. Harness Thread.
2 " Black Thread.
8 Round Head Ivory Screws.

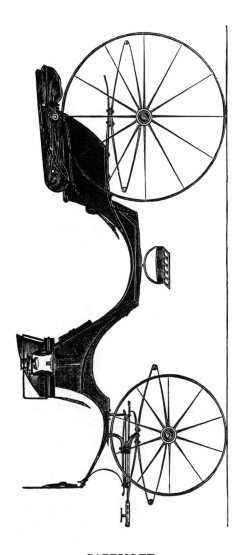

CABRIOLET.

TABLE NO. 23.

Material for Trimming Cabriolet.

WIDTH ON BACK SEAT, 38 INCHES; SPREAD OF TOP, 68 INCHES;
4 BOWS.

129 feet Top Leather.	38 Knobs.
5 " Jap. Trimming.	2 papers Tacks.
12½ " Hard Splits.	¾ ℔. Cord and Twine.
5 " Soft Splits.	¼ " Thread.
18 " Railing.	½ oz. Silk.
44 " Grain Dash.	4 Bows.
7 Goatskins, or 4¼ yards	8 Joints and 8 Props.
Body Cloth.	8 Rivets and 12 Nuts.
7¼ yards Head Lining.	1 set Slat Irons
6½ " Cotton.	5 ℔s. Paste.
4½ " Burlaps.	6 each Buckles and Billets.
1½ " Cambric.	1 pair Cross Straps.
1 " Enam. Cloth.	4 Silver Buckles.
2¼ " Rubber.	1 Center Piece.
4¼ " Broad Lace.	6 yards Webbing.
24 " Narrow Lace.	10 Springs.
1⅜ " Oil Carpet.	6 Pressed Loops.
1½ " Wilton Carpet.	1 Back Light.
¾ " Buckram.	½ ℔. Risers.
14 ℔s. Curled Hair.	1 pair Shaft Straps.
8 " Pig Hair.	1 " Apron Straps.
1½ " Moss.	1 " Roll Up Straps.
1¼ " Wadding.	1 " Evener Straps.
129 Buttons.	1 " Check Straps.
1 gross Nails, assorted.	1 " Dash Straps.
85 Screws, assorted.	1 Whip Socket.

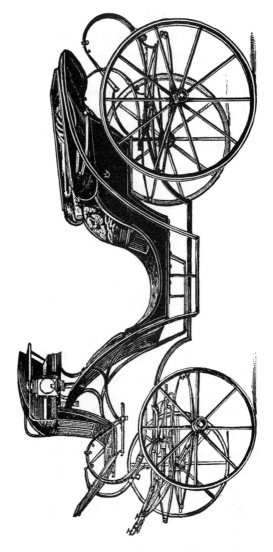

VICTORIA.

TABLE NO. 24.

Material for Trimming Victoria.

WIDTH ON BACK SEAT, 40 INCHES; SPREAD OF TOP, **49** INCHES; 3 BOWS.

75 feet Top Leather.	105 Buttons.
26 " Jap. Trimming Leather.	1 gross Nails.
	$\frac{1}{2}$ " Screws.
51 ft. Colored Leather, or	22 Knobs.
4 yards Body Cloth.	1½ ℔s. Tacks.
9 feet Hard Splits.	$\frac{3}{4}$ " Cord and **Twine**.
6 " Soft Splits.	$\frac{1}{4}$ " Thread.
13 " Railing.	1 pair Silk Frogs.
55 " Grain Dash.	3 feet Molding.
2½ " Skirting Leather.	4 Bows.
4¾ yards Head Lining.	4 Joints and 4 Props.
3 " Cotton.	4 Rivets and 8 Nuts.
6 " Burlaps.	1 set Slat Irons.
1¼ " Cambric.	6 ℔s. Paste.
7 " Enam. Duck.	8 Buckles and Billets.
2¼ " Rubber.	1 pair Cross Straps.
4¼ " Broad Lace.	4 Silver Buckles.
24 " Narrow Lace.	5 yards Webbing.
1¼ " Oil Carpet.	8 Springs.
2 " Velvet Carpet.	8 Pressed Loops.
2½ " Buckram.	1 Back Light.
1 pair Shaft Tips.	1 Storm Curtain Light.
1 Whip Socket.	$\frac{1}{2}$ sheet Straw Board.
12 ℔s. Curled Hair.	1½ ℔s. Risers.
9 " Pig Hair.	1 pair Evener Straps.
1 " Moss.	1 " Roll Up Straps.
1 " Wadding.	1 " Apron Straps.

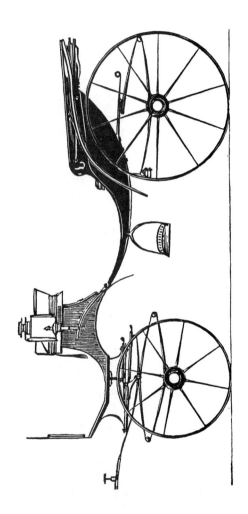

ROUND CABRIOLET.

TABLE NO. 25.

Material for Trimming Round Cabriolet.

WIDTH ON BACK SEAT, 40 INCHES; SPREAD OF TOP, 49
INCHES; 3 BOWS.

78 feet Top Leather.	80 Tufts.
5 " Jap. Trimming.	12 Knobs.
4 " Hard Splits.	6 papers Tacks.
5 " Soft Splits.	½ ℔. Cord and Twine.
32 " Apron Leather.	3 balls Thread.
38 " Grain Dash.	2 skeins Thread.
5 Goatskins.	8 feet Molding.
3½ ℔s. Harness Leather.	1 spool Machine Silk.
7 yards Body Cloth.	3 Bows.
4¾ " Head Lining.	2 Joints and Props.
1½ " Burlaps.	2 Rivets and 4 Nuts.
10 " Cambric.	3 ℔s. Paste.
1 " Enam. Cloth.	18 yards Webbing.
3 " Rubber.	12 Springs.
6 " Broad Lace.	6 Pressed Loops.
36 " Narrow Lace.	1 Back Light.
2½ " Oil Carpet.	2 Cushion Straps.
2¾ " Carpet.	1 pair Shaft Tips.
1½ " Buckram.	1 pair Lamps.
16 ℔s. Curled Hair.	1 Whip Socket.

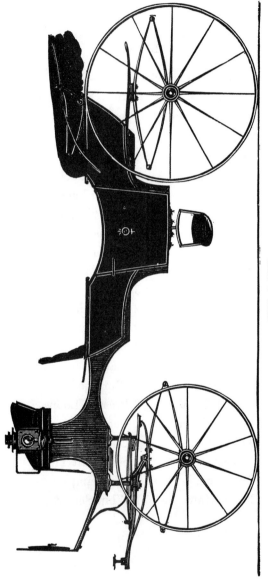

VIS-A-VIS.

TABLE NO. 26.

Material for Trimming Vis-a-Vis.

WIDTH ON BACK SEAT, 40 INCHES; SPREAD OF TOP, 49 INCHES; 3 BOWS.

75 feet Top Leather.
26 " Jap. Trimming Leather.
50 ft. Colored Leather, or 4 yards Body Cloth.
9 feet Hard Splits.
6 " Soft Splits.
13 " Railing.
4¾ yards Head Lining.
3 " Cotton.
6 " Burlaps.
4 " Cambric.
7 " Enam. Duck.
2¾ " Rubber.
8½ " Broad Lace.
32 " Narrow Lace.
1¾ " Oil Carpet.
3¾ " Carpet.
15 ℔s. Curled Hair.
5 " Pig Hair.
1 gross Tufts.
3 yards Wadding.
4 doz. Buttons.
3 gross Nails.
⅔ doz. Screws.
3½ " Knobs.
3½ ℔s. Tacks.

1 ℔. Cord and Twine.
¼ " Thread.
7 feet Molding.
3 Bows.
4 each Joints and Props.
4 Rivets.
8 Nuts.
1 set Slat Irons.
6 ℔s. Paste.
8 each Buckles and Billets.
1 pair Cross Straps.
4 Silver Buckles.
1 Card Case.
5 yards Webbing.
8 Springs.
8 Pressed Loops.
1 Back Light.
1 Storm Curtain Light.
½ sheet Straw Board.
1½ ℔s. Risers.
1 pair Roll-Up Straps.
1 " Apron Straps.
1 Whip Socket.
1 pair Spring-Lock Handles.
1 " Pull Handles.
4 Silver Dash Hooks.

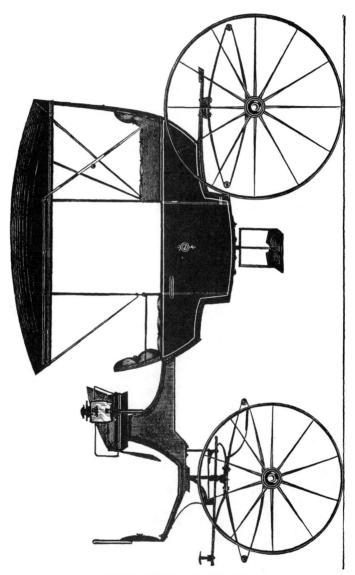

EXTENSION-TOP BRETT.

TABLE NO. 27.

Material for Trimming Brett, Extension Top.

WIDTH ON BACK SEAT, 40 INCHES; SPREAD OF TOP, 51
INCHES; 4 BOWS.

140 feet Top Leather.	1 lb. Cord and Twine.
14 " Jap. Trimming.	¼ " Thread.
15 " Colored.	12 feet Molding.
7 " Hard Splits.	½ oz. Silk.
29 " Railing.	4 Bows.
10 Goatskins.	4 Joints and 8 Props.
8 yards Head Lining.	8 Rivets and 12 Nuts.
9 " Cotton Drilling.	1 set Slat Irons.
3 " " Muslin.	6 lbs. Paste.
4 " Cambric.	8 Buckles and Billets.
1 " Enameled Duck.	1 pair Cross Straps.
3 " Rubber.	4 Silver Buckles.
8½ " Broad Lace.	1 Silver Center Piece.
32 " Narrow Lace.	1 Card Case.
1¾ " Oil Carpet.	6½ yards Webbing.
3¼ " Wilton Carpet.	28 Springs.
6¼ " Slip Lining.	8 Pressed Loops.
19 " Tape.	2 Back and Front Lights.
15 lbs. Curled Hair.	2 lbs. Risers.
5 " Pig Hair.	1 pair Evener Straps.
1 gross Tufts.	1 " Roll-Up Straps.
3 lbs. Wadding.	1 " Apron Straps.
3½ dozen Buttons.	2 Covered Buckles.
3 gross Nails.	1 Whip Socket.
⅔ dozen Screws.	1 pair Spring-Lock Handles.
3½ " Knobs.	1 " Pull Handles.
3½ lbs. Tacks.	4 Silver Dash Hooks.

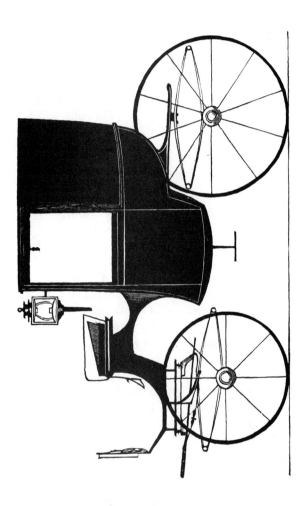

COUPE.

TABLE NO. 28.

Material for Trimming Coupe.

WIDTH ON BACK SEAT, 41 INCHES.

26 feet Jap. Trimming.
2½ " Skirting Leather.
5 " Hard Splits.
3 " Soft "
6 " Railing.
14½ " Grain Dash.
9 Goatskins, or 3 yards
Satin.
7½ yards Cotton Cloth.
6½ " Cotton Drilling.
5 " Cambric.
1 " Enam. Cloth.
2⅛ " Rubber.
16 " Broad Lace.
60 " Narrow Lace.
2 " Oil Carpet.
2¾ " Wilton Carpet.
2 " Braid.
1 Gong Bell.
1 Whip Socket.
1 pair Shaft Tips.
1 " " Straps.
1 " Apron Straps.
1 " Pole Straps.
18 ℔s. Curled Hair.
1 " Wadding.
171 Tufts.
21 Buttons.
1 gross Nails, covered.
½ " Screws, assorted.
2 Knobs.

1½ lbs. Tacks.
¾ lb. Cord and Twine.
1 oz. Thread.
7 Acorn Tassels.
4 Curtain Tassels.
4 Spring Barrels.
5 feet Molding.
3¼ yards Silk.
8 " " Cord.
1 Looking Glass.
2 Bent Beveled Glass.
2 French Plate Glass.
1 foot Galvanized Wire
Netting.
1 Check Cord.
4 ℔s. Paste.
2 each Buckles and Billets.
1 pair Silver Buckles.
3 Bone Slides.
3 yards Webbing.
22 Springs.
1 Back Light, beveled.
1 lb. Risers.
1 set Cushion Straps.
1 pair Frogs, silk.
1 " " ivory.
1 Card Case.
1 pair Lever Handles.
1 " Pull Handles.
1 " Door Handles.

BROUGHAM.

TABLE NO. 29.

Material for Trimming Brougham.

WIDTH ON BACK SEAT, 42 INCHES.

26 feet Jap. Trimming.
2½ " Skirting.
5 " Hard Splits.
3 " Soft Splits.
6 " Railing.
14½ " Grain Dash.
7 Goatskins.
5¼ yards Body Cloth.
⅞ " Black Cloth.
2½ " Cotton Cloth.
6½ " " Drilling.
2 " Burlaps.
4 " Cambric.
1 " Enam. Cloth.
2⅛ " Rubber.
16 " Broad Lace.
60 " Narrow Lace.
2 " Oil Carpet.
4 " Wilton Carpet.
2 " Braid.
1 Whip Socket.
1 pair Shaft Tips.
1 set " Straps.
1 pair Apron Straps.
1 " Pole Straps.
18 ℔s. Curled Hair.
1 " Wadding.
21 Buttons.
183 Tufts.
1 gross Nails, covered.
½ " Screws, assorted.
2 Knobs.
1½ lbs. Tacks.

¾ ℔s. Cord and Twine.
1 pair Silver Eyelets.
1 oz. Thread.
4 Holder Tassels.
3 Curtain Tassels.
6 Acorn Tassels.
3 Spring Barrels.
5 feet Molding.
3 yards Silk.
8 " " Cord.
1 Looking Glass.
4 French Plate Glass.
1 Check Cord.
½ dozen Finishing Screws.
1½ " Sil. " Screws.
1 set Dash Hooks.
4 lbs. Paste.
2 each Buckles and Billets.
1 pair Silver Buckles.
3 Bone Slides.
3 yards Webbing.
22 Springs.
1 Back Light.
2 Side Lights.
1 ℔. Risers.
1 set Cushion Straps.
1 pair Frogs, silk.
1 " " ivory.
1 Card Case.
1 pair Lever Handles.
1 " Pull Handles.
1 " Door Handles.

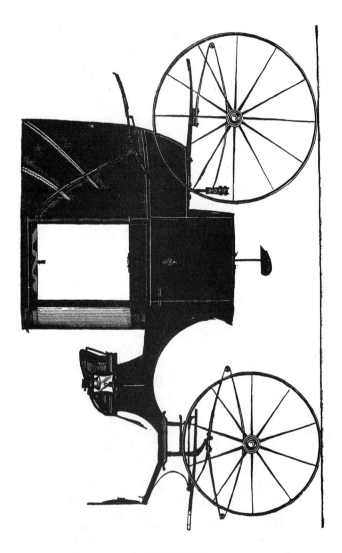

LANDAULET.

TABLE NO. 30.

Material for Trimming Landaulet.

WIDTH ON BACK SEAT, 42 INCHES; SPREAD OF TOP, 28
INCHES; 3 BOWS.

75 feet Top Leather.	$\frac{3}{4}$ ℔. Cord and Twine.
30 " Jap. Trimming.	2 oz. Thread.
2½ " Skirting.	5 Tassels.
5 " Hard Splits.	3 Spring Barrels.
20 " Soft Splits.	4½ yards Silk.
14½ " Grain Dash.	8 " Silk Cord.
10 Goatskins.	3 Bows.
6½ yards Body Cloth.	1 Looking Glass.
4 " Head Lining.	2 sets Joints and Props.
3½ " Doeskin.	2 Rivets and 4 Nuts.
2 " Burlaps.	3 Glass.
10 " Cambric.	2 gross Tufts.
1 " Enam. Cloth.	1 Card Case.
22 " Broad Lace.	1 Bell Pull.
90 " Narrow Lace.	1 Dressing Case.
2 " Oil Carpet.	1 pair Slat Irons
2½ " Carpet.	4 ℔s. Paste.
3 " Buckram.	2 Buckles and Billets.
4½ " Curtain Silk.	4 Slides.
1 set Dash Hooks.	10 Springs.
2 yards Braid.	1 Back Light.
1 pair Shaft Tips.	1 ℔. Risers.
17 ℔s. Curled Hair.	1 set Curtain Straps.
1 " Wadding.	4 ℔s. Harness Leather.
2 gross Tufts.	4 Curtain Gimps.
1 " Nails, covered.	6 Triggers.
½ " Screws.	2 Frogs.
2 Knobs.	1 Whip Socket.
1½ papers Tacks.	1 Gong Bell.

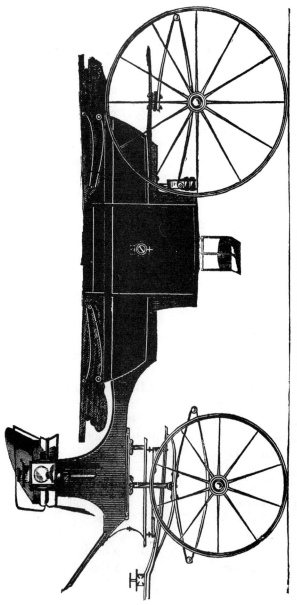

LEATHER-TOP LANDAU.

TABLE NO. 31.

Material for Trimming Landau, Leather Top.

WIDTH ON BACK SEAT, 52 INCHES; 6 BOWS.

120 feet Top Leather.	3½ yards Silk.
20 " Jap. Trimming.	6 Bows.
6 " Skirting.	2 pairs Joints and Props.
36 " Enam. Leather.	4 Rivets and 8 Nuts.
17 ℔s. Harness Leather.	2 Glass.
14 Goatskins.	3 " String Slides.
7½ yards Body Cloth.	1 Whip Socket.
2 " Doeskin.	1 pair Lamps.
10 " Cotton.	1 Looking Glass.
1½ " Burlaps.	1 Card Case.
2 " Enameled Cloth.	2 pairs Slat Irons.
24 " Broad Lace.	10 ℔s. Paste.
100 " Narrow Lace.	6 Buckles and Billets.
2 " Oil Carpet.	1 pair Cross Straps.
2½ " Velvet Carpet.	1 " Pole Straps.
5 " Buckram.	4 Silver Buckles.
½ " Plush.	2 Backstrap Loops.
2 pairs Gimps.	2 Slides.
2 " Frogs.	5 yards Webbing.
3 " Triggers.	12 Springs.
15 ℔s. Curled Hair.	2 Curtain Lights.
8 " Wadding.	1 Pair Silk Frogs.
3 gross Tufts.	2 ℔s. Risers.
1½ " Nails.	1 Set Cushion Straps.
2 " Screws, assorted.	1 Speaking Tube.
4 Knobs.	1 Bell Pull.
3 papers Tacks.	2 Pull-to Handles.
½ ℔. Cord and Twine.	2 Inside Handles.
2 balls Thread.	1 Bell.
7 large Tassels.	1 pair Door Handles.
4 Spring Barrels.	1 " Dickey Seat H'dles.
9 yards Molding.	

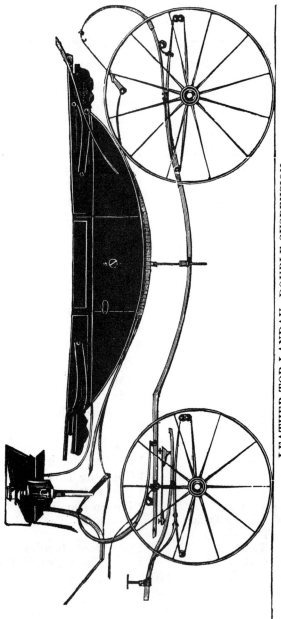

LEATHER TOP LANDAU—DOUBLE SUSPENSION.

TABLE NO. 32.

Material for Trimming Leather-Top Landau.

WIDTH ON BACK SEAT, 46 INCHES.

5½ yards Body Cloth.
1¼ " Curtain Silk.
1⅓ " Dickey Seat Cloth.
⅓ yard Body Cloth (doors).
18 " Broad Lace.
50 " Seaming Lace.
40 " Pasting Lace.
⅝ " Bl'k Cloth (frames).
⅔ " Bedford Cords (cushion bottoms.)
3¼ yards Gum Drill (32 ounces, top cover).
3 yards Gum Drill (22 seat jockey).
1¾ yards Cloth (lining apron).
5½ yards Russia Sheeting.
4 " Buckram.
2½ " Wilton Carpet.
1 " Oil Carpet.
3 " Cambric (b'lk).
2 " Silk Cord (doors).
12 ℔s. Extra White Hair.
8 " Pure Gray Hair.
1 " Cotton Wadding.
6 " Paste.
½ " Tufting Twine.

3½ ℔s. Harness Leather..
1-16 " Harnes Thread.
1-16 ' Black Thread.
1½ " Seaming Cord.
125 feet Landau Top Lea.
46 feet Dash Leather.
5 " Railing Leather.
2½ " Skirting Leather.
28 " Trimming Leather.
12 Goatskins.
2 Tassel Holders.
2 Trigger Holders.
104 Tufts.
6 papers Tacks.
1 Whip Socket and Fastener.
28 Covered Buttons.
28 Japanned Buttons.
6 Pressed Loops.
2 Pole Strap B'kles (1¼ in.).
12 Elastic Button Holes.
3 Apron Fasteners.
2 Curtain Spring Rollers.
½ spool Machine Silk.
5 yards Muslin (brown).
9 " Engl'h Diaper Web.
14 Pillow Springs.
2 Lace Plates.

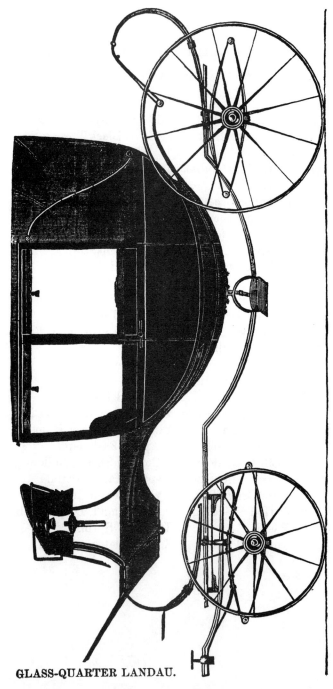

GLASS-QUARTER LANDAU.

TABLE NO. 33.

Material for Trimming Landau, Glass Quarter.

WIDTH ON BACK SEAT, 46 INCHES; 3 BOWS.

105 feet Top Leather.	4 Spring Barrels.
6 " Jap. Trimming.	12 feet Molding.
6 " Skirting.	14 " Diamond Sil. Mold-
33 " Grain Dash.	ing.
5 ℔s Harness Leather.	4 feet Stitch Molding.
8 Goatskins.	1½ Spools Silk.
2 Sheepskins.	3 Bows.
9 yards Body Cloth.	2 Joints and Props.
5 " Head Lining.	2 Rivets and 4 Nuts.
8 " Cotton.	6 Glass Lights.
4 " Burlaps.	2 gross Tufts.
2 " Enameled Duck.	2 Handles.
2½ " Rubber.	1 Card Case.
26 " Broad Lace.	2 Pull-to Handles.
90 " Narrow Lace.	6 lbs. Paste.
13 " Muslin.	4 Buckles and Billets.
2¾ " Oil Carpet.	5 Bone Slides.
13 " Webbing.	2 Long Loops.
3 " Velvet Carpet.	4 Short Loops.
3 " Buckram.	1 Back Light.
5 " Curtain Silk.	1 Gong.
30 ℔s. Curled Hair.	2 Frogs.
6 " Wadding.	5 Triggers.
1 gross Nails.	2 Top Hooks.
4 Ivory Head Screws.	2 Glass Frame Fasteners.
5 papers Tacks.	1 Whip Socket.
6 ℔s. Cord and Twine.	3 Glass string Plates.
1 ball Thread.	2 Lamps.
4 skeins Thread.	2 End Finishers.
5 Tassels.	

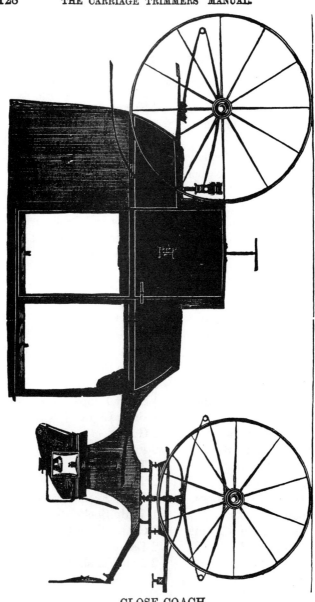

CLOSE COACH.

TABLE NO. 34.

Material for Trimming Close Coach, Glass Quarter.

WIDTH ON BACK SEAT, 44 INCHES.

35 feet Trimming Leather.
6 " Skirting Leather.
60 " Roof Leather.
10 " Railing Leather.
17 ℔s. Harness Leather.
14 yards Body Cloth.
$\frac{1}{2}$ " Plush.
$6\frac{1}{4}$ " Head Lining.
3 " Doeskin
6 " Cotton.
2 " Burlaps.
$1\frac{1}{4}$ " Cambric.
$1\frac{1}{2}$ " Enam. Cloth.
28 " Broad Lace.
110 " Narrow Lace.
2 " Oil Carpet.
3 " Carpet.
5 " Buckram.
$5\frac{1}{2}$ " Curtain Silk.
33 ℔s. Curled Hair.
6 " Wadding.
3 gross Tufts.
$1\frac{1}{8}$ " Nails.
$\frac{1}{2}$ " Screws, assorted.
5 papers Tacks.
6 yards Cord and Twine.
1 ball Thread.
4 large Tassels.
4 Spring Barrels.

5 feet Molding.
2 spools Silk.
1 Bell Pull.
1 Bell.
4 Glass.
1 Speaking Tube.
2 pairs Glass String Holders.
1 Card Case.
1 pair Lamps.
6 ℔s. Paste.
10 Buckles and Billets.
4 large Buckles.
1 pair Cross Straps.
2 Silver Buckles.
1 Back Slide.
1 pair Slides.
$1\frac{1}{2}$ yards Webbing.
12 Springs.
2 yards Carpet Fringe.
4 Pressed Loops.
1 pair Pole Straps.
2 pairs Triggers.
1 " Frogs.
1 Whip Socket.
1 pair Pull Handles.
1 " Inside Handles.
1 Squab Looking Glass and Frame.

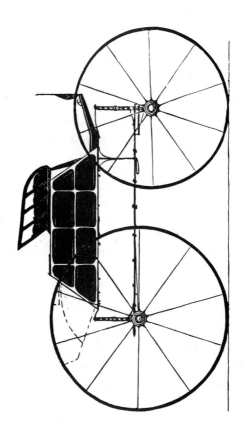

DOG CART.

TABLE NO. 35.

Material for Trimming Dog Cart.

WIDTH ON SEAT, 36 INCHES.

40 feet Colored, or 5 Goat-skins.	$\frac{1}{2}$ gross Buttons.
	$\frac{1}{2}$ " Nails.
6 feet Hard Splits.	$\frac{1}{4}$ " Screws.
4 " Soft "	2 Knobs.
7 " Railing.	$\frac{1}{2}$ ℔. Tacks.
12 " Grain Dash.	$\frac{1}{4}$ " Cord and Twine.
2$\frac{1}{4}$ yards Cambric.	1 oz. Thread.
1$\frac{1}{4}$ " Enameled Cloth.	$\frac{1}{8}$ oz. Silk.
2$\frac{1}{8}$ " Rubber.	4 ℔s. Paste.
1$\frac{5}{8}$ " Oil Carpet.	4 Buckles and Billets.
1$\frac{3}{4}$ " Velvet Carpet.	4 Silver Buckles.
$\frac{1}{2}$ " Buckram.	$\frac{1}{4}$ ℔. Risers.
6 ℔s. Curled Hair.	2 pair Shaft Straps.
4 " Pig Hair.	1 " Cushion Straps.
5 " Moss.	1 Whip Socket.

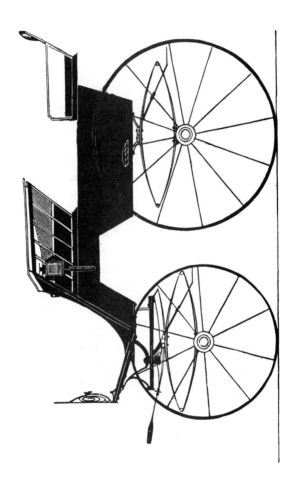

T CART.

TABLE NO. 36.

Material for Trimming T Cart.

WIDTH ON SEAT, 35 INCHES.

28 feet Trim'g Leather.

22 " Grain Dash.

2½ " Railing Leather.

6 " Valance Leather.

2½ " Skirting Leather.

6 " Calfskin Leather.

2¾ ℔s. Harness Leather.

1¼ " Breeching Leath'r.

4 " Best White Hair.

10 " Best Gray Hair.

1 " Seaming Cord.

3 " Paste.

2 1¼-in. Pole Strap Buckles.

6 Pressed Loops.

4 papers Tacks.

⅓ spool Machine Silk.

3 Apron Fasteners.

4 Covered Buckles (⅞-in.)

1 oz. Black Thread.

1½ " Harness Thread.

4¼ yards Body Cloth.

1½ " Russian Sheet'g.

4 " Muslin.

1½ " Enameled Duck.

2 " Wilton Carpet.

1 " Oil Carpet.

¼ " Kersey.

1¾ " Lining Cloth (apron).

3 yards Lace Webbing.

1 Whip Socket.

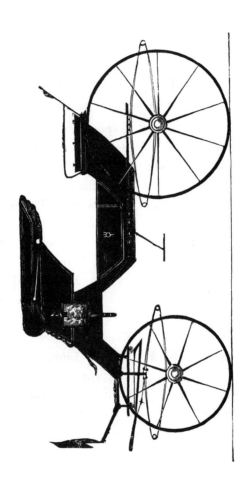

DRIVING PHAETON.

TABLE NO. 37.

Material for Trimming Driving or Mail Phaeton.

WIDTH ON SEAT, 37 INCHES; SPREAD OF TOP, 46 INCHES;
3 BOWS.

75 feet Top Leather.	1 lb. Cord and Twine.
24 " Jap. Trimming.	$\frac{1}{4}$ " Thread.
50 " Colored leather, or	7 feet Molding.
4 yds. Body Cloth.	3 Bows.
9 feet Hard Splits.	4 each Joints and Props.
3 " Railing.	4 Rivets and 8 Nuts.
19 " Grain Dash.	1 set Slat Irons.
$4\frac{3}{4}$ yards Head Lining.	4 lbs. Paste.
3 " Cotton.	8 each Buckles and Billets.
2 " Burlaps.	4 yards Webbing.
$1\frac{1}{2}$ " Enam. Cloth.	8 Springs.
2 " Oil Carpet.	8 Loops.
2 " Velvet Carpet.	1 Back Light.
9 lbs. Curled Hair.	$1\frac{1}{2}$ sheets Straw Board.
2 " Pig Hair.	4 Cushion Straps.
$2\frac{1}{2}$ " Wadding.	2 Roll-Up Straps.
4 doz. Tufts.	3 Dash Straps.
2 gross Nails.	2 Lamps.
$\frac{1}{4}$ " Screws.	1 pair Door Handles.
1 dozen Knobs.	4 Dash Hooks.
3 papers Tacks.	1 Whip Socket.

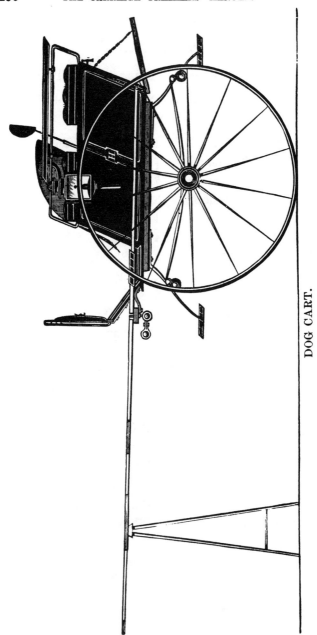

DOG CART.

TABLE NO. 38.

Material for Trimming Dog Cart.

TWO-WHEELER; WIDTH ON SEAT, 35 INCHES.

3 feet Jap. Trimming.	2½ gross Buttons.
20 " Hard and Soft Splits.	8 Screws.
	2 Knobs.
7 " Railing.	½ ℔. Tacks.
1⅜ yards Body Cloth.	⅛ ℔. Cord and Twine.
3 " Cotton.	1 oz. Thread.
1 " Enam. Cloth.	1½ ℔s. Paste.
2 " Rubber.	2 Buckles.
1¼ " Oil Carpet.	2 Silver Buckles.
1¼ " Velvet Carpet.	3 " Dash Hooks.
1½ " Buckram.	1 pair Shaft Straps.
5 ℔s. Curled Hair.	1 " Cushion Straps.
3 " Pig Hair.	1 " Apron Straps.
½ " Wadding.	3 Dash Straps.

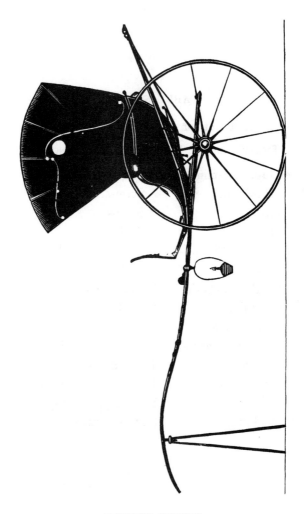

BOSTON CHAISE.

TABLE NO. 39.

Material for Trimming Boston Chaise.

SPREAD OF TOP, 40 INCHES; 5 BOWS.

80 feet Top Leather.	4 each Joints and Props.
3 " Jap. Trimming.	4 Rivets and 6 Nuts.
15 " Railing.	2 Glass.
18 " Grain Dash.	1 set Slat Irons.
3 ℔s. Harness.	1 quart Paste.
3 yards Body Cloth.	2 Brace Buckles.
4¾ " Head Lining.	8 cov'd Buckles.
4¾ " Cambric or Mus.	6 Japanned Buckles.
1½ " Enameled Cloth.	1 Back Light.
2½ " Rubber for Ap'n.	5½ yards Webbing.
1 " Oil Carpet.	10 Springs.
¾ " Velvet Carpet.	4 Pressed Loops.
2 " Buckram.	1 pair Back Stays.
11 ℔s. Curled Hair.	2 Side Stays.
3 " Pig Hair.	1 pair Safety Straps.
80 Buttons	Whip Socket and Clips.
1 gross Nails.	4 Apron Hooks and Rings.
1 " Screws, assorted.	1½ Spools Machine Silk.
10 Knobs.	1 Skein Thread.
4 papers Tacks.	1 Ball Thread.
10 yds seaming Cord and	1 Rein Hook
Twine.	1 pair Shaft Straps.
¼ ℔. Thread.	1 " Hanging Straps.
5 feet Molding.	1 " Apron Straps.
5 Bows.	3 Dash Straps.

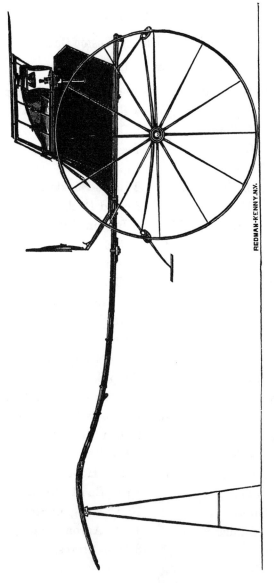

STANHOPE TWO-WHEELER.

REDMAN-KENNY, N.Y.

TABLE NO. 40.

Material for Trimming Two-Wheel Stanhope.

WIDTH ON SEAT, 38 INCHES.

21 ft. Grain Dash Leather. 2 Knobs.

1½ ℔s. Harness Leather. 1½ papers Tacks.

3 yards Body Cloth. ½ ℔s. Cord and Twine.

2 " Cotton Bats. 1 oz. Thread.

3 " Muslin. 2 oz. Sewing Silk.

¾ " Enameled Duck. 2 ℔s. Paste.

1¾ " Oil Carpet. 2 Covered Buckles.

1 " Velvet Carpet. 2 yards Webbing.

9 ℔s. Curled Hair. 1 pair Cushion Straps.

2 doz. Covered Buttons. 1 Whip Socket.

4 " Covered Nails. 1 pair Lamps.

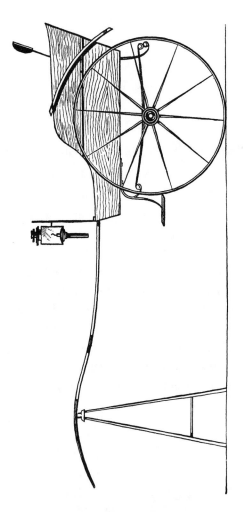

VILLAGE CART.

TABLE NO. 41.

Material for Trimming Village Cart.

WIDTH ON SEAT, 34 INCHES.

2 feet Jap. Trimming.

10 " Hard Splits.

1¼ yards Body Cloth.

3½ " Cotton.

⅝ " Enameled Cloth.

1⅞ " Rubber.

1¼ " Oil Carpet.

1⅜ " Velvet Carpet.

½ " Buckram.

2 ℔s. Curled Hair.

6 " Pig Hair.

2 " Moss.

½ " Wadding.

42 Buttons.

½ gross Nails.

10 Screws.

2 Knobs.

1 paper Tacks.

¼ lb. Cord and Twine.

½ oz. Thread.

2 ℔s. Paste.

2 Buckles and Billets.

2 Silver Buckles.

1 Back.

1 pair Cushion Straps.

1 " Shaft Straps.

1 " Apron Straps.

1 set Dash Straps.

1 Whip Socket.

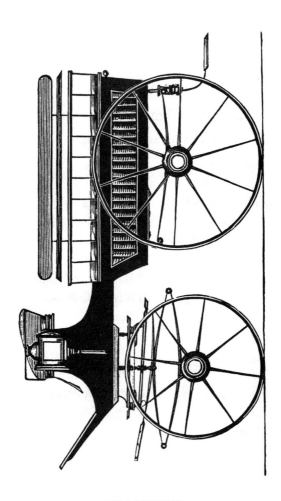

WAGONETTE.

TABLE NO. 42.

Material for Trimming Extension-Top Wagonette.

WIDTH ON BACK SEAT, 36 INCHES; SPREAD OF TOP, 70
INCHES; 4 BOWS.

86 feet Top Leather.	24 Knobs.
12 " Hard Splits.	$1\frac{1}{2}$ lbs. Tacks.
14 " Soft Splits.	$\frac{1}{2}$ " Cord and Twine.
10 " Railing.	1 oz. Thread.
$1\frac{1}{4}$ yards Mole Skin.	10 feet Molding.
$3\frac{1}{2}$ " Body Cloth.	4 Bows.
$6\frac{1}{4}$ " Head Lining.	6 Joints and 6 Props.
5 " Cotton.	6 Rivets and 10 Nuts.
$3\frac{3}{4}$ " Burlaps.	1 set Slat Irons.
6 " Rubber.	4 lbs. Paste.
$6\frac{1}{2}$ " Broad Lace.	6 Buckles and Billets.
39 " Narrow Lace.	3 Backs.
2 " Oil Carpet.	6 yards Webbing.
$2\frac{1}{8}$ " Velvet Carpet.	12 pressed Loops.
2 " Buckram.	1 Back Light.
1 Handle.	2 Side Lights.
5 lbs. Curled Hair.	2 sheets Straw Board.
10 " Pig Hair.	$\frac{1}{4}$ lb. Risers.
2 " Excelsior.	1 pair Curtain Straps.
2 " Wadding.	1 " Roll-up Straps.
$9\frac{1}{2}$ dozen Buttons.	1 " Apron Straps.
2 " Nails.	1 " Evener Straps.
$\frac{3}{4}$ " Screws, assorted.	1 Whip Socket.

For Table of Materials for Trimming a Wagonette
without top, see page 162.

JUMP SEAT.

TABLE NO. 43.

Material for Trimming Jump Seat, Half Top.

WIDTH ON BACK SEAT, 34 INCHES, SPREAD OF TOP, 43 INCHES; 4 BOWS

67 feet Top Leather.	28 Knobs.
5 " Jap. Trimming.	1½ ℔s. Tacks.
2 " Hard Splits.	½ " Cord and Twine.
7 " Soft Splits.	½ oz. Thread.
9 " Railing.	4 Bows.
3 " Grain Dash.	4 Joints.
2½ yards Body Cloth.	4 Props.
4¼ " Head Lining.	4 Rivets.
3 " Cotton.	8 Nuts.
2 " Burlaps.	1 set Slat Irons.
1½ " Cambric.	4 ℔s. Paste.
1 " Enameled Cloth.	6 Buckles and Billets.
2¼ " Rubber.	4 yards Webbing.
1⅜ " Oil Carpet.	6 Pressed Loops.
1⅜ " Velvet Carpet.	1 Back Light.
1 " Buckram.	½ sheet Straw Board.
9 ℔s. Curled Hair.	¼ ℔. Risers.
8 " Pig Hair.	2 Check Straps.
1½ " Moss.	2 Safety Straps.
1 " Wadding.	3 Roll-up Straps.
7 dozen Buttons.	3 Apron Straps.
1 gross Nails, Jap.	2 Shaft Straps.
½ " Screws, assorted.	1 Whip Socket.

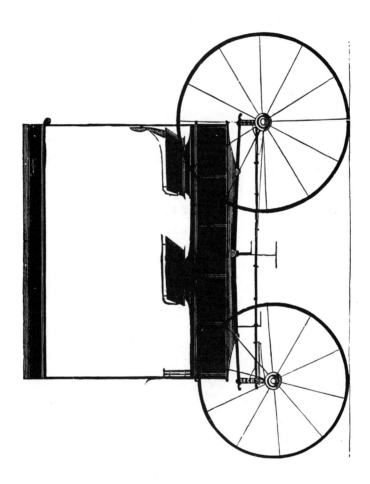

DEPOT WAGON.

TABLE NO. 44.

Material for Trimming Depot Wagon.

WIDTH ON SEAT, 33 INCHES; SPREAD OF TOP, 66 INCHES;
4 POSTS; STANDING TOP.

3 feet Jap. Trimming.	$\frac{1}{2}$ gross Screws.
17 " Hard Splits.	4 dozen Knobs.
17 " Soft Splits.	1 lb. Tacks.
$2\frac{3}{4}$ yards Body Cloth.	$\frac{1}{4}$ " Cord and Twine.
2 " Head Lining	1 oz. Thread.
5 " Cotton.	3 lbs. Paste.
2 " Burlaps.	6 Buckles and Billets.
1 " Cambric.	2 Backs.
2 " Enameled Cloth.	3 Back Lights.
$8\frac{1}{4}$ " Rubber.	6 Side Lights.
$1\frac{5}{8}$ " Oil Carpet.	$\frac{1}{2}$ sheet Straw Board.
$1\frac{7}{8}$ " Velvet Carpet.	$\frac{1}{4}$ lb. Risers.
$\frac{1}{2}$ " Buckram.	12 Curtain Straps.
2 lbs. Curled Hair.	2 Apron Straps.
14 " Pig Hair.	4 Flap Straps.
4 " Wadding.	2 Cushion Straps.
$5\frac{1}{2}$ dozen Buttons.	2 Safety Straps.
1 gross Nails.	2 Check Straps.

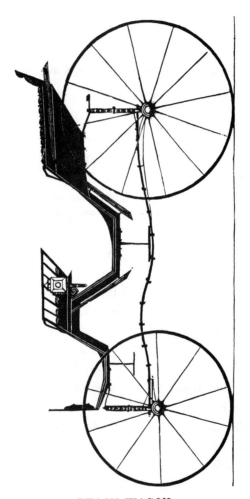

BEACH WAGON.

TABLE NO. 45.

Material for Trimming No-Top Beach Wagon.

WIDTH ON SEAT, 34 INCHES.

3 feet Jap. Trimming.	104 Buttons.
4 " Hard Splits.	1 gross Nails.
7 " Soft Splits.	50 Screws.
4½ " Railing.	2 Knobs.
3¾ yards Body Cloth.	1 ℔. Tacks.
4 " Cotton.	¼ " Cord and Twine.
½ " Burlaps.	1-16 ℔. Thread.
2 " Cambric.	2 lbs. Paste.
1½ " Enam. Cloth.	4 Buckles and Billets.
2 " Rubber.	½ sheet straw Board.
2⅛ " Oil Carpet.	¼ ℔. Risers.
2¼ " Velvet Carpet.	1 pair Dash Straps.
½ " Buckram.	1 " Shaft Straps.
1 Whip Socket.	12 Curtain straps.
5 ℔s. Curled Hair.	1 pair Safety Straps.
6 " Pig Hair.	2 Check Straps.
1 " Wadding.	

PORTLAND SLEIGH.

RUSSO-CANADIAN SLEIGH.

TABLE NO. 46.
Material for Trimming Portland Sleigh.
WIDTH ON SEAT, 30 INCHES.

2½ yards Plush.	1 ℔. Moss.
1 " Enam. Cloth.	3½ dozen Buttons.
1 ℔. Harness Leather.	2 " Nails.
2½ yards Broad Lace.	3 papers Tacks.
8 " Narrow Lace.	¼ ℔. Cord and Twine.
1 " Velvet Carpet.	3 oz. Thread.
2 " Buckram.	1 pint Paste.
1½ ℔s. Curled Hair.	1 Whip Socket.

TABLE NO. 47.
Material for Trimming Russo-Canadian Sleigh.
WIDTH ON SEAT, 29 INCHES.

5½ lbs. Harness Leather.	4 lbs. Pig Hair.
12 feet Grain Dash.	6 yards Wadding.
4 yards Body Cloth.	80 Buttons or Tufts.
2 " Burlaps.	27 yards Cord and Twine.
1 " Enam Drill.	2 lbs. Paste.
5 " Broad Lace.	4 yards Muslin.
48 " Narrow Lace.	1½ " Felt.
2½ " Velvet Carpet.	1 Whip Socket.
8 lbs. Curled Hair.	

WESTERN NEW YORK CUTTER.

ALBANY CUTTER.

TABLE NO. 48.

Material for Trimming New York Cutter.

WIDTH ON SEAT, 27 INCHES.

1 lb. Harness Leather.	¾ yards Velvet Carpet.
1 foot Flap.	1½ lbs. Curled Hair.
7 " Grain Dash.	5 " Pig Hair.
3 yards Plush.	50 Covered Buttons.
1 " Enam. Drill.	1 Whip Socket.

TABLE NO. 49.

Material for Trimming Albany Cutter.

WIDTH ON SEAT, 38 INCHES.

7 feet Soft Russet Lea'r.	2 ℔s. Moss.
1¾ yards Body Cloth.	6 dozen Buttons.
3 " Cotton.	1 " Nails.
¾ " Enam. Cloth.	3 papers Tacks.
1½ " Broad Lace.	¼ lb. Cord and Twine.
19 " Narrow Lace.	3 oz. Thread.
2½ " Velvet Carpet.	1 pint Paste.
2 " Buckram.	1 pair Safety Straps.
2 lbs. Curled Hair.	1 Whip Socket.

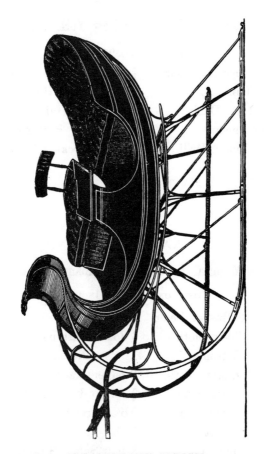

ALBANY PONY SLEIGH.

TABLE NO. 50.

Material for Trimming Albany Pony Sleigh.

WIDTH ON SEAT, 3 FEET 2 INCHES.

7 feet Dash Leather.	$3\frac{1}{2}$ lbs. Moss.
$3\frac{1}{4}$ yards Body Cloth.	8 dozen Buttons.
4 " Cotton.	3 papers Nails.
1 " Enam. Cloth.	4 " Tacks.
$5\frac{1}{2}$ " Broad Lace.	$\frac{1}{4}$ lb. Cord and Twine.
29 " Narrow Lace.	3 oz. Thread.
$6\frac{1}{2}$ " Velvet Carpet.	1 quart Paste.
3 " Buckram.	2 Cushion Straps.
3 lbs. Curled Hair.	1 Whip Socket.

ALBANY SIX-SEAT SLEIGH.

THE ORIGINAL "PORTLAND"—Built in 1817.

TABLE NO. 51.

Material for Trimming Albany Six-Seat Sleigh, no Top.

WIDTH ON SEAT, 3 FEET 5 INCHES.

4½ feet Jap. Trim. Leather.   7 lbs. Moss.

9 " Russet for Wings.   12 dozen Buttons.

9 " Railing.   2 papers Nails.

4½ " Body Cloth.   4 " Tacks.

5 " Cotton.   ½ lb. Cord and Twine.

1¾ " Enam. Cloth.   3 skeins Thread.

11 " Broad Lace.   2 quarts Paste.

34 " Narrow Lace.   2 Cushion Straps.

7 " Velvet Carpet.   1 pair Safety Straps.

1½ " Buckram.   1 Whip Socket.

5½ lbs. Curled Hair.

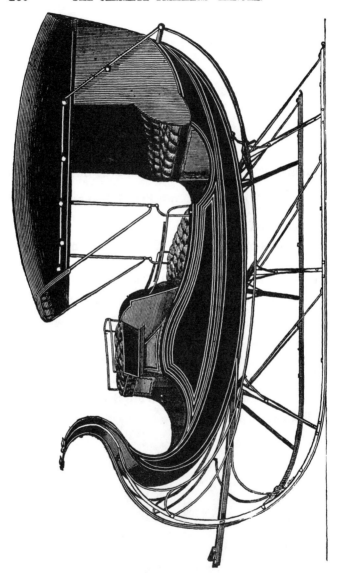

ALBANY SIX-SEAT SLEIGH.

TABLE NO. 52.

Material for Trimming Albany Six-Seat Sleigh.

WIDTH ON BACK SEAT, 3 FEET 5 INCHES; SPREAD OF TOP,
5 FEET 10 INCHES; 6 BOWS.

115 feet Top Leather.	2 papers Nails.
4½ " Jap. Trimming.	3½ dozen Knobs.
9 " Soft Russet for Wings.	4 papers Tacks.
	¼ lb. Cord and Twine.
9 feet Railing.	4 skeins Thread.
8 " Grain Dash.	12½ feet Molding.
4½ yards Body Cloth.	6 Bows.
6½ " Head Lining.	6 Joints and Props.
6 " Cotton.	10 Rivets and Nuts.
5 " Burlaps.	1 set Slat Irons.
5 " Cambric.	½ gallon Paste.
1¾ " Enam. Cloth.	8 Buckles and Billets.
1¾ " Rubber.	4 yards Webbing.
11 " Broad Lace.	16 Pressed Loops.
39 " Narrow Lace.	2 Back Lights.
7 " Velvet Carpet.	2 Side Lights.
4½ " Buckram.	3 Back Curtain Straps.
6 lbs. Curled Hair.	4 pairs Curtain Straps.
7 " Moss.	1 pair Safety Straps.
12 dozen Buttons.	1 Whip Socket.

TABLE NO. 53.

Material for Trimming Wagonette.

WIDTH ON BACK SEAT, 36 INCHES; NO TOP.

5 feet Jap. Trim. Leather.	6 lbs. Moss.
10 " Hard Splits.	2 " Wadding.
15 " Soft Splits.	8 dozen Buttons.
4 " Railing.	$\frac{1}{2}$ gross Nails.
3$\frac{1}{2}$ yards Body Cloth.	$\frac{1}{4}$ " Screws.
5 " Cotton	2 Knobs.
1$\frac{1}{2}$ " Burlaps.	1 lb. Tacks.
2 " Cambric.	$\frac{1}{4}$ " Cord and Twine
1$\frac{1}{2}$ " Enam. Cloth.	1 oz. Thread.
2$\frac{1}{4}$ " Rubber.	12 feet Molding.
5 " Broad Lace.	3 lbs. Paste.
24 " Narrow Lace	1 Silver Handle.
2 " Oil Carpet.	3 Backs.
2 " Velvet Carpet.	1 sheet Straw Board.
1 " Buckram.	$\frac{1}{8}$ lb. Risers.
1 Whip Socket.	1 pair Cushion Straps.
6 lbs. Curled Hair.	3 " Dash Straps.
8 " Pig Hair.	

CHAPTER III.

TECHNICS OF TRIMMING.

GENERAL PRINCIPLES AND CONDITIONS—CUTTING AND TUFT-
ING CUSHIONS AND SQUABS—CHARACTERISTICS OF GOOD
WORK.

Before entering into a detailed description of methods adopted by any one class of workmen, the subject
of carriage trimming will be treated in a general
light, the workman's attention being directed to the
rules or principles, applicable in all cases, whether the
work be of the plainest or most elaborate de-cription.
A thorough knowledge of the rudiments prepares the
trimmer for the work before him, and by the confidence
which this knowledge imparts, he is ·prepared to give
full scope to his genius and skill, enabling him, by continued practice, to reach the highest standpoint of his
profession. These principles are to the trimmer what
the alphabet is to the school-boy, and to attempt to
teach how to trim, by giving directions for specific
styles, without first imparting a primary knowledge of
the art, would be like teaching a child to read before
he knew his letters.

Neither should the trimmer confine himself to the
mere mechanics of his profession. A thorough knowl-

edge of materials, their characteristics, adaptability to specific uses, grade and quality are equally as important as the mechanical knowledge. A study of colors, the effects produced by certain shades when given certain forms, harmony of the whole when grouped, inside ornaments and artistic designs, are all absolutely necessary if the workman aspires to be more than a mere automaton. The artistic studies require a high grade of talent, and necessitate culture from other sources than can be gathered from books, though much that is embodied in this manual would be found useful in that direction.

With carriage trimming, as with all other mechanical arts, success depends upon a fixed primary course of action, to be followed in all cases. Without this it is impossible to work with any degree of uniformity or accuracy. Cushions, squabs and other similarly constructed articles are made up on flat foundations, with fullness upon the top or face sides, the intervening space being filled with an elastic material, which supports the top, gives and preserves the required fullness, and makes an easy seat or rest for the occupant of the carriage. To secure the best results from the use of this elastic material, it is important that the different pieces, such as bottom, facings, linings and tops be so cut and secured as to give the result required; the fullness must be in the top; it is, therefore, important that the exact amount required be determined before cutting or making up; it will not do to leave this matter to chance, if the work is to be executed in an artis-

tic or skillful manner, or of a quality to secure durability in form as well as wear.

In making a cushion, the first act of the trimmer is
to determine the size of the various pieces to be used,
commencing with the bottom ; it must be cut to the
exact size and shape of the seat bottom, but enough
larger than the actual measurement to provide for
wastage from seams in making up ; the under-top, or
false top, as it is sometimes called, must be cut to the
size of the cushion on the top line of the facings, and
the top proper to such a size as will give the required
fullness ; this can be accurately determined ; to do so,
however, the trimmer must first decide on the general
character of the cushion ; if a flat top is desired the
marginal fullness alone is to be provided for ; if tufted,
allowance must be made for each space between the
tufts and for the margins. An examination of fig. 4 will
illustrate to the trimmer the importance of ascertaining
just the fullness required before cutting stock. This
diagram, while giving an extreme illustration of the
point involved, serves the purpose better than it would
were it simply drawn to the exact proportions. In the
illustration the curved lines all come into contact with
the parallel base line. In a cushion the top and under-top are not drawn closely together unless the tufting strings are drawn very tight ; the trimmer must,
therefore, make the necessary allowance for this space.

Referring to fig. 4, A is the line of the under-top,
which must be flat ; B, the top line of the cushion, with
1 inch fullness between tufts ; C, the top line with $1\frac{1}{2}$

inches fullness ; D, 2 inches fullness.   Supposing the
space between H and E to be four inches, the curves a b
and c represent the length of the material between tufts
to give the fullness required ; the length on line a, if the
base is 4 inches long, is $4\frac{5}{8}$ inches, on line b $5\frac{1}{4}$ inches,

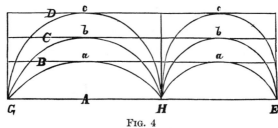

FIG. 4

on line c $6\frac{1}{3}$ inches.   To make up a cushion with four
tufts and six spaces in length, the top must be cut $3\frac{3}{4}$
inches longer than the under-top ; if the width requires
three rows of tufts and four spaces the cloth must be
cut $2\frac{1}{2}$ inches wider than the under-top.   The space
between H and G represents 5 inches ; on this line a is
$5\frac{1}{2}$ inches long, b 6 inches long, c $6\frac{3}{4}$ inches long.   By
following the principle laid down, the trimmer can de-
termine in a few moments the exact amount of fullness
necessary to secure any desired rise to a cushion or
squab, of a square, diamond or other pattern.

Having determined the exact size of the top by
measurement, and made the necessary allowance for
seaming, cut to the form shown by fig. 5, the straight
lines of which represent the under-top, and the curved
lines the form given to the outer lines of the top in order to secure the required fullness, the total fullness
being equally divided between the respective sides and

ends. If a perfectly flat top is desired, cut the top as shown by fig. 6 ; this gives fullness at the corners ; the corner curves begin at the first row of tufts.

In making up cushions the minor details of laying out the forms, etc., constitute the special features. A perfect cushion has a bottom, facings, false top, top and top lining ; in cheap grades the top lining, and in some cases the false top is omitted. The quality of material used, and the character of the work when completed, are the points that govern the trimmer in his operations.

The trimmer's first step is to ascertain the exact size of the cushion bottom, then the flare of seat ends and back ; to do this where the bottom of the seat is not square, make a paper pattern by laying a piece of manilla paper on the seat bottom, and with a sinker mark by tracing around in the corners the exact form of the

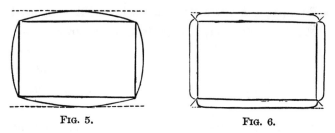

FIG. 5.   FIG. 6.

bottom ; cut out the pattern, allowing enough for seams. To get the bevel of the corners lay a piece of heavy paper against the panel, with the straight edge resting on the seat frame, and with a sinker press the paper into the corner formed by the angles of the seat ends and back ; cut off to the line made by the sinker and the angle will be correct.

In cutting facings, care must be taken to cut to such a width that all, whether flared or straight, will, when in their proper position, be of equal hight, no matter what their angle ; be governed, therefore, by the front facing; cut it to the proper width, and mark the angle that represents the flare of the ends ; the length of the angle line will determine the width of the ends ; when the back of the seat flares more or less than the ends, obtain the width by measuring the angle line on the end facing at the back corner.

If the facings are pasted up for the front use buckram for the body and paste heavy muslin on one side and cambric on the other ; cut these one-half inch wider than the buckram, and allow the edges to project over each edge of the buckram one-quarter of an inch to sew to when joining. For the ends use heavy enamel duck, and paste up with muslin on the unglazed side ; in pasting lay the pasted pieces straight and tack them down ; if this is done they will not draw out of shape while drying. If the facings are made of skirting leather, paste up with muslin on the unfinished side.

In making squabs, whether for backs or quarters, the trimmer makes a cushion, the whole thickness of which is made up by the fullness in the top, there being no facings as with a seat cushion. The first point is to secure the exact shape and size of the squab; this can be ascertained in the same manner as that adopted in obtaining the size of the seat bottom. The parts used are foundation, top and top lining; the foundation can be made of buckram, pasted up with muslin on both sides; or of heavy manilla card paper, pasted up with muslin in the same manner ; it should be cut larger than the space it is to fill, and trimmed to the required size after it is dry ; the fullness of the top can be determined in the same manner as that of the cushions, being governed entirely by the fullness desired and the number of tufts used.

Backs, when springs are used, are made up to the desired form, the springs being properly bridled to the foundation and covered with Russia canvass; tow or moss is used between and around the springs to prevent their cutting through the cover, and to obviate the noise caused by the spring wires coming in contact with each other.

The top or outside covering is made up on a back of muslin, not pasted, the muslin being stretched on a frame and the fullness given to the cloth or leather top, the squab tufted and completed on the frame except on the top edge, which is tacked to the back rail and stuffed at the time of tacking. Special directions for the work in detail will be found elsewhere.

The trimmer, to perform his work artistically, must not aim at ornate designs, or such as do not correspond with the vehicle to be trimmed, or the materials used. The points to be attained are practicability, perfect adaptation, and correct taste in execution, and these without the sacrifice of comfort or durability. Carriages, in which the trimming is much exposed, should not be trimmed with materials that are easily affected by wet or sun, nor should it be of a character to make the cleaning a difficult matter. Seats not covered with tops should be trimmed with plain untufted cushions, and plain falls. Close carriages may be trimmed with more showy materials and in a more elaborate manner, but the trimmings around window and door lights should be of a character not easily affected by the sun's rays.

Cushions and squabs appear much richer when made up soft with tops nearly flat and tufted in not less than six-inch squares than with full four-inch biscuit tops; when made this way there are no folds at the tufts or corners, and the cushions are soft and elastic; the tufts not being sunken but little below the surface, make it much more easy to clean than when sunken low. The production of a soft elastic cushion and squab calls for the highest grade of skill, and the trimmer who is able to select colors and designs which harmonize with the form and character of the vehicle, and to give the touch of an artist to all the minor details, producing a luxurious and comfortable lining for a carriage, may claim a high position as an artist, and if to these qualities he is able to add a high grade of mechanical skill he honors and is honored by his profession.

CHAPTER IV.

SETTING TOPS.

Though the setting of carriage tops is not a part of
the trimmer's work, it is so closely identified therewith
that the trimmer should be capable of directing the
operation, even if he does not perform the work. The
trimming shop alone bears all the odium of a badly-
set top, without the power to correct the fault, unless
the trimmer controls the operation.

There are various methods of top setting, some based
upon correct rules, others upon the whims or peculiar
views of the operator. The plan given in this chapter is one of the best; other plans will be given in
subsequent chapters. The one primary rule that
should never be ignored, no matter what method is followed, is, first of all, to prepare an accurate drawing
of the body and top, full size, as a guide for subsequent operations. Without such a drawing the proportions, pitch and sweep of the top cannot be deter-

mined correctly, and if a perfect top is set without this
guide it is the result of chance.

After having perfected such a drawing, the trimmer
can follow whatever plan best suits his views, providing that in the end the bows are placed in the same
position as that determined by the full drawing. The
leveling of the body must not be overlooked, and when
it is placed upon the trustles it must occupy the same
position that it will when hung upon the carriage part;
this must be ascertained before the body is removed
from the carriage part. A simple method is to provide
a board about six inches wide with one edge perfectly
straight ; attach to it in the center a strip two feet long
and six inches wide, set at right angles with the straight
edge ; this should be lapped in so that faces of the upright and the main piece are flush ; to the upper end of
the upright attach a cord ; to the other end of the cord
attach a heavy plumb bob ; before the body leaves
this is removed from the carriage ; lay the long strip
lengthwise of the body with the ends resting upon the
highest points back and front, marking these so as to
know just where to place the board when leveling in
the trimming shop ; then mark on the side of the board
the position of the line and bob ; if the body is placed
upon the trustles so that the line hangs just as it did
before the body leaves the carriage part, the trimmer
will have no trouble in setting his top correctly.

Fig. 7 represents a square-box buggy, body and top,
in outline, on the draft board for a four-bow top. The
body is placed in the exact position it is to occupy when

hung off on the carriage part. In laying out draw the
bottom line of the body A one-quarter of an inch higher
in front than behind, and square the outline for the top
from this line, then measure up from the top of the seat
frame forty-four inches, and strike top parallel line B.
The rake of the top must next be considered. Where

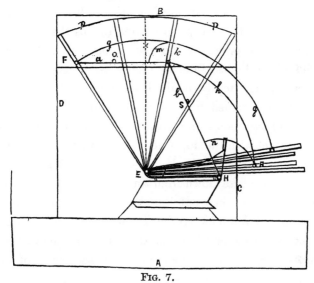

FIG. 7.

the body is 4 feet 1 inch to 4 feet 2 inches long, the rake
for a four bow top should not be less than $3\frac{1}{2}$ inches;
this will give location for the back perpendicular line C;
if the top is full size, 45 inches, measure off 27 inches
from line C for the actual center of the top, and strike
the dotted line X, from which point measure off 27
inches and strike D. Next proceed to locate the front
prop E; its location, as to hight, depends somewhat
upon the construction of the seat end; the prop for a

four-bow top should be about $3\frac{1}{2}$ inches higher than the
back prop iron H; if the back corner is higher than the
front add whatever difference there may be to the $3\frac{1}{2}$
inches, which will give the hight of the prop E; this
space must also be governed by the style of slat iron
used; the point to be attained is a level back bow when
the top is down. Having located the front prop iron,
decide upon the sweep of the top. In this the workman
must be governed by the head room required, which
should not be less than 43 inches on dotted line X; if
a very round top is required, the increased roundness
must be obtained by raising the center bow or bows,
for nothing is more annoying than to have the hat come
in contact with the top when sitting. upright and resting against the lazy back. For a medium top, such as
shown, measure down from top line B, on back line C,
4 inches, and on front line D $5\frac{1}{4}$ inches, then, with a
string; strike top sweep line P, setting the pivotal point
so that the sweep will strike the points on the front and
back perpendicular lines and the exact center of the
top parallel line B, then with a compass space off on
the line three equal spaces, first, however, deducting
one-half the width of the front and back bows, then
strike center lines for the middle bows, and lay out the
bows full size, centering the lower ends to the center of
the prop iron.

If a three-bow top is used, be governed, in laying out
the square, by the same rules as with a four-bow top;
do not give it more than $2\frac{1}{2}$ inches rake, and reduce
the sweep to 3 inches on the back and 4 inches on the

front line. Fig. 8 shows
a three-bow top on a
seat.

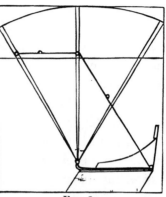

FIG. 8.

The diagram being
ready on the draft-
board, the workman can
readily obtain the exact
length of each bow; to
cut these to the required
length, without measur-
ing each bow, construct
the cutting-frame, fig. 9. This is made of two strips
of hard wood, 4 inches wide and 2 inches thick, in the
form of a square, with the stay-brace 2 inches wide.
The long arm should be 48 inches long, and the short
one about 30 inches long; glue a strip, 1 inch square
and 2 feet 1 inch long, on the long arm, and sink a
straight 24-inch rule in the long arm, 1 inch below the

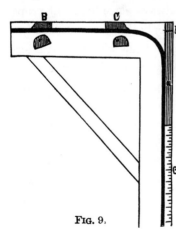

FIG. 9.

face; beyond the end of
the square strip glue on
two strips, 1 by 1½ inch-
es square and 3 inches
long at B and C on the
short arm, and place di-
rectly before them two
eccentric buttons, and
the frame is complete.

In cutting the bows,
place them on the frame
with the upright bearing

against the cleat, *a*, and the two blocks, B and C; tighten the buttons and cut off to the proper length, computing it by counting the two feet from line *b* on *a* and the requisite number of inches on the rule *c* necessary to make up the total; before removing the bow mark the face side and strike a line with a pencil across the top, using the end of block C for a guide; then turn the bow, cut off the other side, and strike a line at block C as before. By this arrangement both ends of the side pieces are necessarily cut to the same length, and the pencil marks across the top give points for obtaining the exact center, regardless of the irregularities of the bent corners. The bows may now be secured to the slats and rounded; it is, however, a good plan to put but one screw on each bow, and set the top up before finishing.

A top frame is always desirable, as by its use the utmost accuracy and uniformity can be secured. The blacksmith does not always place his front props in exactly the same position on both sides, and slat irons are not always true; defects of this kind do not interfere with setting tops correctly when a frame is used.

Fig. 10 represents a very complete top frame. A, the main post, is of ash, 6 inches wide and 2 inches thick. The base B is heavy, and not less than 1 foot wide. The forms B B are also of ash of like thickness; these are secured to the post by two heavy hinges, *b b*. Slats 1 inch wide are sawed into the forms, as shown. The bow supports A are of heavy 3-inch band-iron, notched at the top for the bows, and slotted at the lower end; these are held in place by thumb-screw bolts, with T heads, the bolt passing through the seats in the forms and bow-irons; they are easily adjusted to suit any form of top or number of bows. The bow-iron on the post is made like the others, and held in place by a bolt provided with a thumb nut; this bow-

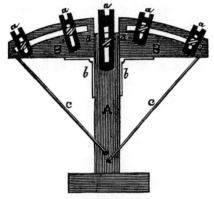

FIG. 10.

piece should be made so that it can be raised four to five inches. The form pieces are held by the two hooks *c c*; dowels should be inserted at *d d*, to prevent the sections of the form getting out of place. When not in use the securing hooks can be released, and the form sections allowed to drop down against the post; this form answers for a three, four or five-bow top. A much cheaper frame can be made by making forms B of one piece, and securing it permanently to the upright, and driving nails on the curve for the bow supports.

As soon as the top is set, screw on the top props,

and obtain the length of the joints and position of the knuckles. A great many blacksmiths depend upon the string, but the plan is a crude one, and is far from being accurate. Fig. 7, page 173, illustrates a simple and perfectly accurate method. The top props, being located on the draft-board, strike lines a and b, which represent the lower lines of the joint when set, then with a compass, with the points of the stationary arm resting in the center of the slat-iron bolt E, and the point of the loose arm set at prop iron F strike circle g. Next set the stationary point at E as before, and the movable point at prop iron K strike line h; these lines represent the line of travel described by the prop irons when the bows are falling, and locate their positions when the bows are down. To find the position of the knuckle of the front prop, set the stationary point of the compass in the center of prop iron K, and the movable point where the line g intersects the face of the bow and strike line m; then divide the space on line a, between F, and point where line m intersects line a into two equal parts, and the center will be the point for the center of the knuckle for the front joint. For the back joint set the stationary point of the compass upon the center of the prop iron H, with the movable point at R where line h terminates on the bow, and strike line n, then divide the space on line g between points K and where line n intersects line g, and the center S will be the point for the center of the knuckle for the back joint. This plan gives level joints when they are folded down, which is the only correct position. This rule works equally well for three, four or five-bow tops.

Before the bow support is removed slats should be screwed on to hold the bows in their proper place while being trimmed. Fig. 11 shows a top supported by the strap A connecting the bows, and B, the brace, which

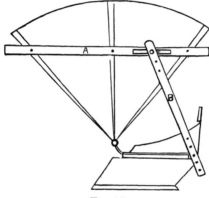

FIG. 11.

keeps the bows from falling either way. The strip a is secured by screws, care being taken to make the holes in the bows at the points where the curtain knobs are driven in. The lower end of the brace B is provided with holes, through which the prop iron on the seat can be inserted. The slat A is slotted to allow the top of the brace B being moved to adjust the brace to the exact length; a T-bolt, with a thumb nut, binds the two together.

Another plan is to fit a curve to top of the bows so as to secure them in the proper position, and to fix the

top in its proper place by means of strong cords tied
back and front.   This, however, is less secure, and
more troublesome than the plan illustrated.

CHAPTER V.

COVERING DASHES.

How to cover a dash or wing so that the leather
will not wrinkle or lose its luster, is one of the unset-
tled problems of the trimming shop. Almost every
trimmer has his theory, and all have known what it is
to meet with failure, as well as with success, and that,
too, without any apparent change in the manner of
performing the work. A method, if correctly followed,
should always produce uniform results, and if successful in one instance, should be alike successful in all,
and a failure to accomplish like results in all cases is
due to defects in the material, or is the fault of the
workman.

The primary point is the proper selection of leather;
unless care is taken in this particular, all attempts to
overcome the evil will prove failures. The best leather for the purpose is " grain dash ;" it owes its superiority solely to its being made of the outside split of
the hide, containing, therefore, the grain fiber and the

strongest part of the parallel fiber, the thin, firm portion next underneath the grain. The japan is put upon the split side, leaving the strongest and most pliant portion of the leather as a backing. Owing to the closeness of its texture, grain dash is not affected by heat or moisture as quickly as " split dash," which accounts in part for its retaining its form when on a dash or wing.

The impression prevails to a considerable extent that grain dash is tanned and finished in a different manner than splits ; this is a mistake ; the tanning and finishing is alike in all cases where the quality is the same. A heavy hide will furnish three splits ; the outside, or hair side, is finished in " grain dash " as described, and two splits finished as " split dash ;" the main split, the one next to the grain split, is generally returned to the vat and retanned to insure a perfect tannange. The only difference, therefore, in the tannage or finish of the two kinds, is such as exists in the general manner of performing the work in different factories.

The next consideration is cutting the leather. For all crooked dashes and wings the fiber should run crosswise, and as nearly as possible parallel with the frame of the dash. If cut on the bias, as shown by the dotted lines F, fig. 12, it is impossible to prevent its wrinkling after it is put on. Leather can be fitted to a hollow form much more evenly with the fiber running lengthwise than when it runs crosswise, but straight dashes or wings may be covered with the fiber running

in either direction, providing the fiber runs parallel
with the bars of the frame.

Another point to be observed is to have the leather
as nearly uniform in texture as possible ; if the flanks
or soft parts are to be used, cut the entire piece from
such parts, if possible. A dash covered with leather cut
from the flank, as shown by A, fig. 12, though it be
from the poorest part of the side, will work much bet-

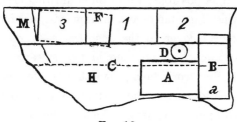

FIG. 12.

ter, and give a better result, than when covered with
a piece cut as shown by B ; in the latter, some of the
leather is from a poor part of the flank, while the other
portion is from the best portion of the side. The lower
part, a, will stretch and shrink more easily than the
upper part, and, no matter how smoothly the leather
may be put on, it will soon wrinkle and bag.

The best portion of a side is that from the back down
to the dotted line C, a strip eighteen to twenty inches
wide, it being the most uniform in texture and grain,
omitting, however, the hip knurl, D, a small piece from
four to six inches in diameter, which should never be cut
into a dash cover. The pieces 1, 2 and 3, in the order
named, are the choice pieces of a perfect side. The

shoulder flank, H, though not so firm and fine as the back pieces, if the side has been well finished, is superior to the back flank A. The neck portion, M, forward of the irregular line, is sometimes so wrinkled as to show through the enamel; when this is the case it should not be cut into a dash cover.

The leather being correctly cut, the next step is to draw it on. With some trimmers this means stretching it as much as possible; with others drawing it smooth, both having the same object in view, viz., producing a perfectly level cover to the dash frame—a result not easily accomplished, not one in twenty, even of the dashes on fine work, being smooth. Stretching, however, serves to increase rather than diminish the difficulty, as it opens the pores, and makes the leather more susceptible to moisture than when in its natural state, besides adding a new annoyance in the japan "flatting," and becoming uneven in shade. All that is necessary is to draw the leather hard enough to take out the bagging and leave it perfectly smooth when stitched.

Soft, pliant, finely japanned leather can be drawn on dry, but if it is harsh and bony, as is often the case with a middle or "main" split, owing to its not being retanned after it is split, it must be dampened a little all over; dampening a narrow strip on the edges is the worst thing that can be done, as the stretch is then all thrown on a small portion. In dampening it should be remembered that patent leather is not curried with oil and grease like harness leather; owing to this it absorbs water on the plain side so quickly that it is an easy matter to wet it to such an extent as to damage it greatly. In dampening use a large sponge; fill it with cold water and squeeze it until the water ceases to drip from it; then pass it over the leather; the fiber of the sponge will retain enough water to dampen the leather all that is necessary. Baste the leather on and stitch close to the iron bars, and in stitching be sure to pass the awl through perfectly straight; if this is not done the stitches will draw the leather and produce small wrinkles, which, in time, will spread entirely across the dash

With a view to saving time some trimmers stitch as many seams as possible on the machine, the dashes being made with loose cross bars in order that the cross seams may be stitched in this way. This will answer for common work, but for no other; a dash stitched in that way, partially by hand and partially by machine, will wrinkle, owing to the difference in tension, no matter what other precautions may be taken.

In trimming the edges the trimmer should use a very sharp knife, and, if possible, cut true enough to obviate the necessity of going over it a second time, and cut as close to the stitches as possible without endangering the strength of the stitching; take off the sharp corner with a corner tool, then black with iron black, and when dry rub with a bone slicker, and polish with a silk rag. If the leather has been cut smooth and the black is good no other coloring material is required.

CHAPTER VI.

SEAT FALLS AND BACKS.

Seat falls may properly be divided into two classes, hard and soft. The first are those made up on a foundation of hard leather, pasted buckram, duck or other firm material. The latter are made up on soft leather, heavy enameled duck, or other thick, firm, but pliant material. Hard falls are used upon nearly every class of vehicle, while soft falls are mainly confined to victorias, some styles of phaetons, and heavy close carriages. The variety of styles is very great; of the hard ones, the plain bound, the welt and the pipe are, however, the most popular. The plain-bound

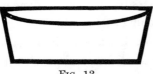

FIG. 13.

fall, fig. 13, much used for outside seats, is made up on a foundation of leather, with the cloth pasted on the flesh side. The cloth is cut large enough to allow its being turned over the ends and bottom edge ; it is pasted to the back, and, when dry, stitched by machine, thus forming a good cloth binding. When bound in this way, a crease should be made in the leather, about one-quarter of an inch from the ends and bottom, stitching in the crease or on the outer edge.

Another binding is of thin railing leather, cut wide

enough to allow it to wrap the edges of the fall, showing one-quarter of an inch on the face side, and width enough on the back to receive the stitches which secure the front edge of the binding. This strip of binding leather should be blacked on the flesh side and edges, and then pasted on the fall, the stitching being done after the paste is dry. A plain valance of patent leather, or of leather covered with cloth and bound in the same manner as the fall, is used to finish the top edge.

FIG. 14.

The welt fall is used more than any other ; it is made up in a great variety of patterns, and can be adapted to almost every kind of a vehicle. The most popular

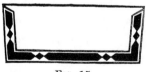

is made with blind underlays of a plain or ornamental pattern, as illustrated by fig. 14. The foundation is made up of hard leather or other firm material ; the welts are of leather or heavy felt, cut to the required shape and pasted to the body. After the paste is dry the entire surface, welts and all, is covered with good, smooth paste, and the cloth cover is pasted to the body, care being taken to rub the cover well in

FIG. 15.

around the welts, so as to preserve their exact outlines. After the paste is dry, the cloth may be stitched around the welts if desired. Welted falls are sometimes ornamented with an underlay of black patent leather; in this case a piece of railing leather is pasted to the body

FIG. 16.

of the fall, and the cloth is pasted to the body, except at the ornament; this is drawn upon the cloth, and, when the paste is dry, it is stitched in outline, after which the cloth is cut away by a sharp-pointed knife. Fig. 15 illustrates a fall with a patent leather underlay. Valances may be used if desired; they should be plain, a little stitching around the edge being all that is necessary.

When duck, buckram, or other textile fabric is used for the foundation, it should be shrunk before using; to do this cut the foundation a little larger than required, tack it to a board and moisten; allow it to remain on the board until it is dry. If treated in this

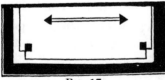

FIG. 17.

way it will not shrink or wrinkle after being made up. Pockets are sometimes placed in the fall; when this is done an extra flap is necessary, as the pocket must not be exposed. Pockets are attached in two ways; one, the outside pocket, as shown by fig. 16, made of the same material as the fall, or of morocco or enameled leather; the other, the back pocket, of leather

placed on the back of the fall, the opening being near
the top of the fall, fig. 17; the latter plan allows for a
larger pocket than the former. The flap, fig. 18, may
be made plain, and similar in pattern to the main fall,
or it may be pleated or piped; it should be made

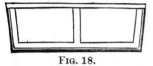

with some fullness where the
pocket to be covered is on
the outside. In all cases
where a flap is used the
body of the fall should be plain, a border welt being
all that is necessary.

FIG. 18.

The pipe fall, fig. 19, is the least popular of any, but
it is used to a limited extent on phaetons, cabriolets,
etc. The foundation is made up the same as for the
welt fall, the piping is cut to the required shape, out of
heavy enameled duck or pasted buckram. When the
latter is used the back must be covered with muslin,
the cloth cover is pasted to the plain side; the pipe is
finished flat, and when completed the edges are cat-

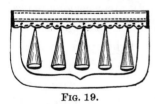

stitched together. They are
then placed upon the fall
and securely fastened at the
top and bottom, and, if very
long, in the middle; hoop
iron is sometimes used to
maintain the form of the bottom.

FIG. 19.

Welted falls are sometimes made up on soft leather,
enameled cloth or heavy duck. When blind welts are
used they are cut out of heavy felt, or other thick, pliant material, pasted to the body in the same way as

with hard falls.   The cloth face is pasted to the body, but not to the top, of the welts ; the cloth should be stitched to the body close to the edges of the welts. The pleated fall, fig. 20, however, is the principal soft fall.   It is made of heavy duck, covered on the back

FIG. 20.

with black muslin, and on the face with cloth.   The coach lace is stitched to the body, and the plaits laid after the stitching is completed.   When the plaits are laid so that the folds on the back come together they are cat-stitched with heavy thread to hold them in place when they do not meet; each fold is loosely sewed together with strong thread.

Occasionally soft falls are finished with piping in place of plaits.   When this is the case the body is made in the same manner as for plaits, but no longer than the seat front, the piping being sewed on.   The piping is made of heavy duck.

Quilted and corded falls, fig. 21, are occasionally used

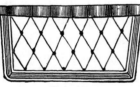

FIG. 21.

on ladies' phaetons and similar light park vehicles. They are made up on a firm foundation, with welted edges.   When quilted, a thin layer of curled hair, or a single layer of cotton is laid upon the body, filling the space between the welts, the cloth laid on loosely over the cotton or hair; after tufting or quilting by machine the edges are pasted to the welts and back, and, when dry stitched. The vallance is made by laying a strip of cotton bat on a leather foundation, covering it with cloth and stitching across at intervals of three or four inches and around the edges. A corded fall is made by pasting the cloth to the back, and, when dry, stretching cords across the face and securing the crossings by tufts or buttons, backed with muslin, faced with cloth and trimmed with lace, sewed on in the same manner as in the body. The piping, whether straight or conical, is then formed by being cut to the required width and shape, the edges cat-stitched together and then secured to the body in the proper place. When soft leather is used in place of cloth, black muslin pasted on the back, the lace is pasted on, and, when dry, stitched; otherwise the operation of making is the same as when cloth is used. Falls are abandoned on coupes, broughams and other heavy vehicles, a squabbed or welled piece about two inches wide being used instead. It is made up on heavy leather and is tacked to the front edge of the seat bottom. It is necessary when this is used to put a cushion stick on the top at the outer edge of the seat bottom, and to put a board against the under side the full width from the seat rail out to the edge of the bottom boards. When the fall is not used the carpet, rocker, trimming, etc., extend back the full depth of the seat.

SEAT BACKS.

The designs given herewith are for light work. Figs. 22 and 23 are suitable for surrey wagons, dog

carts, light piano-box wagons, etc. Fig. 22 : Make
the back upon pasteboard, cut in shape to fit the lazy-
back, allowing it to extend three-eighths of an inch
over each end, the width of the back generally ranging from five to eight inches. Curve the bottom
line with the top, leaving it one-half inch wider
in the center than at the ends ; lay off the back
before cutting out, in order to have a straight line
to work from, as shown by dotted lines ; lay off in
squares and punch holes for the buttons with a No.
3 punch ; next cut the cloth, allowing three-quarters
of an inch to each square both ways, and punch

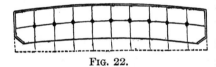

FIG. 22.

holes for the but-
tons. Press the
folds with a hot
iron, then lay the
cloth on a smooth board wrong side of cloth up, and
line with a layer of cotton cut one-half inch less all
around than the size of the cloth ; paste around the
edges of the cloth, and lay white muslin over the
cotton and press it down all around with the hand to
make it adhere to the cloth. Then tack out on the
board to dry. When it is dry remove it from the
board, place it on the bench right side up, and take a
stitch at each hole made for the buttons, to hold the
cotton and muslin in place while being worked, and it
is ready for the buttons. For sewing in the buttons
use tufting twine and a saddlers' needle ; fasten the
twine well at one end of the back, then stick the needle
through the hole in the back and the cloth, and through

the eye of the button, then back again through the same hole, and so on until the buttons are all in. Care should be taken not to cross the thread or run the needle through the thread, as that will prevent it from slipping. The buttons being sewed in, stuff up the bottom row of biscuits and sew down around the edge, then cover the back with bow leather, bind with bow leather across the ends and bottom of back; tack the back to the lazy-back; when tacked fast stuff up the top row of biscuits and finish on top of the lazy-back with a cord and flat welt.

Fig. 23 is made in four pieces, and is made up upon

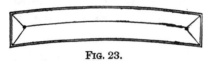

FIG. 23.

the lazy-back; the lazy-back should be made not less than four inches wide. In making up draw a line through the center of the lazy-back, brad a half round rattan molding on the mark, leaving it three inches shorter at each end than the lazy-back. Sink the brads and sand-paper the molding off smooth, paste a strip of bow leather over the molding, crease it down close around the same. While this is drying cut out the cloth for the rolls; allow two inches for fullness in the width and cut three inches longer than the lazy-back, line with cotton and muslin the same as described for fig. 21; this prevents the hair from working through the cloth and gives it a smooth appearance. When the cloth rolls are dry tack them close to the cord with the wrong side of cloth up, and draw them tight along the cord when tacking them down, then tack the rolls to the outside edges of the lazy-back and stuff up with curled hair; when the rolls are stuffed out to the ends and tacked down put in the points at each end; they may be put in with bow leather or cloth. Cut bow leather the required shape, trim off the edges, fold over and paste down, then fasten at the point with a tufting nail; stuff up and tack to the end of lazy-back; cloth may be drawn over the bow leather one-half inch smaller than bow leather, showing a one-quarter inch cord on each side of the points; finish around the edge with a cord and a flat welt.

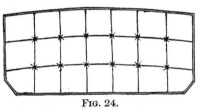

Fig. 24 is called a biscuit back; the material used in trimming is leather. First get out the

FIG. 24.

foundation or rough lining, for which some use pasteboard, others use three-ply of buckram pasted together with good flour paste and tacked out on a board to dry; when well dried out cut in shape to fit the seat and lay off in squares, as shown in drawing; divide the back with a compass in seven equal parts lengthwise and three the other way, and punch holes where the lines cross the place for the buttons with a No. 3 punch; lay off the leather, allowing one inch fullness to each square both ways, and allow one and one-half inches extra across the top to finish on the lazy-back. Sew in the buttons with tufting twine, as described in fig. 1; take a stitch at each plait to hold in place while

stuffing. Stuff up the middle and bottom row of biscuits, then sew down across the ends and bottom, carefully laying the plaits; sew the back lining across the
bottom on the right side of the back, and turn up over
the back and baste across the top and ends, thus forming a binding across the bottom; then bind the ends
of the back with bow leather, or with the same material
as used in trimming; tack it to the lazy-back and
finish stuffing the top row of biscuits; lap the plaits all
down and lay them with the stuffing-stick before stuffing up; the plaits running up and down should be all

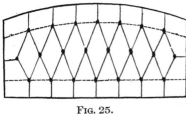

FIG. 25.

laid one way, and
care being taken to
lay them straight;
make the finish on
the lazy-back with a
cord and welt.

Fig. 25 is a dia-
mond back; it is made upon the same kind of foundation, and is fitted to the seat in the same way as fig.
24. To lay off a diamond back, space off with the
compass in eight equal spaces and draw lines across
the back, then draw a line across two and one-half
inches from the bottom of the back, and one the same
distance from the top, following the same curve as that
of the top of the back, as shown by dotted lines; with
the aid of those lines no trouble will be experienced in
laying off a diamond back. Lay off the material used
in trimming in the same manner, allowing one and
one-half inches for fullness in the width and one inch

in the length of the diamonds; if cloth is used line with cotton and muslin, as previously described, and proceed in the same manner as with leather.

In a subsequent chapter the making of falls and backs will be treated more in detail, and other illustrations given.

CHAPTER VII.

STUFFING CUSHIONS—COVERING GLASS FRAMES AND BOWS.

MATERIALS USED FOR STUFFING—THE STUFFING STICK—COTTON OVERLAY—CLOTH FOR FRAMES—PASTING ON—PASTE LADLE—BOW COVERS—STITCHING—WELTS AND BINDING.

Success in trimming depends much upon stuffing the various parts so as to preserve the most minute pattern, giving firmness enough to insure retaining the shape and yet be soft, even and elastic. To do this calls for the exercise of skill on the part of the workman and the use of the best materials. The only stuffing material that makes this result possible is the best quality of curled hair, but as this is looked upon as too expensive for use on any but first-class high-priced vehicles, other materials must take its place. The second best is a second grade hair and clean, fine moss; the latter, if well cured and cleaned, is superior to the inferior grade hair, and it may be employed to a good advantage on medium grades of work if the trimmer knows how to use it. An expert trimmer will make a much firmer, elastic and durable job with first quality moss than a less skillful man will with the best of curled hair, a result due entirely to the manner of filling the cushions or squabs. A good job, if elasticity is to be the guide, cannot be made by stuffing with cheap hair, excelsior or rowen ; these articles are unfit for use, excepting where hard cushions, etc., are called for.

The American workman prides himself on his independence and disregard for the old way simply because it is the old way, while persistently adhering to old customs. This is noticeable in the zeal displayed in favor of the stuffing-stick, a useful and indispensable adjunct to the trimmer's kit, but an article that should be in its place under the work bench oftentimes when it is in use. A soft job such as is popular in fine work cannot be done with it, while for hard stuffing there is no such thing as success without it. The superiority of hair is due to its elasticity ; when it is placed by the stuffing-stick it is frequently broken and so matted that its elasticity is but little more than that of less expansive material ; each handful as it is forced into place becomes a wad entirely detached from that around it, which cannot act freely and makes it impossible to produce smooth, soft work, excepting in small forms. There are places, however, where the stuffing-stick must be used, as by no other means can the stuffing be satisfactorily performed, but where this is the case care should be taken to work the hair in without making it up into small wads.

The soft, elastic, luxurious cushions are not filled by using the stuffing-stick ; in them the hair is laid, that is, the curled hair is placed upon the foundation and evenly spread over the surface. In this way the trimmer can see how to distribute it evenly over the entire surface, and prevent the formation of small wads. A little experience will enable the trimmer to determine the amount of hair necessary to produce a full, firm and elastic cushion. Cotton may be used to overlay the hair, to prevent the ends working through the cloth. Where a lining is used the cotton should be placed upon it; a good lining, however, of itself will accomplish the same purpose as the cotton; but when the latter is used it should be done sparingly, as cotton is non-elastic, and it readily mats down and packs the stuffing under it.

In using the stuffing-stick it is not necessary that small handfuls be worked in separately; a large, loose body of hair may be worked in and not broken up into wads, if the trimmer will exercise proper care. There is no necessity for packing the hair in corners in order to fill them. Let the corner be filled by working the stick on the bottom or lining and afterward adjusted, by a slender needle, through the seam or lining. A copper wire three-sixteenths of an inch in diameter, with the end flattened out to the required width and ground so as to remove all sharp corners, makes a good stuffing-stick, and one that can be rolled up and carried by the trimmer with his kit of tools.

COVERING GLASS FRAMES.

The carriage builder experiences a great deal of trouble from cloth-covered glass frames; the cloth either comes loose from the wood, tears or cuts on the edges, or meets with some other mishap, arising from imperfect manufacture or careless use. The trimmer is generally made the scapegoat, and whether he wills it or not he must bear the burden. This being the case, he should see that the frames are properly made; if they are not the trimmer cannot cover them properly.

The points of construction that most interest the trimmer are, first of all, a correct and ample groove for the glass; in "routing" out this groove, body makers too often use a cutting tool with acute angles, for the purpose of making room for the cloth; this is a mistake, as in such a shaped groove the glass has but a narrow side-bearing. The proper shape of a groove is perfectly square, just such a one as would be made by a saw, with the edges slightly rounded to prevent their cutting the cloth. The groove should be about one-quarter of an inch deep, and wide enough to allow for two thicknesses of cloth, in addition to the glass; allowance should also be made in constructing the frames for two thicknesses of cloth at the joints; when this is done the trimmer can turn in the edges over the shoulders of the tenons and mortises. When no allowance is made there is nothing to hold the edge of the cloth in place but the paste.

The most durable frame is made with the mortises in the end pieces. This is important on the bottom bar, as the bearing in that case all comes against the shoulders, and the tenons not being subjected to any

strain are not liable to break off, as in the case where
they are on the cross pieces.   Then, too, the top edge
of the frame presents an unbroken appearance, as the
cloth extends entirely across and overlaps on the side
which is buried in glass frame groove in the door ;
the ends of the cross pieces should be slightly trenched
to permit the cloth being lapped, and made more secure
by the use of a few gimp tacks.   The frames may be
made with long tenons which pass entirely through the
mortises, or with stub tenons and shallow mortises, a
little more than half way through the slat, secured by
a long, slim screw running through the solid section
under the mortise and into the end of the tenon ; where
the bar is one and one-quarter inches wide the screw
should be two inches long.   When the frames are
made with the mortises in the cross-bars the screws in
the top bar may be put in after it is covered, but in
that case the screw heads should first be covered with
a piece of the cloth from which the cover to the frame
is cut.

In covering cut the cloth lengthwise, and just wide
enough to allow it to entirely encircle the bar and lap
at the bottom of the glass groove ; lay the cloth out on
the bench and spread on the paste with a paste ladle
having a slim strip of india rubber on the edge, as
shown by fig. 26, or one with a serrated edge, as shown
by fig. 27.   The rubber is decidedly the best paste stick
for all purposes.

Spread the paste evenly and heavy, as the wood will
absorb more than the cloth ; lay the strip to be covered

on the cloth far enough from the edge to allow the fold
to reach the bottom of the glass groove ; turn the strip
over, lap the cloth around it, draw it smooth and rub
the edges down into the groove, using an ivory slicker,
except at the corners, where an awl may be used advantageously ; rub the cloth slightly with a slicker and
lay aside until dry; then trim off, put in the glass ; if

FIG. 26.   FIG. 27.

the frame is made with full mortises, tack the corners
with gimp tacks.   Good paste is an absolute necessity.
Ample directions are given on page 55 for making
wheat or rye flour paste, which will answer for all general purposes ; but rice paste, made by mixing rice
flour in cold water, and then slowly boiling it until it is
thickened up, gives a paste that is nearly transparent
when dry, and of such strong adhesiveness that it is
almost impossible to remove the cloth, it is also less
easily affected by water.

COVERING BOWS.

The covering of bows for curtain tops is an important part of carriage trimming, as the work is exposed
at all times and subjected to constant wear, and unless
well done the top presents a shabby appearance.   The
rounding and finishing of the bows is not a part of the
trimmer's work, but he should see that it is well done,

or he cannot produce a good job. In factories where machinery is used the bows are rounded to a pattern, and all are necessarily alike, but these are few in number, and the mass of trimmers realize no benefit from that source. Bows should be rounded to a true oval, and taper; if neatly rounded all will be alike, and the trimmer can cut all his covers to one pattern; otherwise a separate pattern must be made for each bow or leather will be wasted.

Cut the covers from heavy railing leather, lengthwise of the hide; dampen on the plain side, and wrap the bow; tack the leather, top and bottom, on the inside; paste the edges and set up the seam with smooth draw nippers, and stitch while the leather is moist; or, set up with the nippers, and put tacks at intervals to hold the leather in place, and clamp the seam full length with a wooden clamp made of two pieces of hard wood about one inch thick and one and one-half inches wide, and joined by about four set screws; set the screws tight and allow the clamp to remain on until the leather and paste are dry; then remove the clamp and stitch. The use of this clamp insures a straight seam and a hard edge; the lower end around the iron can be stitched before the clamps are put on if desired.

Stitching by machinery is gaining favor, and where the bows are properly finished the work can be well done, but, where the bows are not finished uniform in oval or taper, each cover must be fitted separately or much trouble will be experienced in getting the covers smooth and tight. The same appliance to a sewing machine as that used for stitching leather-covered buckles after the leather is dry could be used for stitching bow covers after they have been clamped, in cases where the slat irons are not riveted together; in all other cases where covers are stitched by machinery the leather should be cut to a pattern to fit each bow. The seams should be on the back edge of the front bow and the front edge of the back bow; those on the intervening bows may be turned either way, but preference is given to the seam on the back edge.

The joining seams are not ornamental and they give the bows a heavy appearance; this has led some trimmers to place the seams on the inside of the bows directly in the center of each; this gives the bows a fine finish, but, from some unexplained cause, this plan has never become popular. Trim the edge of the seam as near the stitching as is safe; black it with vinegar black, and burnish with a bone slicker.

The plain finish on the outside of the bow can be relieved by folding the cover lengthwise on a line with the center of the outside of the bow, and stitching together by machine; if a heavy welt is desired insert a layer between the folds and trim off on the inside after stitching. Another plan is to lay a welt instead of a fold; this is done by working the leather into a trench made of the required size for the welt in a board, dampening the leather and rubbing it in with a wooden slicker of the required shape; after the leather is creased fill the trench on the back with a strip of felt pasted in, and when dry trim even with the face of the leather.

CHAPTER VIII.

DETAILED DIRECTIONS FOR TRIMMING A TOP BUGGY.

SETTING THE TOP—OBTAINING LENGTH OF JOINTS—MAKING
CUSHIONS—CUTTING OUT AND COVERING TOP—MAKING AND
PUTTING IN HEAD-LINING AND MAKING CURTAINS.

In giving the chapters devoted to detailed descriptions of methods, rotation of work, etc., the author has deviated somewhat from the plan of the manual as outlined by other portions of the work. The object in so doing is to give a plan, which may or may not be followed, as a guide to beginners. No two trimmers will work exactly alike, yet time is gained by adopting some one system, whether it be as laid down in this treatise or some other one equally concise. The haphazard trimmer is sure to be a slow and careless workman, while the one who adopts a regular system works more rapidly and is less wasteful than his companion. The trimmer, therefore, who reads these chapters can gain from them a general idea of rotation of work, and if not adopting the one here laid down can arrange from it one that will meet his particular manner of working.

This chapter is devoted to the practical details of

trimming a buggy, using a three-bow top, as it is the most popular style. The trimmer often finds that the blacksmith has spoiled the top by not placing the goose-neck, A, fig. 28, in the proper place to secure the correct length and have a plumb center-bow. To do this properly take a strip of board with the length of top marked upon it and a center mark representing half the length of the top; place one end two and one-half inches over the shifting rail at the back; the cen-

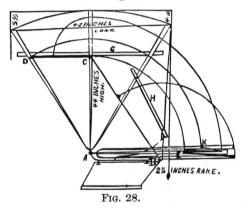

FIG. 28.

ter mark on the strip gives the exact position for the goose-neck, A; the location of the pin on the goose-neck is very important on three-bow tops, as the center bow must stand plumb.

Set the center bow first, the distance between the under side of the bow and the seat frame being forty-four inches; then set the back bow four and one-half inches lower, and the front bow five and one-half inches lower when in their proper positions than the center, thus giving the top one inch more drop in front than at the back; there should also be one inch more space between the front and middle bows than between the middle and back bows. When these are up, place the bows square and secure them by nailing strip, G, across the inside about where the props will come, and strip, H, from the back bow to the lazy-back, as shown in the diagram. Lay a straight edge on the front bow and measure seven inches from the under part to the straight edge on each side, and mark the bow with lead pencil; then put the straight edge on the side of bows, front end to the mark made on front bow, and level the straight edge with a spirit level; the body having previously been leveled, mark across each bow, put the front prop on with the center directly on the line made, and the back edge to the back edge of bow ; place the back prop one-quarter inch above the mark, to allow for the drawing up of the top in front while trimming.

Take the length of joints after the props are on, having a board prepared for the purpose by making four straight lines about one inch apart; drive four 16-oz. tacks, one on each of those lines, one and one-half inches from the end of the board; take the length of each joint and drive a tack for each, putting the long ones on the outside lines and short ones on the middle lines; this done, remove the strips, G and H, from the bows, first measuring between the middle and back bows at the bottom edge, and mark the distance on the back bow for reference. Throw the bows back and proceed to determine the position of knuckles in the following manner : With a string take the length of the long joint from the board from B to C, as shown on diagram ; place one end at B, the other at E, draw the string out doubled until the lower part is parallel with the back bow ; twist the string at the point where it is doubled and take the measure of the short end and mark it on the board, driving a tack to locate it ; obtain the length of the short joint in like manner by measuring from C to D and doubling from E to K, marking each joint right and left for the sides to which it belongs.

To trim the body get out the rough lining, cut the cushion bottom of duck one-half inch larger than the seat both ways, lay it on the seat, and with a lead pencil mark all around the edge and front, cut one-eighth of an inch in full; on the front at the center allow three-eighths of an inch, and cut a true sweep from end to end, making it one-quarter of an inch full; this will be found an improvement on straight fronts, as cushions are liable to draw in on the front while being tufted. Cut buckram for the back, allow one inch in length, and width enough to come within two inches of the bottom of the seat ; cut two-ply and paste heavily with two-ply of heavy wrapping paper ; dampen the paper with a moist sponge before laying it, rub or slick well, and tack it out to dry ; cut the cushion front either of enameled or split dash leather, or buckram, two inches wide ; paste Russia sheeting, or stout muslin, on both sides ; cut three inches wide to form a lip on both sides, tack out to dry ; rough out the back stays of two-ply buckram and one of sheeting, paste heavily and put steel stay one-half of an inch from the

edge, doubled end one inch from bottom between the
layers of buckram; slick well and tack out to dry; cut
fall of duck to fit the flare of body and of the proper
width.   Fig 29 is a good pattern for a top buggy.

The cushion front being dry, fit it to the flare of the
seat and cut off the lip to one-quarter of an inch in
width, then cut the end and back facings of duck; lay

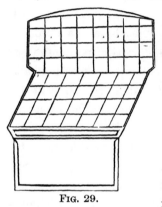

a piece for the end facing
against the seat panel, bottom edge to the seat, mark
both ends with lead pencil
for flare, lay the work on
the bench, and put the front
facing to the front of end
facing, which will give the
width of the end facing,
making it one-quarter of an
inch wider back than front;

FIG. 29.

lay the back facing in and mark the flare, then lay the
end facing to the back one, which gives the width of
back facing, which is generally about three and three-
quarters of an inch at the center.

To cut the false top, lay the material on the bench,
and with the cushion bottom, which has one-quarter of
an inch round in front; mark the front by it, giving the
same shape; this line is made one-half of an inch from
the edge, to allow for turning over; then lay the front
facing on and mark the length on the top, and square
both ends from these marks; lay on the end facing,
using the top edges, bottom edges outward front corner

to the marks; lay the back facing on at the back end of the facings; this is usually longer than the front facing, to allow the ends to extend over the squared lines equally; move the end facings to meet those of the back. The inside of the facings on diagram, fig. 30, represents the false top, with the design as laid off upon it; the facings are then marked, the front with

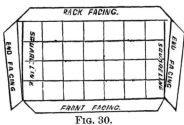

FIG. 30.

lead pencil opposite each line, as a guide to lay the plaits, the end and back with chalk; then cut and fit the back and lay off as per design of back cushion

and fall. Cut the cloth, laying it right side up on the bench, straighten the edge, then with a compass obtain the size of blocks on the back, and allow three-quarters of an inch for fullness; count the number of blocks lengthwise, and lay off that number on the cloth, marking with French chalk; about fifteen inches up from the edge mark off the same crosswise, allowing seven-eighths of an inch, and mark the lines each way with a straight edge; next lay off the cushion top in like manner, allowing similar fullness to the blocks; lay off the roll; the width on the back is marked one and three-quarter inches, the cloth is cut three and one-half inches, the cushion facing two and three-quarter inches wide; lay the fall on and allow three-quarters of an inch on the bottom and ends. All of the above is cut with nap of cloth running toward the front or down on roll and back, and front on cushion top, and down on cushion front and fall; the remaining cloth is cut into welts for cushion, flat welt, seat binding and welts for back; the strip of cloth on side is used for seat lining, back and end facings for cushion. Cut the welts one inch wide.

With a No. 2 punch make holes at all the cross lines on the back and cushion top for the buttons; also at the end of lines at the edge of cloth, to serve as a guide for turning down the plaits; turn the right side of cloth to the bench, and put on two layers of cotton, trim off one-half inch from the edge, put paste all around the edge, and lay thin unbleached muslin over the cotton, patting down well to make it adhere to the paste. Back and cushion top is treated in the same way; trim off the muslin close to the cloth; put cotton in the roll, but not in the seat lining; turn the back right side up, and with a needle and thread take two stitches at each button hole to hold the muslin, cotton and cloth together, while the back and cushion are being made up. Paste out the fall, cut the risers from pieces of horse blanket goods, or thin grade of rug carpet; never use leather, as it cuts through before the cloth is half worn out; cut the riser one and one-eighth inches wide, and place it around the fall, as shown in the design, fig. 30, one-quarter of an inch from the edge, the point at the top one and one-quarter inches down; having fitted these lay them aside.

Paste up the duck solid, lay paste on heavily, but evenly, remove all lumps or skins; be particular to see

that the edges have not been missed. After the paste
has been laid with the stick, double together a piece
of muslin and make a sort of swab, with which smooth
the paste, rubbing all over, then lay on the risers,
pressing them down with the hand; lay on the cloth,
nap running down even with the top, dividing equally
over each end, and rub lightly with a slicker, toward
both ends and bottom, from the center; rub out all
wrinkles, and be careful that none are made after rubbing; draw the cloth over the risers, rub down along
the edge, and tack out on a smooth board to dry;
paste out the cushion facing riser, cut to suit the flare
at the ends, lay paste on the facing, lay the riser on
straight, pat down with the hand, and immediately lay
on the cloth and rub down on both sides of risers until
it has adhered to the facing, then turn it over and trim
the cloth at the end, allowing one-half of an inch to
turn over for pasting to the back; tack out on a board,
cloth side out. While these are drying stitch the dash,
then put in the seat lining, tack the welt of railing
leather around the seat, wet the leather and use small
rattan cuttings at the corners to square them; use $2\frac{1}{2}$-
ounce tacks, and be careful not to split the edge of
seat; when tacked all around set the leather, with a
tickler, close to the rattan.

The seat lining having been cut to the right flare,
turn in one-quarter of an inch on the ends of back lining
and stitch on flat to side pieces; tack to the seat, on
the inside, then put paste around the seat panel and
lay on a thin layer of hair; draw the cloth up and tack

on top of seat close to the welt; sew three strips of welt together by overseaming; measure around the seat and back for the flat welt, tear it off and with a hot iron turn one-quarter of an inch down on one side, and stitch close to the edge thus turned down; tack the welt close to the leather, welt wrong side up, paste heavily and turn over, putting a gimp tack at each corner, about three more along the back and two on the sides; rub down with the slicker.

Make up the back; punch holes in the buckram for the buttons, using buttons or tufts to correspond with the color of the cloth, drawing them in with tufting twine; sew up the ends and top, laying the plaits to the marks on the back; turn the end plaits so they will lap down; the top ones all one way; sew the corded welt along the top, the nap of cloth welt to run down to correspond with that of back; then sew on the roll, the nap also running down; stuff from the bottom, filling the top row first, turning the plaits in, each one as they are stuffed; when the bottom row is reached sew one square at a time and stuff, beginning at the right hand corner; when all is done, trim off around the edge and cover the back with "mole skin," putting a layer of cotton over the buckram to prevent tufting strings from showing through; baste the "mole skin" to the buckram, trim off and blind sew the turnover welt around the edge; attach the back rail, put the shifting rail on the seat, cover the back with "mole skin," then tack the back to the rail with 10-oz. tacks, being particular to secure the ends in a perfect manner.

It is best, when possible, to unscrew the arm rail and put on the buckram, and screw the rail down upon it; when secured turn up the roll and tack it to top of rail one-half inch from back edge; when tacked within six inches of the end stuff from both ends to the center, tack three inches more toward the ends and stuff again, finish out the ends, put on a corded welt, the cord toward the front, nap running the same way, the back edge of welt one-half inch from back edge of rail; this welt should be lined with muslin or canvas; blind tack the stitched flat welt close to the corded welt, paste heavily, turn over and slick down; let it extend about an inch under the end of back rail, and tack the corded welt. Cut the cord out when the corner is reached, to make a flat finish on the bottom, and the back is finished.

Remove the fall and cushion facings from the board, stitch around the inside of riser; cut a piece of enameled leather two and one-quarter inches wide, paste it along the bottom edge of fall, lay on the leather and trim the ends to the edge; paste the cloth all around, turn over the hem, cut the corners and lay away to dry; stitch the front facing around the risers, stitch the front facing to the end facings by laying the front on the end, lapping over one-quarter of an inch, stitching through both; sew up the back corners, turn and hammer down, baste the cloth welt along the front and sew close from the front corner around the ends and back; make a line with French chalk, to stitch by, three eighths of an inch from the inside edge of riser,

following the shape at the corners; stitch all around
the hem, trim off the cloth and use a stick one and one-
quarter inches wide, three-sixteenths thick, oval to
sharp edges on one side, and of proper length; slit the
leather on the inside of fall about three-quarters of an
inch from the end, insert the stick, sew up the slit and
paste the fall to the front facing; then cut two straps
of stout enameled leather four and one-half inches long
and one and one-quarter inches wide, punch a hole in
one end with a No. 4 punch, black the edge and back,
baste them to the front facing; sew in the bottom on
the front only, then sew in the top, beginning at the
middle of end facing, with the front to the right; use
strips of canvas same width as the welt to line it with—
this is better than the ordinary muslin, being stiffer
it makes a more solid welt; commence at the center,
sew the welt firm to the first mark or the one nearest
to the back corner, when that is reached lay a plait in
the top about one-quarter of an inch wide, making the
lap to turn front; this is the starting point from which
to commence to sew on the top; if the corners of the
cushion be square, cut the top rounding at all the corners, and when the corner is reached lay about three
small plaits while sewing around; lay the plaits at each
of the marks on the facings, all one way and as near
the same lap as possible; the front and back should be
laid one way, the ends to lap toward the front; when
the top is sewed in around to the end, stop within two
inches of the front corner and sew the welt on to meet
the other end; cut the cord just at that point; cut off

the welt one-half inch longer for a lap; be careful when making laps not to make any on the front, as a splice does not look well in so prominent a place; there are three plaits on the end that is left open, and only one is sewed in the top; sew in the false top more like basting than sewing, leaving opening for stuffing; then turn the cushion, being particular that all the corners are pushed out, go all around and press the welt out, turn and hammer with a small mallet all the corners, hammer the bottom in like manner, then blind-sew the bottom in, and the cushion is ready to be stuffed.

Pin the cushion to the bench with a cushion awl in each corner, the front to the edge of the bench, the fall hanging down; fill the bottom first, packing in solidly; when full sew the false top to the welt and fill the top; put a little bunch of hair in the corners first, then fill along the end, then sides, stuffing evenly and not hard; when full blind-sew the top in, laying the plaits at the marks on false top; remove the awls; commence tuft-ing at the center of the cushion on the middle row; draw them down tight upon the false top, all alike; when all are in, with a round awl turn in the plaits, by putting the awl under the plait and lifting it, which will cause it to fall into position. Turn the cushion over, top to the bench, with the back out, and with the fist hammer the back and end facings in to make them flat; turn over and brush off with a whisk broom. Measure from the front edge to the hole in cushion strap, and also the distance the strap is from the end of cushion; make a corresponding measurement on the seat and put in two screws to knob the cushion to—round heads are preferable.

Cover the bows, with the seam on the back one facing front, those on the front and middle bows facing back; let the covers on front and middle bows cover the bottom of prop. Set up the top, put on the joints, leaving off the thimbles, put on the nuts; get two pieces of five-eighths poplar, one-half inch longer than the spread of middle and back bows; saw down on each end the bevel of the bows one-half inch deep, leaving a lip one-eighth thick and one-quarter long, to keep the stick from slipping up when the top is jarred. Tack webbing the full length of top, first on middle bow about fifteen inches from the center; draw to the back bow, placing the stick directly under the webbing, with the lip under the bows, and draw as tightly as possible—then draw to the front bow; get two strips of poplar one and one-half inches wide, five-eighths of an inch thick and about two feet ten inches long, cover about five inches of the ends with cloth and the same in the center; take seaming cord, twice the width of top in length, put a slip knot on one end, then put the sticks on the outside of bows just below the props, holding them up tight, but not to spring the bows; level the body, and measure down two and one-quarter inches from center of front props and mark with chalk; obtain the center of bows by measuring from one prop to the other, over the top of bows, and mark with lead pencil; put a straight edge at the chalk mark on front bow, level it and chalk each bow by the straight edge ; from these marks get the center of back bow.

The center piece of the head lining for 39-inch bows is cut twelve inches wide ; to determine the exact width of the latter, measure from the center of the middle bow fifteen inches ; the distance from that point to the prop will give the width of quarter piece. Draw the quarter pieces on the bows, tacking to front and back bows, nap on the inside ; cloth on outside of bows, nap running down ; lay the center piece doubled on the bench, get the middle lengthwise, from the center to front ; cut five-eighths of an inch off the front and back, which gives the sides five-eighths inch round ; cut straight from center to front and back, notch the front and back at the center, and lay the top piece on the center marks on the bows ; put in tacks to hold it, then draw the four corners down and tack ; mark the quarters with French chalk on all the bows, at the edge of center piece; mark on both edges of center bow, from one prop over the top to the other ; these lines are to sew the strips to ; remove the cloth and lay the quarters on the bench ; strike a straight line from the center marks front and back, and cut off at that mark ; put a mark on front to designate it, sew the quarters to center piece by machine; begin at the center and sew toward the ends, keeping the center marks together ; press the seams open with a hot flatiron ; sew strips on the marks and tack to both sides of the center bow ; allow the head-lining to hang in that position while the top is being stuffed, then draw a strip of web across the corner of bows about three inches below the other strips ; draw stout unbleached muslin, yard wide, over the round of bows, allowing the top edge to lap four inches over the upper strip of webbing ; tack down as far as the front prop on front bow, and a corresponding distance on the back bow, then tack about two inches apart on center bow to within four inches of prop ; lay on paste heavily over the upper strip of webbing, and as low as the muslin is tacked, being careful to put no paste on the bows ; lay on the hair as far as pasted until a nice full round is obtained ; keep the hair off the bows ; put a thin layer on the sides or bottom edge, but gradually thicken toward the top, making the hair nearly perpendicular on the sides, running up to a sharp corner ; then draw the lower half of the muslin over the hair and tack down ; if any hair should be pressed over on the middle bow, work it off by passing a tufting needle through the muslin ; sew up the upper edges of muslin so that the hair cannot shift toward the center ; draw up the head-lining and tack it to the front and back bows, and trim it off along the bottom one inch above the line of the side quarters.

Cut duck one and three-quarter inches wide for inside lace, and fit in with a tack at the back and front, the bottom edge three-eighths of an inch above the line of bottom edge of quarter, the black side of lace to the head-lining ; with a lead pencil mark the bows across the lace ; cut risers one and one-quarter inches wide and fit on the lace, cutting to go between the marks on lace, thus leaving a space the width of the bow in the middle and leaving a space at the ends for the front and back bow ; cut strips of cloth four and one-half inches wide ; lay paste on the white side of the duck ; lay on the risers, then the cloth, with nap running toward the bottom, just enough cloth at the top for a hem, say three-quarters of an inch ; put no paste on the risers ; rub the cloth down close to the risers and paste down over the back on the bottom edge ; paste just enough to hold the cloth to the edge, leaving the rest loose. When dry, stitch around the risers along the bottom, then turn the cloth down and

[Outside Finished.]

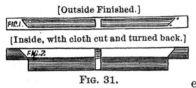

[Inside, with cloth cut and turned back.]

FIG. 31.

stitch along the top and ends ; cut the cloth down close to the stitching, at the ends and middle, so it may lay back to receive the head-lining when the lace is in, and just enough to clear the bows, fig. 31 will more fully show how they will look when finished.

Put these in position by placing the lace on the middle bow first, so as to have the vacant space in the center directly on the bow, having the seams of the head-lining to correspond with those at the end of risers ; tack these temporarily and draw the ends to the front and back, making the bottom edge three-eighths of an inch above the line of quarter ; then remove the tack from the center and hold a straight edge up to the bottom edge to insure accuracy, and drive two covered nails, one each top and bottom, directly on a line of the stitching, and two in the front and

back ends, as shown in the diagram; cut the head-
lining close to the bows, nearly to the top edge of lace;
turn the edge back over the lace, spread on paste
heavily and put the head-lining back upon it, and rub
down well; let the remaining cloth hang until the
dusters are pasted in upon finishing up the top. Cut
the back lace of split dash leather ; rough out three
inches wide the' shape of back bow ; tack to the bow,
leaving enough on top for a cone ; mark with lead pencil
on both top and bottom of bow, also at the bottom
edge of side lace. [Fig. 32 shows the shape and style
of riser.] Lay it on the
bench and measure from
the inside mark one and
seven-eighths inches, and
cut to that mark ; cut the

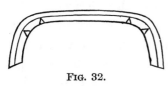

FIG. 32.

ends one and one-eighth inches wide, the shape shown
in diagram ; the top three-eighths of an inch above the
mark, until the bend is passed; then cut to the mark
down the sides; cut the risers one and one-eighth
inches wide ; notch them at the corners, as shown ;
paste a piece of cloth on the back part of ends, say
eight inches long, to cover them ; trim off the edges
and paste the other side ; lay on the risers one-quarter
inch from the edge ; lay on the cloth ; cut the shape of
piece, with nap running down ; rub down close to the
risers ; turn over and put paste on the cloth, extending
below for hem ; slit at the sharp round, so it will turn
over nicely.

Cut a strip of welt from the head-lining cloth one

inch wide; a piece of muslin the same width to line with; tack this with seaming cord to the back bow, commencing at the bottom edge of side lace; continue around the lower edge of bow, and finish off at the lower edge of the lace at the other side. The roll-up strap, fig. 33, may be made of light bridle leather, or two light pieces of patent leather pasted together, or enameled and patent leather pasted; mark off by

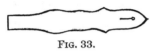

FIG. 33.

the pattern and stitch one-eighth of an inch from the edge; this pattern is twelve inches long and one and one-eighth inches wide at the broadest points; four straps should be used to a buggy.

Cut the front valance from harness leather one and one-eighth inches wide; put into water to soak; get the shape of the front bow by placing a board against the bow with bottom edge one-half inch below the mark made for the bottom of side quarters, and outline the bow with chalk mark; bend the leather to this mark, tacking it at intervals of four inches, except around the bend, where the tacks should be closer together; set away to dry; stitch the back laces, and tack on to back bow, allowing the top edge to extend one-quarter of an inch above the bow, the ends to meet the bottom of side lace; tack on with six-ounce tacks, using cloth-covered nails at the ends, as the heads of plain tacks will show.

Cut the back straps six and one-half inches wide and punch a hole, with a round awl, one inch from the bottom, and one-eighth of an inch from the edge through the steel stays ; secure them to the bows with one tack in each at proper distance apart; if twenty-four inches at the bottom, set them twenty-four and one-quarter at the top, spacing at equal distances from the center; mark the bow and punch the two remaining holes for knobs to correspond with those in the rail ; remove the quarters and ascertain the length required for the bottom of stays to cover full one-half inch of seat panel; one and one-eighth inches from the

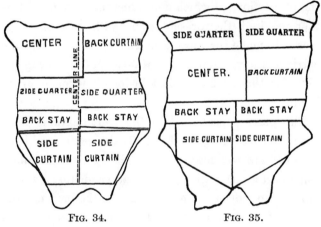

FIG. 34.   FIG. 35.

knob holes will generally suffice ; cut off the ends, allowing one-half inch at the top.

To cut the leather for these stays sweep a place on the floor and spread a sixty foot hide out straight, finished side up, and mark as shown by one or other of the diagrams figs. 34 and 35, deviating when necessary to avoid patches.

Every sixty foot hide will not suffice for a top, while there are some fifty-seven feet hides that will ; there are various conditions which operate to determine the size; some seats are six inches high on the sides, others are but four and one-half inches, increasing the length of the side curtains one and one-half inches; then, again, some trimmers turn up three inches for hem on side quarters, while five-eighths of an inch is sufficient, as other material can be used to line with; three-quarters of an inch is all that is required for the hems to the back stays. As regards the size of tops, the proportions of which determine the amount of leather required, the present style with side bar buggies is to make the top low and long, so as to give the carriage a low, squatty appearance, but in cutting the hide for these, what is lost in length is made up in hight.

The plans represented in the two diagrams have each their advantages. In fig. 34 the center and back curtains are cut first, the butt being nearly square, side quarters next, giving firm leather for them, avoiding the most of the flank. In fig. 35 the butt is more irregular, but in some cases the round of side quarters is such that they can be cut advantageously, thereby saving from one-half to one inch; there is some flank at one end of the quarter, but the most of it will trim off on the front, and what remains is no great detriment to the top, while the space gained insures the cutting of the entire top out of the hide; but if any piece must be left out, let it be one of the back stays, as they can be made up of smaller pieces than any other part.

After the hide is cut lay the back stays upon a smooth board, and with a sponge dampen around the edge ; paste heavily, but lay it on smoothly and all over, removing all lumps, as they will show through the leather ; then lay on the buckram, rub it down well with the slicker, but never rub the leather on the enameled side ; turn the hem and rub down until it has adhered to the buckram ; use an oiled rag over the slicker so as not to injure the enamel. Cut the corners at the bottom so that when turned and pasted they will be flat ; when pasted lay one on the board, enameled side up, and with an oiled cloth oil the edge all around, and with a three-sixteenth creaser line the stay ; measure two inches from the edge on both sides, top and bottom ; mark with the point of a tickler, and by a straight edge ; having first oiled the leather, mark heavily with the tickler from the top to the mark at the bottom, on both sides, also the bottom line across to meet the side ones ; make a second line one-quarter inch from the first, making a double crease all around the stay, except at the top, then with a round awl pierce the leather through the hole made at the bottom of the metallic stay, which is for the knob, and with a tape, measure the distance from the outside hole in the rail up to the mark on the back bow at the bottom of side quarter ; add one-half inch and measure the same distance from the hole at the bottom of stay on the side which contains the metallic stay, and dot it with chalk just half way between the crease marks ; then divide that distance into three spaces, and dot each

with chalk, being particular to mark them for their
respective sides, with the metallic stay outward; pierce
the leather and metallic stay with a round awl at the
marks for the knobs ; use riveting knobs and cut the
shanks off to one-quarter inch long and insert them in
the hole in the stay, having a hard piece of wood under
them when driving to prevent the metallic stay from
spreading ; when riveting lay a heavy piece of flap
leather, glazed size up, on the bench to prevent the
knob from slipping, and to prevent injury to the japan;
no knob is put in the bottom hole at this time, that being for the knob to secure the rail to the stay when finished ; make a hole opposite each knob, just inside the
double crease, with one-half-inch tongue punch, through
the leather only ; then take one-half inch chapes, two
and one-half inches long, scarf the ends and punch a
hole in the center with the tongue punch ; black and
crease ; put the chapes on one-half-inch buckles ; insert a one-half-inch loop-set under the leather, through
the hole in the stay ; double the chape, remove the
loop-set and insert the chape with the tongue of the
buckle up; insert an awl into the hole at the buckle,
and force it up to its place; rub the leather down
around the chape ; drive a two and one-half-ounce tack
through and clinch on the bench iron to hold the
chapes until they are stitched ; put on the loops, six
each, for the stays and back curtain; these are made
of pieces of bow leather five and one-half inches long,
doubled, pasted together, creased over sets and dried ;
those for the stays should be one and five-eighths

inches long with five-sixteenths inch at the open, and half that at the closed end; those for the back curtain one and one-half inches long, creased over a three-sixteenths-inch set; stitch them on the stays by machine, then trim off and black; the stays are then ready for the lining.

The cloth being cut, lay it right side up, and draw a line with French chalk one-half of an inch from the edge, and six and three-eighths of an inch from each end; lay the stay on, enameled side down, and mark the bottom by the stay. Press the cloth with a hot iron, turning it over at the chalk lines; cut cotton batting (two layers if thin), five inches wide and three inches shorter at each end than the stay, spread paste here and there along the stay to keep the cotton from slipping, lay on the cloth, baste all around the cloth nearly flush with the edge of the stay; stitch on by machine, draw out the bastings, put riveting knob through the metallic stay at the bottom, and insert in the outside hole of the shifting rail; draw the stay up and put a tack at the top.

Cut a slit in the back lace at the level of the bow for the metallic stay; cut down one inch below the top of the bow on each side of metallic stay to allow it to pass through the slit easily; draw up tight, and with chalk mark at the top of bow; " break " the back joint and draw the back stay up so the chalk mark will be one-quarter inch above the bow, lap the metallic stay over on the bow, and secure by ten-ounce tacks, driven about two-thirds the way in; "spring" the joint, and if it draws the back stay up tight without bulging the bow it is right; care is necessary in adjusting back stays, as the back bow once sprung spoils the top; if the back stay should be loose draw the tacks and tighten up, and when correct drive the tacks in, and turn down the metallic stays and break them off; be careful that there are no rough edges. Put the stays up square, by ranging them with the bows and by measurement; the strain on the stays must be uniform, or the back bow will be drawn out of range.

Fit up the back curtain, the bottom even with the bottom of the back stays; mark at each buckle with chalk for the straps, and at the double creases on the bottom, top and sides, as a guide for the hem; punch for knob holes with a round awl, allowing five-eighths of an inch for a hem, and cut the bottom to the sweep of shifting rail; black the edge, and cut stay pieces of enameled leather, for the bottom three inches wide, and long enough to reach from hem to hem, then cut the pieces for stays, under the billets, four inches long and two and one-half inches wide; scarf all around on the enameled side; put paste on the enameled side and place pieces at the billets, the stays on the inside of curtain. Paste the bottom stay in, and double crease the bottom to correspond with the bottom of the back stays. The billets are one-half inch wide and four and one-half inches long. Black and crease the billets, lay the points even, and draw a line one and one-quarter inches from the back end across all, then mark the curtain two and three-quarter inches from the edge

for the back end of billets, the center on the mark
made when the curtain was fitted, put a tack in the
back and front through the hem to hold them while
they are being stitched on the machine; begin at the
back end and stitch along the side to the mark on the
side, and down to the back end; stitch on the loops,
first attaching them with two or three tacks; begin at
the hem and stitch one-sixteenth of an inch from the
edge of the billet down around the loops, stopping at

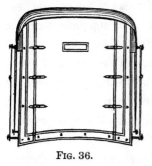

the hem on the side; trim off
and black the edges and put
in the lining; paste all around
one-half inch wide close to
the hem, and full width on
the bottom; trim off the cloth,
turn and rub the hems down,
take a stitch at the corners to
keep them in position, mark

FIG. 36.

the rings for knob patches, stitch them, stitch the hem
and punch the knob holes.

To put in the glass get the center of the curtain and
measure eight and one-half inches from the top to the
center of glass; be sure that it is straight; put up the
roll-up straps, tack two one and one-half inches each
from the edge of back stays, and the other two four and
one-half inches from them; knob on the back curtain
at the bottom, draw it up and put four tacks along the
top; hang it square and without wrinkles, baste along
the top, trim off, and the back is complete.   Fig. 36 is
a back view of the quarters and back curtain.

To fit the top lay the side quarter pieces over the bend of the bow with the best leather back ; tack front and back to hold them in position ; put a tack at the back and front edges of front and back bows at the line of bottom of side quarters ; drop the leather down five-eighths of an inch below these tacks for a hem; with a pointed knife slit the leather. to fit over the props ; remove the nuts, take off the joints, and put the leather over the props; put the joints on again, draw the leather up smooth and put tacks at the bottom hem on front and back bows ; double the top piece together and sweep the edges five-eighths of an inch from end to end ; lay it on the top, center to the center of bows; draw on smooth across the bows and put a tack at either side on the middle bow ; then with chalk mark along the edge of the top piece upon the side quarters, and crosswise on the middle, front and back corners of bows, as a guide when putting together; with a chalked line strike a line for the hem at the bottom of side quarter ; pass the leather around on the back stay ; mark down along the edge of the back stay, allowing one inch to pass under the stay ; mark from the prop on the front bow along the edge of bow to the bottom line of quarter ; trim off the surplus leather above the prop ; remove the quarters; then mark with chalk, on the enameled side, one-eighth of an inch above the line at the center over the middle, front and back bows, and mark a true sweep from front to the middle and from middle to back bow ; the line thus made is often too full and irregular ; a little practice will enable the trimmer to determine the fullness necessary to have the welt nearly straight when finished ; a full top will wrinkle sooner than a tight one, but much depends upon the quality of leather used. If hand-buffed a close cut may be made, but if machine-buffed more fullness must be allowed. Lay a straight edge on, touching the mark at the front and back bow for the hem ; slit the leather in front toward the front prop hole to within one-eighth of an inch of the line along the bows ; dampen the leather and turn down the hem. Cut two strips of duck three and one-half inches wide the length of the quarters ; paste along the bottom of quarters two inches up from the hem, and solid the full width of the duck back of the back bow ; lay on the duck and rub smooth with the slicker ; then cut a triangular piece of cloth and paste on at the back above the duck ; trim off at the front even with crease of hem, and cut two strips of cloth four and one-half inches wide for dusters ; paste on top of the duck in the same manner ; rub the hem down all around and crease the edge, and two inches up from the edge run a double crease. Cut two strips of enameled leather for welts one inch wide ; dampen and double together ; rub down with an oiled cloth and hang up to dry.

Fit the front valance by pointing a few tacks in it along the front bow ; cut off the ends at the bottom of side quarter ; take it off and round off the inside corner, and with an edge tool trim the corners all around on the black side ; lay the valance on the enameled or bow leather which is used for covering ; mark

all around the edge and cut five-eighths of an inch outside of the mark; dampen and lay black side of valance down and baste; notch around the sharp curve
and corners to prevent straining when being turned;
oil the edge and crease around the bottom and two
and one-half inches up on the top edge, or about on a
line with the front prop, which is as far down as is necessary to stitch by hand; stitch by machine as far as
creased; remove the bastings, center the valance, put
that line to the center on front bow, and tack on with
four-ounce tacks about one inch apart, allowing the top
edge to extend one-quarter inch above the top of the
bow as a lip to stitch to; tack down to within four
inches of the end, and baste the muslin together at the
top edge of padding.   Cut the welts for top with sharp
cutting gauge three-sixteenths of an inch wide; stitch
the side quarters along the hem, and one row at the
double crease; trim off the hem and black the edge.

Punch the holes for props back and front, and cut
out the cloth or dusters from the top to the prop hole,
the width of hole to allow for passing over the prop.
Cut the back close to the back bow; scarf the back
edge of the quarter to allow it to pass into the back
quarter under the cloth; they are then ready to be
basted together; center the side quarter to the center
of the roof piece, the front of roof piece to the front of
quarter; insert the welt also at the center, and with a
No. 4 three-square needle, and No. 40 spool thread,
overseam with half-inch stitches toward the ends, keeping edges even; when basted crease the edge with one-

eighth of an inch crease as a guide to seam up by ; fold
the top and put it in the horse ; take the bite close up to
the welt ; use No. 25 spool thread, double, well waxed;
harness wax can be used if desired ; good beeswax,
however, answers every purpose ; avoid wrinkling the
seam, which is easily done by jerking the thread ; use
as fine an awl as will work, and place about four stitches
to the inch ; slicker the stitching down flat on both
sides to rub out any draw that the stitching may have
made ; take between the thumb and fore fingers a
sponge that is well filled with water, and dampen the
top of the welt as far down on the edge as the stitching; open the top and slicker the top of welt by rubbing,
to slightly flatten the welt; clean the enameled side
with a rag, and throw the top over the bows; remove
the nuts from the props all around ; break the front
joints, slip on the top, put on the thimbles and replace
the joint ; draw the front of top over the front bow
about one foot, which will make it easier to put on ; go
to the back of the top, grasp the leather at the seam,
give a gentle jerk backward at each seam to draw the
top back into position ; put the leather over the back
props, leaving the thimbles loose until the back is secured ; draw back at the seam and tack the front; then
return to the back and draw down on the sides to meet
the line on the bow for the bottom of the quarters ; put
a tack at the bottom, another one-half inch above the
upper row of stitching ; loosen the thimble at the front
prop and draw front, and at the same time screw the
thimble up tight to hold the leather in position ; treat

the back prop in the same way; put a tack at the hem
to keep it in place until it is dry and set; pass to the
back and cut the top into the outside corner of back
stay; turn the top back; loosen the cloth lining from
the stay by cutting the stitching as far down as the
edge of side quarter; draw the cloth up and tack it to
the bow; insert the back end of side quarter between
the lining and stay, and stitch through the same holes
as far as possible; baste the top on, front and back;
trim off, dampen and draw the front up over the top;
run the tickler along on the back edge of front valance,
and crease the front; bind the back; rub down in like
manner; stitch, trim off and blacken; put a black nail
at the end of front valance, and at the end of welts on
front and back bows, and top of back curtain through
the hem; draw the tacks at the hem on side quarters,
and spread paste on the inside lace; draw down the
cloth duster against it and rub well. Spread paste on
the cloth on the inside lace; turn up and rub well;
put four knobs in each bow, one one-half inch below
the edge of side quarter, and two in the front bow;
tack up the side curtain, the hem at the top on line
with the upper row of stitching on side quarters, and
at the double crease on back stay; mark for the knobs
with chalk; carry the upper back corner back on the
outside of side quarter and tack to back-stay; mark
where it strikes the double crease, and cut a slit straight
up on the line of lower prop at the shifting rail to allow the curtain to go over; mark down the edge of
front bow and close under the prop; with a round awl

pierce a hole at the corner where the side quarter enters the back stay, as the curtains divide there and the
back part goes outside ; take off and pierce all the
marks for knob patches ; allow one inch outside the line
of front bow, the bottom even with the bottom of back

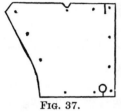

FIG. 37.

stay. Fig. 37 shows the side curtain finished.

The curtains are pasted out
with enameled leather patches inside; the pieces for the bottom
back corner are large enough to
cover prop hole and two knob holes, the upper back
corner one knob and the slot, which is not cut until
the curtain is finished ; stitch around this slot when
hemming and make the ring one-half inch across ;
punch a hole with the knob-punch, and cut straight up
from that ; this completes the buggy trimming in detail.

CHAPTER IX.

DETAILED DIRECTIONS FOR TRIMMING AN EXTENSION TOP.

Previous to giving the instructions for trimming an extension-top phaeton, a brief reference will be made to the many ill-proportioned tops that are seen everywhere. The fault, however, cannot in all cases be traced to the trimmer, as the foundation is laid, and, in many instances, the top is set without consulting him, and must be trimmed as brought to him, whether good, bad or indifferent. To locate this defect, go into the smith shop and ask the blacksmith where he is going to place the goose-necks and eyes for the middle bows. He will, in most cases, answer: "Well, I guess I will put one about here and the other about there." He may have a slight idea about door room, but the location of the front and back bows never enters his mind, and, owing to ignorance, he fails to properly locate the two middle bows, or to understand how the whole top should be set. His is the starting point, and an error by him cannot be remedied in the future.

First decide upon the length of the top. To do so

take a straight-edge six feet long and lay it across the seats, as shown by fig. 38, allowing it to extend three inches back of the back seat panel, and not less than seven inches forward of the front seat, increasing the distance in front if necessary. Lay a short, straight-edge across the back seat at the front corners, and measure from the back end of the long to the edge of the short one ; supposing the distance is twenty-one inches, mark it on the long, straight-edge; then measure a like space for doorway, and also between the front and middle bows; if that should not bring the mark up to seven inches forward of the front seat, increase the spacings, but get the goose-neck at B for-

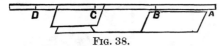

FIG. 38.

ward of the front line of the seat frame ; if neces-sary it may be placed one inch back of the top corner of seat panel, giving a run of about three inches. An extra long top may require the goose-neck to be placed plumb with front of seat, while on an extra short one it may be placed back of the seat corner; on an extra wide seat it should be placed well back, so that when the bows are spaced off equally the front bow will not project more than ten or less than seven inches forward of the front seat. The bows must be equally divided with three inches rake at a, making the spaces equal. B and C, Fig. 38, show the positions of goose-necks for the middle bows. The above is a correct rule for the trimmer and the blacksmith to follow.

To set the top place the body on the trestles in a

level position; put on the shifting rail, if there is one; take strips of five-eighth inch poplar, one and one-half inches wide, and erect the frame work as shown by fig. 39, securing the upright piece on the back by a thumb screw; then place the horizontal strip three feet nine inches above the front seat bottom, level and secure it to the back upright, and set up the front piece; mark at *a*, four and one-half inches from the top, and place the plumb bob at that point inside of strip; place a wedge between the strip and the back; loosen the screw, and

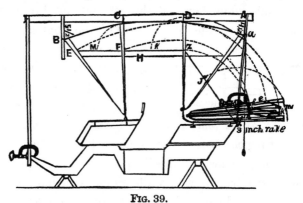

FIG. 39.

by the wedge regulate the rake to three inches; then measure the length of top on the horizontal strip, and nail on strip B; mark five and one-half inches down on it for the top of the front bow; then divide the space between A and B into three equal spaces, C and D; locate the middle bows; place the front inside bow at C; measure from the seat up on each side; to level it mark and cut off one-half inch above the slat-iron rivet; when replacing put a one-quarter inch block on top of the bow, to lower it below the back inside bow to equalize the round, the front bow being one inch lower than the back; otherwise the bow at C would appear higher than at D; put up the bow as directed; place the slat-iron in the center of bow; put screw at top and bottom; set up the back inside bow at D, without the block; then the back one with the top at *a*, and the front one with the top at B; put on strip H on both sides a little below the prop line, on the inside; nail to the back bow, and see that the bows range before nailing to the front; range the middle bows and nail them.

To locate the props, place a straight edge across the front of front bow six inches below the inside edge; mark with lead pencil at E; then place the straight edge on the side, with front end at E; level it and mark on the back bow; raise the straight edge one-quarter inch above this mark, and mark the inside bows; the line is raised at the back to overcome the draw by the back stays, as they pull the top back a trifle; place the center of the prop on the line in the center of the back inside bow; screw it on; place the center of prop on the front inside bow one-eighth of an inch below the line, and one-quarter of an inch below on the front bow; the props are lowered when put on; the bows work up by trimming; if the props were put on level the middle prop would not line when trimmed, owing to the front bow pulling up; in some cases even more than one-quarter inch may be necessary; all depends upon the play allowed to the joints, and the trimmer should know whether the tops are fitted loose or snug, and be governed accordingly.

Take the length of joints upon a board large enough to hold the whole six joints; measure from center to center of props, and allow one-sixteenth of an inch in the length of each if they fit snugly, and one-eighth of an inch if any play is given; take the measures; mark for right or left, as the case may be; take down the frame work, and throw the bows back, as shown by Fig. 39.

Determine the position of knuckles with a good string which will not stretch; take the length of long joints from h to z from the board, and place one end on the center prop-iron at h and the other at z; draw the string out and double at j, the position for the knuckle, the lower half on a line with the back bow; lay the string upon the board, and drive a large tack to mark for the knuckle; take the length of middle joint from the board from z to f; place one end of the string on the center of the prop at z; the other at f; draw out and double at k; bottom half on a line with the bow; put the measure on the board; mark the front of joint and take the measure from that end, as the knuckle often comes very near the center of this joint, for an error may occur if the front is not marked; take length for the front prop from f to e, and mark for the knuckle upon the board; it can then be sent to the smith shop, and the bows to the woodworker to be rounded.

To make up the body lining cut three-ply of buckram for the back and one fall, and for the other fall Russia sheeting or ticking; paste them well; slicken until no blisters appear, and tack out on boards to dry; cut the cushion bottoms of duck, one-half inch larger than the seats; lay them on the seats with back edge even with the back of seat panels; equal fullness at the ends; put a tack in each end; mark close to the seat panels with a lead pencil, and the front by the edge of the seat; allow one-quarter inch on each end over the marks, and the same on the front at the ends, and round off to one-half inch in the center.

Cut a paper pattern one-half inch wider than the broad lace; cut off to the flare of the seat, and cut end facings of duck by it front and back, making the necessary allowance for the flare; the width must be governed by the front facing; fit the miters correctly; facings can be used as a guide for cutting the false top, using tick, Russia sheeting or thin muslin canvas; cut the false top as directed in the previous chapter. Cut the falls to fit the rockers, allowing for the carpet or other covering, and the exact depth from seat to the floor; the falls may be sewed in the cushion or tacked to the seat, and finished on top with roll stick covered with cloth; lay the falls on a board, bottom to the front, and mark all around with chalk; then lay on broad lace, right side to the board, beginning at the right hand top corner; let the lace extend one-half inch above the chalk mark; put one two and one-half ounce tack in each corner; draw to the corner below, and tack on the edge of the lace; turn the corner sharp, and draw the lace to the next corner; drive a tack close to the corner on the edge of lace, and at the inside corner double up the lace and put a tack in both sides of the corner; then draw to the inside corner and tack; don't drive the tack all the way in until the lace is turned and the corner brought up sharp; then draw the lace down straight; double at the outside corner and tack; at the lower bottom corner turn sharp, and point tacks along the bottom to the other corner, and proceed as before, when they are ready seam up each miter, as noticed, and cut the lace down to within one-quarter inch of the seam; when opened and hammered gently the lace is ready to be put on the foundation. Fit the buckram for the back, the bottom to fit snugly upon the top of back cushion riser; fit to the seat corners; then cut straight up to the end of back, allowing one-eighth of an inch on each end; for the back lay the buckram on the bench; square up the ends, and cut off to the marks on ends and top; draw a line two inches from the top for the roll.

To paste out the cushion fronts cut the broad lace five inches longer than the front facing pattern; tack on a board one inch apart; cut strips of buckram five-eights of an inch narrower than the broad lace, and strips of cloth five-eighths of an inch wide the length of facings, one for each of the four sides; paste the facings heavily, avoiding all lumps; lay the buckram in the center and a strip of cloth on either side; rub with slicker, but do not rub the cloth hard, as it will work up and not adhere; it is best to pat the cloth down with the open hand; the cloth extends a full one-quarter inch over the edge of lace for a lip to sew to; paste buckram and cloth heavily; lay on Russia sheeting or tick; slicker down well; lay aside to dry.

To cut the cloth for body lining, spread the cloth right side up on the bench, nap running down; lay the

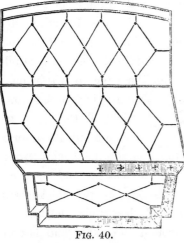

buckram back on the cloth; allow one and one-quarter inches on each end; mark the exact width of buckram, the bottom of back to the edge of cloth; mark along the top with French chalk; lay off the design on the buckram, and on the cloth without fullness, as shown in fig.

FIG. 40.

40; cut the roll for top of back three and one-half inches wide; lay the false tops on the cloth, allowing one inch fullness in length and one-half inch in width, and cut the cushion tops; lay off the design on the false tops, and on the cloth, without fullness; the points of diamonds should be two and one-half inches from the edge; mark the lines with French chalk; cut the cloth for the back for the front seat, if the rail is three and one-half inches wide, six and one-half inches wide; cut the cloth for the falls, allowing one inch at each end and at the bottom, to pass under the lace, measuring from inside of broad lace, and lay off, as

shown in fig. 41. Cut the seat linings from the strips
left from the falls; cut the end seat linings with nap running front; the cushion facings will serve as patterns
for the bottom and flare; the width can be obtained
from the seat panels; cut the back seat linings one
and one-quarter inches shorter than the facings, as the
cloth will stretch that much in length; stitch by
machine with silk. Fold the back, cushion tops and
falls on the chalk marks, right side out, and stitch
scant one-eighth inch from the edge to within one-

FIG. 41.

quarter inch of the tufts;
stitch all the lines as
shown in fig. 40, to form
the diamonds; when stitched lay on the bench wrong
side up; point a tack in the corners and at each
seam, and draw out straight; lay on two thicknesses
of cotton; cut one-half inch less than the top all
around; spread paste around the edges, and lay on
unbleached muslin; pat it down with the hand; remove the tacks; turn the top over and tack again; take
a stitch through cloth, cotton and muslin at the spaces
left for tufts, and trim off the muslin; lay cotton on
the falls to the edge of the broad lace; paste close up
to the cotton; draw on the cloth, the seams to the
points of the lace at the rocker, the same distance
from end and top; pat down all around; when dry
enough to handle put in the tufts at the intersection of
lines or seams; tie them on the back; lay the fall on
black muslin; cut one inch larger on ends and bottoms; lay paste on the right side, and turn the muslin

up over the edges; paste for the lace; lay on the edges of lace to the edges of fall, and finish by stitching around both edges.

To make the back lay off as shown in fig. 40. Cut strips of muslin four and one-half inches wide; double the edges together; put them to the edge of back, and baste four and one-half inches from the edge; begin at the right-hand bottom corner; baste to the left; fill with hair; baste and fill the end, then along the bottom edge of the roll and across the other, and this forms a roll all around the inside of back; cut a piece of muslin two inches larger than the back, and baste along the bottom; paste a little, and lay well-picked hair on the buckram about six inches thick; draw the muslin over from the bottom; press the hair down with the open hand; baste the muslin along the top; pull the muslin even, so as to make the back smooth; baste the ends; put on a layer of cotton; draw the cloth over the seams to the marks upon the back; baste all around; draw in the tufts lightly to make the back as level as possible; trim the edges, and baste seaming-lace across the top at the bottom edge of roll; baste the roll on close to the seaming-lace; line the roll with cotton, leaving one-half inch on each side; cover with muslin, pasted on the edges; sew the roll on strong; cover the back and bind around the edge with seaming-lace; cover the back rail and tack on the buckram solidly with fourteen-ounce tacks; tack the roll to the rail; stuff, close up the ends, and tack seaming-lace around the rail, one-quarter inch from the edge, beginning one inch under the end of the back on the bottom; finish with pasting lace.

To make the cushions, stitch the facings close to the edges; fit them to the flare of seat; fold the lace the exact flare, but do not cut it if it can be avoided; piece the side facings to the front and back facings by machine; sew the seaming-lace around the ends and back on bottom of facings; baste on the front and fall; sew in the bottom on the front only; baste the lace around the top, and sew it in; baste in the false top, leaving one end open eight or nine inches for stuffing; turn the cushion and blind-sew the bottom in; if the fall is not attached sew the bottom in all around first, and turn the cushion through the opening; secure the cushion to the bench by four round awls; fill the bottom, and sew the false top to close the bottom; settle down; then fill the top; tuft and draw the tufts down even with the front facings.

The back to the front seat, fig. 41, is made on pasteboard or three-ply of pasted buckram, cut to the size of the board; mark a line through the center; lay on small rattan; tack fast from the under side; line the cloth with muslin; mark the center with French chalk; lay on cloth, nap running down, the chalk mark directly on the rattan; baste and stitch both sides of the rattan; cut the rattan one inch short at each end; draw the cloth tight through the center; tack to the back, draw up the edges and tack to the rail; stuff and close the ends; cover the back of board with bow leather, and finish with seaming and pasting lace.

To put in the seat lining, put a bow leather welt over small rattan around the seat frame; secure with two and one-half ounce tacks, pointed inward, to avoid splitting the seat; dampen the leather, and rub close to the rattan with the tickler; sew the seat linings together by machine, taking a small seam; turn them right side out; lap the back on the front, and stitch down close to the edge of lap; blind-tack to the seat panel, beginning at one of the back corners, and draw while tacking all around; if well pasted about one-quarter inch up, the welt makes a good stiff foundation to tack to. Paste the seat panels and lay hair all around quite thin up to the edge of panels; draw the linings up at the corners first, without disturbing the hair, and tack the top close to the leather welt; trim off and finish with pasting lace.

The bows being rounded and pointed, take their diameter top and bottom, allowing a full one-quarter inch on each side, and obtain the length of each; cut out and scarf the bottom ends; dampen the cover; turn up the bottom about three-eighths of an inch, and rub down; tack to the bow at the bottom with three-ounce tacks, the seams on the inside edges of the bows, the front and middle, and the back and middle covers facing each other; draw them snugly at the bottom, covering the bow one-quarter inch full at the bottom; point a tack in each side; draw up and set two tacks at the top; even the edges, and tack about four inches apart on each side close up to the crease; then with the tickler crease close to the bow, keeping the edges even ; stitch close to the bow ; trim off close ; black and polish ; a little tallow will be found useful for polishing.

To put in the head-lining, put the bows all on the back seat, and while down, see that the joints fall correctly ; when right, set the top up ; put two strips of three-quarter-inch poplar, one and one-half inches wide, the full length of top just below the props, on the outside of bow, covered with cloth, to prevent them scratching the leather ; fasten them by passing a cord, with a slip knot, over each one between the front and middle bows, and draw tight enough to keep the sticks from slipping ; extend a cord across between back and middle bows ; the sticks keep the bows straight on the sides, and also prevent their spreading ; plumb from the back bow, and give three inches rake ; cut two sticks with ends the same bevel as the flare of bows ; put them between the middle and back bows, and tack at the ends to keep them from slipping ; place them about where the seam comes in the head-lining ; when all are in position center the bows, and measure from the center to the bend, and about two inches down on the bows if the corners are flattened ; mark and measure the same distance on the middle bows from the center outward, and one inch less on the back and front bows ; if the middle bows measure sixteen and one-half inches from the center each way, make the front and back to measure fifteen and one-half inches ; tack web to the back bow on both sides, the edge to the mark of seam line ; draw to the front and tack ; tack to the marks on the middle bows.

To cut the head-lining spread the cloth on the bench; measure over the bows from back to front, and mark the length one inch less on the cloth; cut thirty-two inches wide for an ordinary top; measure from the seam-line marks on the middle bows to the props, and cut one side-quarter piece, as the cloth is not wide enough to cut the other piece; the remaining strip, nine inches wide, will serve for the inside laces; cut the other side-quarter piece; center the top piece by folding and notching, and lay it over the bows, the notches to the center marks on the bows; point tacks three inches apart along the front and back bows; draw on the side-quarter pieces to meet the top piece on the center bows, and lap over at front and back; keep the cloth straight and smooth along the bottom; point tacks as before; mark the edge of back middle bow with French chalk on the inside from prop to prop; on the front middle bow mark the front edges; on front and back bows at the seam line on each piece, then along the edge of bow; lay each piece on the bench separately, and by a straight-edge mark from the line of the front center bow to the mark at the front, and then the back, and cut to those marks; sew up on the machine, the marks corresponding; designate the front before removing the cloth from the top; press open the seams with a hot flat-iron; for strips for sewing to the head-lining use good, smooth list; if rough or coarse, take strips of cloth; if the cloth is thin, double it and sew by machine with silk in the bobbin; baste the strips on at the French chalk marks, and stitch along by the bastings ; tack to the bows, first on the inside of back middle bow, then on the front middle one ; leave the head-lining in that position, and put on a piece of webbing about three inches below the other across the corners of bows ; tack on two pieces of unbleached muslin one and one-half inches longer than the top, allowing the top edge to extend four inches over the upper strip of webbing ; tack as far down on the bows as the props will admit of.   Lay paste on the muslin to the upper edge of the upper

FIG. 42.

strip of webbing, and down to within an inch of the top props ; lay the hair well picked, in small quantities, until all is covered ; build up to a sharp corner above the level of the bows ; make it very thin on the sides and build straight up with the bows ; draw the muslin up over the hair ; tack to front and back bows ; draw up on the middle bows ; draw up the head-lining and tack front and back.

Cut two strips of duck one and seven-eighths inches wide, the length of top at the props, for side lace ; fit them in, marking at each bow in the center ; mark the front ; cut the risers one and one-quarter inches wide, as shown by fig. 42 ; paste and lay the risers ; lay the cloth on them, the nap running front, the cloth four and a half inches wide on the top edge, or enough to turn over for a hem ; pat down with the hand and rub with the fingers close down to the risers ; when both are pasted turn them ; paste along the edge a space of one-half inch ; turn the cloth and pat down ; when dry stitch all around the risers; when the top edge is stitched, lay back the cloth that turns up from the bottom ; measure from the center of front prop down on a plumb line two inches ; put a straight edge to that mark and level by a spirit level; dot at the back bow and raise the straight edge one-quarter inch ; mark all the bows with chalk along the straight edge, and put in the side lace on the inside, the points of center risers to the center of middle bows, the bottom edge one-quarter inch above the line of bottom edge of side

FIG. 43.

quarters; tack the ends to front and back bows, and secure by covered nails; trim off the ends; cut the head lining close to the edge of bows, nearly to the top of lace ; push it in over the top of lace, and cut the cloth on the lace down to the bottom hem ; spread paste on the lace smooth and heavy from the top to the hem at the bottom ; pull the head lining out over and rub against the lace; if too wide trim off close down to the hem; this can be best done when the cloth is cut to turn up over the lace ; rub down when the paste is on.

Measure six and three-quarter inches for the back lace—fig. 43—from the outside corner of rail on each side ; mark the center with chalk and divide ; measure each way from the center on bow and add one-eighth of an inch; the back lace is in three pieces; the center one is cut to fit in between the marks for the back stays, while the ends extend to the edge of side lace, and cut to show the same width, adding the width of bow and three-eighths of an inch at the top as a lip to stitch to. Cut pieces of split dash leather; tack the corner pices to the bow, and mark around with lead pencil on both sides; from the inside mark measure one and seven-eighths inches; cut the corners round, and allow three-eighths of an inch on the top and corners; cut the middle and risers the same as for side lace in width, and put on as shown, the nap run-

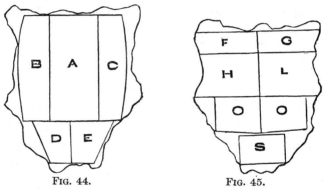

FIG. 44.   FIG. 45.

ning down; lay on the risers, then the cloth, and pat down with the open hand; turn the cloth at the bottom and paste; stitch around the risers; trim off the cloth close to the stitching; secure to the back bow full one-quarter inch above the top with 6-ounce tacks.

Trim the back stays with the metallic stay pasted in one edge seven inches wide; let the stay extend one-quarter inch outside the corner of shifting rail; pierce a hole through the metallic stay for the knob, the stay extending below the rail one-half inch; the buckram should extend one inch below; put the top inside edge to the mark on the bow, mark with lead pencil on the inside of stay along the bow, pierce all the holes for knobs, allowing enough on the bottom to cover the edge of seat panel, and cut off at the top, allowing one-half inch above the mark.

To cut the leather for the top take two hides, from fifty-five to fifty-seven feet each, spread them on the floor, and mark off as shown by figs. 44 and 45. A, fig. 44, roof piece; B and C, side quarters; D and E, front curtains. F and G, fig. 45, back stays; H and L, door curtains; O, quarter curtain; and S, back curtain.

This plan cannot always be adhered to, but the roof pieces and side quarters should be cut as shown in fig. 44, no matter what else may be got out of the hide; these pieces may be shifted further front if the hide will admit of it, and the back stays cut from the back end, but hides measuring less than sixty feet are seldom of a shape to permit a change. When all are cut paste out the back stays on a smooth board, and with a sponge dampen about one inch for the hem all around; lay the paste all over smooth, as all specks and lumps will show through the leather; lay on the buckram, rub down with the slicker, oil the hem on the enameled side, turn over and rub down the hem until it adheres to the buckram; crease the edge; oil about two inches from the edge, and make a double crease one-quarter of an inch apart two inches from the outside edge and two and one-quarter from the bottom; measure the distance from the knob on the shifting rail for bottom of quarter on the bow, making one inch less on the stay; punch a hole through the leather for the knob at the bottom of the metallic stay; divide that distance into three spaces, and punch a hole with a round awl through the metallic stay midway between the double and outside crease; cut riveting knobs off to one-quarter inch and drive them in; turn the stay over and put the head of the knob on a piece of heavy flap leather, enameled side on a bench iron and rivet the knobs.

Punch holes for the buckles with a one-half inch tongue punch, the hole directly opposite the knobs and on the inside of double crease line; cut chapes two and one-half inches long, punch a hole with tongue punch half way of the chape; scarf both ends; black and crease, insert the buckles, open the hole (which should be punched through the leather only), and insert the chape doubled until the buckle is close up to the leather; put the bench iron under it and drive two and one-half-ounce tacks through, and clinch; five or six tacks, properly clinched, will hold without sewing; sew on the loops.

Cut the cloth for linings seven and one-half inches wide; make a line for hem or turn-down three-eighths of an inch from one edge; then measure six and three-quarter inches to the other side, and mark with French chalk; lay on the stay, enameled side down, and mark along the bottom for the turn-down; then, with a hot iron, press the hem down all around; lay two layers of cotton six inches wide on the stay, and baste the cloth down all around, the cloth as near to the edge of the stay as possible ; then stitch by machine all around; pull out the bastings ; measure from the inside knob-hole on shifting rail up to the bottom of back rail, on the buckle side of each outside of double crease ; lay a five-eighth-inch strap, three inches long, on the cloth side, lengthwise with stay, and stitch two rows across the middle ; this, when the stays are up, is tacked to the bottom of back rail, to hold it up when the top is thrown ; put the knobs through the metallic stays and set them up ; cut the cloth and buckram away from the metallic stay at the top to an inch below where it strikes the bow ; cut a slit through the back lace for the metallic stay ; insert it, and draw up and mark the stay at the top of side lace each side, spring the back joint, pull the bow back, and give the stays one-quarter-inch draw ; punch three holes through each metallic stay, and drive 14-ounce tacks half way in ; tighten the joints, and if the stays are tight, drive in the tacks ; drive 14-ounce tacks in along as far as the double crease.

Fit up the back curtain, the double crease to that on the back stay ; tack in the four corners; mark at the double crease, top and bottom, also along the bottom edge of back stays, and at the tongues of buckles ; mark for the knobs, remove it, and hem outside the marks made at the bottom of stays, and at double-crease marks ; black the edge, wet and turn down the hem, paste a lining three inches wide along the bottom, and lining pieces two by four inches where the straps go ; turn the curtain over, oil, double crease to line

with creases on the bottom back of the straps. Cut the
billets four and one-half inches long, point, black and
crease ; put these directly on the marks made at the
tongue of buckles, the points two and one-half inches
from the edge of curtain ; then put on the loops high
enough for the billets; stitch by machine ; trim off and
black, line with cloth, trim off, turn down the hem and
stitch; sew the rings for knob holes ; punch, and slit
one-quarter inch for knobs ; put the center of back light
nine inches from the bow; put up four roll-up straps—
two, two inches from the edges of the stays, and others
four and one-half inches from these ; knob on the curtain, draw up square, point tacks along the top to
keep in position, baste and trim off.

To fit the top, lay the roof piece on the bench,
double the two edges together, enameled sides in, put
a tack at both ends to hold in position, then cut a true
sweep of three-quarters of an inch from one end to the
other ; lay the side quarters on the top, the best leather
back; tack front and back ; draw the leather down to
the props, beginning at the front, three inches from the
bottom ; slit with a knife, right at the prop, straighten
the leather and draw to the other prop and slit that
two and one-half inches from the bottom, then the
back one; remove the nuts, take off the joints and slip
the leather on, replace the joints, put a tack in front
and back bow on the outer edge and on the mark
made for bottom of quarter as a guide; draw the
leather on smooth at the bottom, point a tack at
the bottom line; when both quarters are on, put on the

roof piece, the center to the center marks on the bows, draw tight, draw up the side quarters on the middle bows, and tack; draw the roof piece over and tack, then with a sharp piece of chalk mark along the edge of roof piece, and across the center of each bow on roof and side quarters alike as a guide when putting together; draw a chalk line across the bottom from the tacks, and make a line for turning down the hem; mark up the front bow to the prop at the back, turn the leather on the stay loose, but not baggy; mark with chalk top and bottom on the double crease; take them off; strike a straight line from bow to bow; cut to a true sweep, allowing three-eighths of an inch at the center between the bows, over the straight line, regardless of the lines made by the edge of roof piece; allow one-quarter of an inch over the bows at the middle, and one-eighth of an inch at the ends; cut in to the mark in front of the front prop for the hem; dampen and turn the hem to that and the dots at the back. Cut strips of duck, three and one-half inches wide, full lenth of the quarter, and strips of cloth five inches wide for dusters; paste the duck on first; paste on the leather two inches wide from the hem; where the back bow strikes the quarter paste solid; paste on a triangular piece of cloth above the duck; this stiffens the quarter back of the back bow; paste the cloth on the duck; oil the hem, crease and make a double crease two inches from the edge of quarter, but not up the back end. The welts are got out of pieces cut from the quarters; wet and turn down, oil and slicker.

Cut the valance from harness leather one and one-fourth inches wide ; wet and bend on a board the shape of the bow ; fit to the front edge bow and cut off at the bottom of quarter round the inside corner, and cut bow leather the same shape as valance, two and three-quarters of an inch wide ; dampen and baste the cover on, nicking a little around the inside curve to make it bend nicely ; when covered, crease and stitch around the bottom two and one-half inches, and up the ends ; remove the bastings, and center the valance to the center mark on the bow, and tack with 6-ounce tacks ; leave a full one-quarter inch above the bow all around to stitch to ; stitch the quarters, trim and black the edges, and punch the holes for props. Cut the welts a scant one-fourth inch wide ; baste the roof piece and quarters together, holding the quarters in front, marks to correspond ; holding in that position works the full-ness in. When basted crease for the stitchers ; sew up by hand with awl and needles, using four strands No. 32 ball thread, doubled, or three of shoe thread; do not pull the stitches tight enough to draw the work, as that will spoil the set of the top ; when stitched lay flat on the bench and rub with the slicker on both sides of the seams to smooth them ; open the quarter from the roof and rub down on top of welt with the enameled side to the bench.

Cut the duster cloth at the prop holes to allow it to pass over the props ; sew the muslin together along the top ; draw an extra piece of muslin across the top ; tack to the front and back bows, and baste along the edges ; thirty-two inches is wide enough for this; put on the top, commencing at the front props ; pull over the front so as not to strain it when on the two front props; draw backward by taking hold at the seams; put on the middle props and draw back again, then draw to the back props and put them on; draw down on the back bow and pull to the mark of bottom edge of quarter, tack there to hold in position, then draw back half way between the bottom edge of quarter and the seam, and point a tack there, at the seam, and in the middle of roof; draw the front down and out; screw the thimble up tight; tack at the bottom, then draw at the seam, and tack also in the center of roof. Slit the front valance cover opposite the end of hem on side quarter, and tack the valance as far down as can be reached ; baste the top to the valance, crease down with tickler and trim off; round a strap three-fourths of an inch wide, point both ends, wet where they bend around the corners of bow, insert as far as possible under the valance; dampen the opposite corner and draw up over the top ; point tacks along to hold it; oil the edge and crease around on the front for stitching ; run the tickler around the back edge; turn the quarter around on the back stay to meet the double crease lines ; pull up enough to make the quarter straight along the bottom ; baste along the top, trim off and put a binding of enameled leather over it ; stitch from the double crease on side quarter through the back stay two and one-half inches up with a good, solid thread ; then stitch on front and back, trim off and black; put a black nail in the ends of front valance, one at the top of back curtain on each side, one in the side quarter one-half inch above the upper row of stitching, and another three inches above that ; then paste the dusters in, push up the cloth and lay paste on the inside lace ; draw down the duster against the lace, and rub every part well ; spread paste on the lace cloth and turn up and rub down well ; put in the knobs, four in the top of back bow opposite the roll-up straps, one in each bow one-half inch below the bottom edge of side quarters, and two in the middle bows, one as near the bottom of back middle bow as possible ; drive a tack in the front seat for the knob directly opposite the front middle bows ; divide into three spaces ; drive two knobs in the bow and one in the seat; that in the seat, however, should not be put in until the body has been varnished ; drive another at the front corner of the seat; tack up the front and quarter curtains high enough to reach the second row of stitching on the side quarter when hemmed.

Cut diagonally for the props on the front curtains, and slit for the lamp prop ; mark for the knobs, the curtains to come as far front at the bottom as the handles will admit of. The quarter curtain is slit straight up from the lower back prop to the top of the prop iron, fit it around on the back stay loose, and mark for the knobs. The door curtains are fitted after the others are taken off ; these extend to the handle in the door at the bottom, and on a line with the others at the top ; punch for knob holes with round awl at the bottom of the curtains, allowing one and one-half inches below the knob holes and on the front at the top, and finish the top at the bottom of side quarters; black the edge, wet and turn down the hem. Cut patches of heavy enameled leather one and one-half inches square for the knob holes, and paste the black side to the curtains; for the lamp prop hole in the front curtain cut a piece two inches wide and long enough to reach from the bottom to an inch above the hole; paste it on; when finished slit the curtain; paste a stay piece in the lower back corner of the quarters large enough to cover the back knob hole, the prop hole and the knob on the other side, if more than three inches; line with cloth, pasting well on the patches to keep the cloth from slipping while the rings are stitched on the machine; paste along the edges of curtains, pat the cloth down and trim off at the hem, turn down the hem, and make the rings for knob patches one inch in diameter; for lamp prop hole make a ring according to the size of hole required for the prop iron, mark two straight lines from the ring to the hem three-sixteenths of an inch apart, stitch around the prop hole and down to the hem again; for the lower prop hole, on the quarter curtain, make a ring according to the size of gum used; for one and one-quarter inch gum, make a ring one and five-eighths inch, stitch the ring when the curtain is being hemmed, and stitch the ring for knobs before hemming.

CHAPTER IX

MISCELLANY.

BISCUIT CUSHIONS.

If the seat is straight, or has very little flare, cut the cushion bottom one-eighth inch smaller than the seat bottom ; but if the flare is one and one-half inches or more, cut the bottom one-quarter inch larger all around. The cushion bottom, when made up, should be carefully fitted to the seat, and of full size, but if made too large the front facing will cramp when placed in position, spoiling the appearance of the cushion. After the bottom is fitted, obtain the flare of seat by cutting a piece of pasteboard the width of front facing ; two and one-half inches is the common width. (See fig. 46.) Bevel the end till it fits the bevel of seat, and with a square draw the line from B to C ; from this the width of the end and back facings can be obtained, also the size of false top or division. A to C is the width of end and back facings.

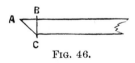

FIG. 46.

For ordinary cushions cut the front facing two and one-half inches wide and four inches longer than the bottom, or enough to allow for the flare ; then cut a

strip of split dash leather three-eighths of an inch
narrower all around than the facing, paste on the riser,
then paste on the facing and a strip of muslin over the
back ; this makes a stiff facing and leaves a soft edge
to sew to.   Ascertain the width of the end and back
facings by measure from A to C (in fig. 46), which will
be about three inches ; paste up same as front facing,
but without risers ; cut the back facing three-eighths
of an inch higher in the center, with a true sweep.   Cut

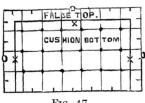

FIG. 47.   FIG. 48.

the false top, by laying the cushion bottom on the
material used (see fig. 47); drive a tack at each corner
to prevent slipping, and measure from A to B in fig.
46, the flare of the seat.   If the flare is one and three-
quarter inches, the false top should be one and three-
quarter inches larger than bottom at the ends and
back only, as there is no flare in the front ; where the
front facing flares back on the top, cut off the false top
in front as much as the facing flares back.   Set a compass with points at A and B (fig. 46) and define lines
O from lines X, and mark out the false top outside of
bottom ; lay off the size of biscuits, commencing on
lines O.   Space off as near square as possible, then
with a round awl punch holes where the lines cross for

the buttons, marking the bottom and false top at the same time ; fit the facings to the bottom, getting the flare with pattern (fig. 46) ; lay them on the false top, and if correct they will fit the false top as well as the bottom.

Lay off the material used for the top proper, allowing one inch fullness to each square both ways, and punch holes with a No. 3 punch for the buttons. If the top is of leather it is ready to be sewed up, but if of cloth press the plaits with a hot iron ; lay on one or two thicknesses of cotton one-half inch less all around than the cloth ; paste the edge of cloth and put on the muslin lining ; trim the edge and take a stitch at each of the holes for bottoms to hold the cotton and lining in place. To sew up, begin by first stitching together the corners of the facings with narrow welts ; then cut welts of the same material one and one-eighth inches wide to cover the cording, and with a glover's needle and a well waxed thread sew in the cushion bottom, sewing the cord in at the same time ; leave a hole open at one end to stuff up the bottom.

Baste the top proper to the false top ; first get the center between the plaits, as shown by dots in figs. 47 and 48, then place the dots on cushion top on dots on false top, and hold in place with a stitch to divide the fullness evenly ; lay the plaits and baste, leaving it open across the back. The top being basted to the false top, sew in across the front and ends, leaving the back open to turn the cushion through, but sew the welt firm to facings, as the top is blind-sewed to the

welt. The top being sewed, turn the cushion and sew
the false top in across the back; draw tufting twine
through the four corners of the cushion, making a loop
two and one-half inches long by which to fasten it to
bench, bottom side up. Stuff the bottom up from the
end, through the opening; draw the cushion out square
and smooth, but not too tight; keep the stuffing up

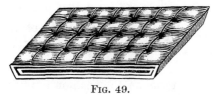

even; level it by
treading upon it;
remove it from its
fastening, turn
over and stuff the

FIG. 49.

top. Draw in the front row of buttons, and stuff up
front row of biscuits; draw in the next row of buttons
and stuff and sew on till the top is all stuffed; close
the back by blind-sewing the top to the cord, laying
the plaits as they are reached. Fig. 49 shows a biscuit
cushion completed.

How to Make a Cheap Cushion.

Obtain the size of the seat bottom, then cut the
cushion bottom to the size required, of enameled duck,
six inches longer and three inches wider than the seat
bottom, as the end and back facings and bottom are
all cut in one piece, as shown in fig. 50—A, the cushion
bottom, B B B, back and end facings, and· E, front
facing; lay it in the seat and gather up the facings in
corners, as shown in fig. 52; cut out as shown by fig.
50, C C; draw a line around the bottom of seat, dividing the cushion bottom from the facings; paste strips

of buckram three inches wide on the back and end facings, and two-ply of buckram one and seven-eighths inches wide and one inch shorter than the front on the front facing ; when dry sew two straps, 1 and 2, fig. 50,

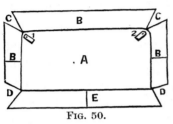

FIG. 50.

in the back corners for fastening the cushion to bench while stuffing; paste a riser of harness leather five-eighths of an inch wide on the stiffening of front facing. Cut the front of the same material as the cushion top two and one-half inches wide, and paste on over the riser ; crease it down close all around and paste a strip of calico over the back of the facing. Fig. 51 shows the front facing with riser on.

To cut out the top of the cushion measure across the facings, and cut the top two and one-half inches larger both ways than this measurement ; draw lines through the center of the top both ways ; place them at the

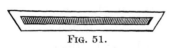

FIG. 51.

lines on facings, to evenly divide the fullness and prevent the cushion top drawing. Fit the front facing to the bottom and seam up the corners, C C D D, with a welt; stitch with a heavy waxed end and two needles. Cut the welts to cover seaming cord one and one-eighth inches wide.

When the front facings are sewed to the bottom across the front, and the corners all stitched, sew in cushion top, baste the covered cords to the facings,

fold the welts around the cord, having both edges even
with cushion facings; sew in the top, sewing close to
cord.   Place the center marks on the cushion top at
the marks on facing, and hold in place with a stitch;
then draw the fullness to the corners and lay a plait;
leave an opening at one end eight inches long to turn
the cushion through, but sew the cord firm to the
facing, for when the cushion is stuffed the top is blind-
stitched to the cord.

To stuff, draw tufting twine in the front corners and
make a loop three inches long; then draw out square
on the bench, holding it in place by round awls, driv-

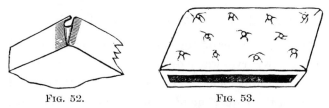

FIG. 52.   FIG. 53.

ing them through the straps in the back corners and
loops in the front.   Use a stick four feet long, round
at one end for handle and flat at the other end, with
notches cut in to hold the stuffing.   First fill the corners, then stuff up even, holding the left hand on cushion top to detect hollow places or lumps; put in but
little stuffing at a time, as otherwise it will work uneven
and lumpy.   A nice soft cushion is the pride of any
trimmer. The fillers used for stuffing this kind of cushions are moss, tow, lawn hay, or rowen and excelsior.

When stuffed and the ends sewed up it is ready for
tufting.   To do this lay the top off in squares or dia-

monds with a piece of soft white chalk ; punch a hole
where the buttons go with an awl, dust off the chalk
and draw in the buttons with a twine, using a tufting
needle made for that purpose.   Thread the top button
on the twine, then thread both ends of twine through
the needle and draw through the cushion ; take off the
needle and thread on a button, tie in a slip loop and
draw up the twine, press the top button down with
elbow ; draw the twine up tight, turn the cushion bottom side up and tie in two knots, drawing the knots
under the buttons ; draw all the buttons in a like manner, and the cushion is completed as shown in fig. 53.

PUTTING IN HEAD LININGS TO STANDING TOP CARRIAGES.

Mark the center on the front and back end rails, and
on the two curves which divide the top into three parts,
the head lining being tacked to these.   Cut strips of
oil cloth three-quarters of an inch wide and tack them
to the inside of the rails, on the line for the seaming
lace ; cut the cloth one inch longer than the inside of
the roof ; mark for the curves to which it is to be attached, and sew strips of cloth scant three-eighths of
an inch inside of these lines ; double the strips and
tack to the curves—the fold of the cloth at the center
lines on the curves ; use 2 or 3-ounce tacks, commencing in the center and tacking each way toward the side
rails ; draw tight while tacking.   Tack to the ends,
drive the first tack in the center ; the cloth must be
turned under and drawn tight ; proceed the same as
with the center ; finish by tacking to the guides on the

top rails, then tack on the lace. Head linings of other goods are put in the same way, excepting that the nailing strips on the center are serged on with fine silk, so that the stitches will not show through.

TOP FOR FREIGHT WAGON.

Fig. 54 illustrates a top for heavy express or other freight wagons. The bows are heavy, being three-quarters by one and one-half inches, and finished smooth all over, painted or covered; joints are dispensed with, two round iron bars being attached to the

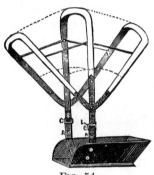 middle bow on each side, having hooks at the ends, which are caught into eyes on the back and front bows. The top is supported by pivots at A to stationary standards, B. Clamps, C, hold the top up when in the position shown; these rest on a lip at L; when

FIG. 54.

the top is lowered the hooks are loosened and the clamps slid up. The top is covered with muslin, duck or other light material, down to dotted lines on the bows.

SUMMER TOPS.

Light tops for summer use are popular in many localities. These may be covered with prunello, merino, buff linen or enamel cloth.

The bows for these are set in every respect the same

as for leather, but as there is no stuffing to hold up the corners they should not have more than three to four inches round, the latter only on large tops. The bows may be covered with leather up to the line of the prop irons, and with the material used to cover the top, on the bends and top, this should be drawn on and tacked on the top of the bows; if another covering is preferred, use the same material as that of the top cover; cut to the right size, allowing for a seam, and stitch up on a machine wrong side out; pinch the seam open, turn the cover and draw it on the bow, with the seam inside, and cover the center the same as when leather is used on the bows. Cover the stay web and back stays with the same material as the top cover; catch the edges together on the top, or turn the edges over and stitch on a machine about one-quarter of an inch from the edge; in nailing on the stay webs, place them so that they will hide the seams that join the side quarters and top. Cut the side quarters three inches wider than they are required to be when finished; then cut a piece of plain leather two and one-half inches wide, paste the edge of the quarter, half inch wide to the leather, and when the paste is dry fold the leather in and stitch on both edges; this gives a strong, firm edge to the side quarter. Buckram or muslin may be used in place of the leather if desired. Finish the front and back by nailing a welt on each bow and blind-stitch on, or with a valance front and bound back, as with other tops. Cut all the curtains and back quarters wide enough to allow for turning the edges over twice, making the seam when stitched one-half inch wide ; if knobs are used for securing the curtains to the back quarters cut off the shanks ; cut out patches of patent leather, and make a hole in the center large enough to allow the heads to pass through, and stitch the patches to the back quarters ; or use small bone or rubber buttons without shank eyes, sewed on in the usual way, and work button holes in the curtains ; knobs can be used on the rail. These tops are not lined, and are light and durable.

SPONGING OF CLOTH.

The sponging of cloth is indispensable in the trimming shop. Cloth in an open carriage is so much exposed that every precaution known to the art should be used to prevent shrinkage. In large shops the cloth is sponged in the piece, but there are smaller shops where no more is purchased than is needed for a single job, and the trimmer is compelled to sponge it—and all trimmers should know how to sponge the cloth, whether in the piece or in smaller quantities.

Piece-sponged goods have their face refinished, which looks equally as well as before it was sponged, but the process of refinishing materially affects the sponging, as the cloth is stretched, and a portion of the fullness taken up in the process of sponging is lost ; such cloth will again shrink when exposed to the weather. This is not apparent in heavy cloths, as they do not stretch in the same proportion as light cloths, and there are ten pieces of light cloths used where there is one of heavy for top cloths.

Body linings are seldom sponged, except in the piece; cloths that require the closest attention are American and German; these are often sold under fictitious names, especially in lower grades; the name is only given to the cheap goods. Such cloths should in all cases be sponged, for their shrinking qualities are in some cases beyond comprehension. English cloths, while they do not shrink as much as others, should not be exempt from sponging.

To sponge for a buggy top, take heavy unbleached muslin, such as is used in lining the cloth of body-linings five yards long; place it in a pail of water; if new use warm water, and allow it to soak until it is wet through; spread the cloth down doubled, the face sides together, in a clean place; remove the muslin from the water and squeeze so that it will not drip over the floor, leaving in as much water as possible; spread the muslin over the cloth, equal distances over each side; lay a wooden roller two or three inches in diameter at the end of the cloth, and roll cloth and muslin together; keep the cloth and muslin smooth, drawing and rolling tight to prevent wrinkles; lay aside for three or four hours, then unroll and hang on a line to dry.

Cloth falls of the body lining should be sponged by laying the cloth on the bench wrong side up, wetting a clean sponge, saturating the cloth with water, putting on all that the cloth will take in; then lay it on muslin and iron while it is yet wet; when dry it is ready for use.

Bow Trimmers.

The edge of the leather cover to bows is always unsightly, and if not finished neatly it contributes in no small degree to condemn the whole trimming. A

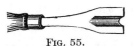

skillful workman may trim the edge true with an ordinary knife

FIG. 55.

or an edge tool, but all will find a gauge an advantage in time spent and perfection of work. Fig. 55 illustrates a tool made for this purpose. It is of steel, with the cutting edge on the crown of

the raised center, the sides being flat and smooth; the one shown trims the edge round; the cutting edge may be flattened if preferred. Fig. 56 illustrates a

FIG. 56.

guard, to be used with an ordinary knife; the guard is made of metal, polished. This is a cheap and convenient tool.

Moths.

There are several distinct species of minute moths, which, in their larval state, are destructive to materials used by carriage trimmers. They are known as the leather moth, the cloth moth, the carpet moth, and the fur or skin moth. The first is particularly destructive to morocco and similar leathers. The cloth and carpet moths live on cloth and woolen stuffs. The fur or skin moth lives on furs.   All make cases or cells of the material on which they live.

The insects which breed these moths appear in our climate in May or June, at which time they lay their eggs, dying immediately afterward.   The eggs hatch out in fifteen days, and the grubs at once commence gnawing such substances as are in their reach, at the same time making their cells with the fragments. Some species attach these cells or cones to the articles they live upon, others travel in them from place to place.   The worms carry on their work of destruction during the summer months ; in the spring they change to chrysalides, and in twenty days thereafter they are transformed to winged moths.   They fly around in the evening, settling into dark closets, folds of cloth, etc. While in the winged state they shun all pungent odors, and it is at this time, and only this, that camphor, tobacco or other moth preventives are of value; when in the larval state they will feed upon the very articles which are so sure a protection against the winged insect.   Light and air are their enemies ; let them alone in the darkness and they do their work most effectually ; disturb them and they cease their ravages. The surest way to exterminate these pests is to subject them to heat and light, during the early part of June. The course pursued by fur dealers is to whip every article as often as once a month, sweep up the dust and destroy it.   The goods in the trimmer's stock room should be treated in the same way, taking the additional precaution to distribute camphor and tobacco freely during the season while the insect is on the wing.

MAKING LACE FALLS.

To make a lace fall, cut out a piece of duck a little larger than the size required for the fall; tack it out on a board, and wet it with a sponge and let it dry.

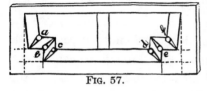

FIG. 57.

While the duck is drying, lay the fall off on a board, as shown in fig. 57; then draw the lace around the edge with the wrong side of lace up, and hold in place with tacks; gather up the fullness in the corners at *a b c d e* and *f*, and sew together with a glover's needle and a stout waxed thread; when the miters are all sewed together, trim off and hammer or iron them down with a hot iron; cut out the piece of enamel duck which has been shrunk, leaving enough

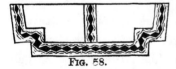

FIG. 58.

goods across the ends and bottom of fall to form a narrow hem; paste on the cloth, putting paste only where it is covered with the lace, and paste the hem over; paste on the strip of lace through the center (see fig. 58) first, then paste on the border; do not get paste on the cloth where it is not covered with the lace. Tack the fall out on a board, and let it get thoroughly dry before stitching; stitch in a strip across the bottom for the fall stick; may be finished

across the top with a valance or covered stick.   Fig. 59
is a fall for light work, and is made on enamel duck,
with a harness leather riser around the fall inside of

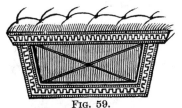

FIG. 59.

the lace.   Place a layer
of cotton between the
cloth and enamel duck,
inside of the riser;
shrink the cloth well
before using; paste the
cloth well around the edge, but do not put paste inside
of the riser.   Stitch two rows through the center both
ways, one-quarter of an inch apart, with silk, a little
lighter shade than the cloth; draw a rosette tuft
through the center, and sew the fall in with the
cushion.

To Make Paste.

To make the common every-day paste for the trimming shop, where one or two trimmers are employed,
have an iron pot, with a convenient handle, holding
from two to three quarts; put in nearly a quart of
flour to make a pot full, stir enough water in to form
a stiff dough, and with a paddle stir and beat until all
the lumps have disappeared; then stir in water gradually until it is reduced to the consistency of cream;
cook over a slow fire and stir continually, to prevent its
sticking to the bottom; do not remove it from the fire
until all is well done.   If these instructions are fully
carried out the paste will be smooth and stiff; be careful in mixing, for if once too thin the flour cannot be

freed from lumps. Heavy paste is needed for leather and rough linings, where buckram is much used, while on some other places thinner paste will work; heavy paste will not spread evenly on cloth, or on the muslin of buggy tops, owing to the soft foundation.

Seasons have a great effect on paste; in winter it may be made thin on account of its keeping sweet, while in summer it sours and becomes thin, and often worthless; alum is a very good thing to put in paste in summer, and rosin is good the year round. The best flour does not make the best paste; where flour is bolted fine the glutinous substance is nearly all abstracted, which destroys the adhesiveness of the paste; coarser flour is the best.

The class of work requiring the best paste known to the craft, is glass frames and hammer cloths, which are exposed to the weather. To make a paste of that quality take rye flour, and to every quart of flour add a heaping table spoonful of powdered rosin; mix well together, then add water to make a stiff dough; then thin to the consistency of very thick cream; cook until well done over a slow fire; stir all the time. Rye flour requires more cooking than wheat. A paste made this way has powers of resisting dampness that is not possessed by glue, and is very elastic; it is the best paste known.

MAKING APRONS.

In making aprons very little paste should be used, as paste readily absorbs moisture, and, by molding, causes the apron to rot. If the lining is basted on no paste is necessary, and the apron, when made, will be less likely to rot than when made in the old way.

Case and Box Loops.

Trimmers, as a rule, pay but little attention to the making of loops, and it is no uncommon thing to see a top to a high-priced carriage defaced by half a dozen or more loops that have been carelessly made and put

on ; in fact the greater portion of good loops seen on carriage tops are metallic, or what is known as the patent loop—a hand-pressed

FIG. 60.

leather loop. These each supply a needed want, yet there is a sameness about them that is not acceptable to most carriage manufacturers.

Loops may be made of patent or plain leather ; the latter are the best, though not quite as showy when new as the former. Patent leather loops cannot be pressed hard enough to make them durable without destroying the enamel. The finest loops are made of a fine grade of leather, known to the trade as "loop leather." This leather is curried with very little oil; if of good quality it is solid, but the grain is fine and mellow ; these qualities are absolutely necessary in order that the creases or forms on the loop can be sharply defined ; if the grain is harsh and coarse, or the leather soft, it is impossible to set creases by hand, or to prevent the pressed creases losing their sharpness when working with the finished loops. When buying, therefore, select a light, well-tanned hide, with a fine, mellow grain and solid body; uniformity in thickness is not necessary, or even desirable, as the thickness of leather required is governed by the size of the loop.

Tempering the stock so that it will work well is one of those little things that is too often overlooked, be-

cause of ignorance of its importance; if not properly d o n e n o amount of work can

FIG. 61.

correct the evil

wrought. The leather should be put into cold water, and be allowed to remain therein until moistened entirely through, but not long enough to become soaked; then remove it and hang it up until it is surface dry; if, when apparently dry on the surface, it sheds moisture on bending, it is too wet to work.

A perfect loop must have the corners full, with a

compressed grain. To secure this, cut the l o o p leather about one-fourth of an inch wider than the com-

FIG. 62.

bined width and depth

of both sides of the loop-stick, for a one inch loop, increasing or diminishing as the loop exceeds or falls short of this size.

In making pressed loops stitch the loop leather to the curtain or on the strap, using bristles instead of

needles for long loops ; insert the loop-sticks, screw up
the side clamps, and press in the top ornament by a
die, with a strong screw press, such as that used by
harness makers ; such presses are seldom used in a
trimming shop, but no one having used them, or made
loops in the way described, will use any other method.

Hand-creased loops are attached the same as the

pressed loops ; the
loop-sticks are in-
serted and the sides
pressed up with
clamps, the fullness

FIG. 63.

in the top being worked down and outward so as to
secure full corners ; when the leather is set down to the
loop-stick, mark off the pattern and crease out with the
proper tools, kept hot by laying them on a metallic box
heated by a gas jet or alcohol lamp ; when the pattern is worked up, remove the wooden loop-sticks and
insert hot iron ones, being careful not to have the irons
hot enough to injure the leather ; then color the leather
with iron and vinegar black, and work over the pattern with a warm slicker until the leather is dry ; this

gives a fine polish ; if
the color is not good,
apply a coat of hat-
ters' black, and rub
with a silk rag. A

FIG. 64.

loop creased and colored in this way never requires
varnish to give it a finished appearance.

The illustrations, figs. 60, 61 and 62, show different

styles of case or curtain loops; 63 and 64, patterns for check and other strap loops. Where pressed loops are used the edges must be perforated for stitching, as shown by figs. 60, 61 and 62. These patterns will not answer for patent leather loops, the figures being too fine for the enameled surface.

DECEPTION IN CLOTHS.

One of the "tricks of the trade" is to give piece-dyed cloth the same appearance as wool-dyed, by removing the color on the edges by acids, which gives a yellow shade to the part touched by the acids, in this way imitating the selvage on wool-dyed cloth. The deception is a good one ; many buyers are misled by it. The true character of the cloth can be determined, however, if examined ; the real list on wool-dyed cloth does not have a fine nap, like the body, while the acid list has the same finish as the body, differing only in color. Nor is the list always of uniform width and color.

FINISHING PLAIN STRAPS.

Plain leather straps on carriages are seldom finished as they should be. The edges are too often rough and uneven, the grain looks coarse, and the holes for the buckles are not blacked. To finish a black strap properly it must be moistened before working, by being placed into cold water and allowed to remain therein until the leather begins to look white, from the grease forced to the surface by the water. Then remove it, and hang it up until it is surface dry. If the leather has not been well curried, give it a coat of of neatsfoot oil and tallow, and allow it to remain over night ; then remove the surplus grease, and rub both sides with a glass slicker. In either case, fit up and stitch before the strap is thoroughly dry. When dry, trim the edges smooth with a sharp knife, black the edges and flesh side with vinegar black, and rub with a bone slicker ; punch the holes for the buckles, and black the insides ; run a creaser along the edges, and a stitch-wheel over the stitches ; black the strap with hatters' black, and, when dry, rub thoroughly with a silk rag ; do not varnish a new strap.

Door Stops.

Where ordinary door hinges are used, "stops" are necessary to prevent the door opening so far as to come in contact with the wheels or parts of the body. A plain stop is made of stay web, covered with leather or coach lace. A much better stop is made of a saw-blade steel, one inch wide, covered with coach lace. The steel has "T" heads at each end, and is secured to the door and standing pillar by means of loops, sufficiently large to allow the steel to slide through when the door is being closed, or by fastening one end to the door, carrying the other end around to the inside of the standing pillar, over a small tube roller. In the latter case the stop-loop should set well back on the pillar, and a small guide-loop be placed over the roller to prevent the "stop" leaving the roller. The "stop" should work easily, so that when the door is closed, it will pass under the fall, or back under the seat, out of the way.

SUPPORTS FOR BODIES.

It is absolutely necessary that the carriage body to be trimmed should be held firmly in a level position; ordinary trestles are inconvenient, owing to the difficulty in leveling up. Fig. 65 shows a device which is at once simple and effective; it consists of a pyramidical box, made of one-inch whitewood, with a flattened top of two-inch ash, through which there is a hole having a coarse thread cut in it which receives the supporting screw; the screw is provided with a small pin in the top, which, when in use, passes

FIG. 65.

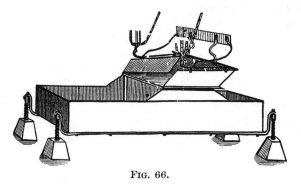

FIG. 66.

through the bolt hole in the body loop. Four of these, placed under a body, as shown in fig. 66, will hold it firmly in place, and by turning any one or more of the necessary screws it can be leveled without trouble.

DRIVER'S CUSHION.

This cushion is made on a frame with two triangular pieces for sides, the top being cut to a slight curve; the back ends are cut to the same flare of the seat; the bottom, back and sides are securely fastened together; the front is strengthened by a strip about two inches square, the top of which is shaped to the sweep of the sides; stay web is stretched across the top, both ways, and interlaced; before securing all the web the box should be well filled with moss; after the web. is tacked draw over a piece of burlap, lay on the necessary amount of hair and cover with muslin; cover the sides and back; make up the top with rolls two inches wide at the back and one-half inch wide at the front; blind tack the top in place; a welt should be tacked on all around the top.

PICKING CURLED HAIR.

Owing to its elasticity, curled hair is the best material in use for stuffing cushions, etc. This elasticity is due to the curl put into the hair by being twisted into a hard rope; the curl thus imparted remains after the rope is untwisted and when loosened up, providing the work is properly done. The only way yet known is to untwist the rope and pick the hair by hand. Machines have been introduced for this purpose, but they break the hair more or less, and straighten it to a considerable extent, thus impairing its elasticity. Picking by hand is slow and tedious work, but until some machine is devised that will untwist the rope and separate the hairs, without breaking or straining them, handpicked hair only should be used in carriages.

A Gipsy Top.

This class of top, fig. 67, is not so much in vogue as  formerly, but it is used to a limited extent in some parts of the country. The back quarter, which is the distinctive feature, is generally stitched to the back stay, and nailed to the back bow. It can be made adjustable by knobbing it to the back quarter stay and the bow. The inside may be lined with plain cloth, or with a thin quilted squab.

FIG. 67.

Curtain Straps.

Curtain straps are not looked upon as among the ornamental fixtures of a carriage. A neat strap for a buggy is made of patent leather, covered with cloth on the inside, and stitched with dark silk, one-eighth of an inch from the edge. Ornamental forms do not make the most desirable straps, nor does fancy stitching improve them. Plain, neat straps, which corres-

pond in color with the trimming, are always **prefera-**
ble to the more elaborate patterns.

BACK CURTAINS.

The prevailing fashion is to make all back curtains
of carriages to roll up, but, as these are objectionable
to many persons, knobbed curtains have been substituted. For these the back is finished with a narrow
fall, as shown by A, fig. 68; this fall is about two

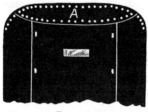

inches wide in the center,
and cut to a sweep, as
shown; the knobs for the
top of the curtain are driven
into the bow under this fall,
or the top of the curtain is
furnished with hooks similar

FIG. 68.

to apron hooks, which hook into eyes attached to the
bow. This arrangement does away with all curtain
straps, and gives a neat finish to the top with or without a back curtain.

INTERIOR FIXTURES.

The interior fittings of carriages have become a very
important element in carriage trimming, the selection
and arranging of which calls for good taste on the part
of the trimmer. These fixtures consist of card boxes,
looking glasses, toilet boxes, fan and parasol holders,
package boxes, call bells, cane and cigar holders, and
cigarette and cigar boxes. Of these, card boxes, toilet
boxes, and the holders for fans, etc., are exposed to

view. The card boxes are generally attached to the doors; they are of ivory, celluloid and rubber, in colors, metal or leather covered, with morocco to match the trimming. The latest style of box is made in two parts; the back, which contains the cards, is securely attached to the door, and the front is hinged at the bottom to the back, and secured at the top by a spring. This contains a silicate slate, with three or four leaves, and a pencil, making a convenient memorandum book. Small willow baskets are also used as card cases.

Toilet boxes are usually attached to the front part of a coupe, or other close two-passenger carriage; when used in other carriages, which, however, is seldom, they are set into the quarter squab, or other convenient place, and covered with a small squab. These are made of rosewood or ebony, highly polished, or of other wood covered with leather. They are sufficiently large to hold a comb, brush and other small toilet articles, and a looking glass. The latter is generally hinged at one of the upper corners, and is dropped into the box on its edge. Parasol, umbrella, cane and fan holders are of metal, leather covered or polished, and ivory. One style is a sectional ring, hinged to a plate, by which it is secured to the side or front of the carriage. This ring is made of metal, covered with leather; one section of the ring is hinged by a spring to the other at the back, near the securing hinge. This ring, owing to its being hinged, will accommodate an umbrella as well as a parasol, and not appear heavy when not in use. The plain ivory ring, hinged, is a popular style. Fan holders are little ornamental spring catches, which clasp the ring or cord of the fan ; they are placed against the standing pillar or one of the bows. Hooks for canes and parasols are of ivory, or metal covered. These are screwed to the front at the top in coaches, etc., and below the first window in coupes, two being used, upon which the cane may be laid.

Looking glasses have long been in use; they are commonly placed in the center of the quarter squabs, or in the back, over the back window, either stationary and covered with an adjustable squab, or to a frame the outside of which is covered with a squab. Either arrangement is inconvenient. A better arrangement is to put the glass into a frame, using two glasses, back to back, and secure it to the hinge pillar by a triple-hinged bracket, covering it, when not in use, by a small squab. The glass hinged in this way can be brought down directly in front of the occupant of the carriage, and be adapted to a two or four-passenger vehicle.

Cigar and cigarette holders are little round, long boxes, conveniently placed. The top opens so as to form a tray; they will hold two cigars. Another holder is an adjustable hook, with a lever arm, supported by a spring; the hook clasps the cigar and holds it in place.

Package boxes are little trays, placed in the neck of a coupe or other vehicle of its class. They are divided into small compartments.

CHAPTER X.

HAMMER CLOTH SEAT.

A hammer cloth seat is the most elaborate in use,
and its construction calls for the exercise of skill and
taste on the part of the workman. It is made up on
a frame constructed for the purpose. Fig. 69 gives
the top view ; fig. 70 is the end, and fig. 71 the back
view ; fig. 72 shows the bottom with the corner blocks
in position, and figs. 73 and 74 show the frame when
completed, the corner lines being canted down, the dotted lines representing the position of the pipes. The
body of the frame is made of ash, the blocks and side
forms of whitewood. The frame needs to be strongly
made and covered with glued canvas; it is secured to
the boot by thumb screws, as shown in figs. 70 and 71.
The frame may be made with the back and front hollowed, as shown in fig. 69, or straight on the back as
shown by fig. 71. The ends may be straight on the
top or hollowed out, as shown in fig. 81. The making
of the frame is no part of the trimmer's work, but he

should know how it should be made in order to be able
to carry out any special plan of construction. The
cushion is made up on the frame, either full stuffed or
with springs, but it should be made quite flat. Before

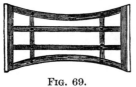

making up the cushion all the
bodies of the pipes, side and
end pieces should be fitted. The
pipes should always be cut to a
pattern, the general shape of

FIG. 69.

which is shown by figs. 75 and 76, the large pattern
being that of the corner pipes, and the small one that
of the small pipe ; the latter, however, is not used on

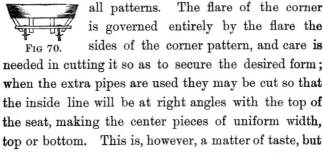

all patterns.   The flare of the corner
is governed entirely by the flare the
sides of the corner pattern, and care is

FIG 70.

needed in cutting it so as to secure the desired form ;
when the extra pipes are used they may be cut so that
the inside line will be at right angles with the top of
the seat, making the center pieces of uniform width,
top or bottom.   This is, however, a matter of taste, but

it is necessary to decide upon
the style before cutting the patterns.

FIG. 71.   Cut the pipes and center pan-

els of pasteboard ; cover both sides with linen, glued
on to the pasteboard ; bend to the desired form while
wet, and tack to a board to dry ; when thoroughly dry
apply two coats of priming, mixed a little thinner than
that used on bodies. When the paint is dry, glue to
the inside another piece of linen ; this should be quite

heavy—heavy sail cloth or buckram pasted up two-ply;
or split leather can be used in place of the pasteboard if preferred. When all parts are prepared as

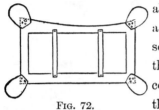

above, place the frame upon
a high trestle, secured firmly
so that it will not move while
the forms are being fitted on;
cover the frame with cloth,
then fit all the pieces, tack

FIG. 72.

and mark so that no mistake will be made when joining the parts. This being done, remove all and paste
on the cloth ; some trimmers paste only at the edges

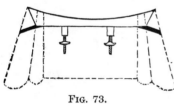

and across the ends
where the cloth is to be
covered by the trim-
ming ; when the paste
is dry tack the pieces to
the frame ; reverse it

FIG. 73.

and sew up the seams with heavy waxed thread ; stay
all the pipes on the back with straps sewed to the joining seams. The fringe and other trimmings are sewed

on next, after which the valance (if one is used) is put
on, and the top is then finished off. The cushion top
is then put on, and cord or

FIG. 74.

seaming lace blind-tacked on to cover the seams.
Some of the plainer styles of hammer cloths are bound
and stitched around the bottom, and trimmed with
broad lace set up from the edge ; this necessitates

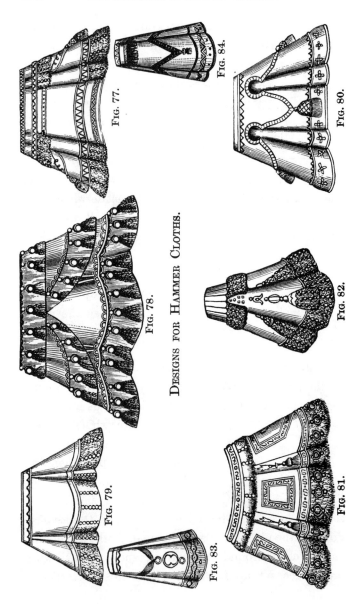

DESIGNS FOR HAMMER CLOTHS.

FIG. 77.

FIG. 84.

FIG. 80.

FIG. 78.

FIG. 82.

FIG. 79.

FIG. 81.

FIG. 83.

much care in stitching. After the cloth is finished on the outside, a good coat of paint should be applied to the inside ; when fastened on the boot the corners should be secured so as to prevent the cloth swinging.

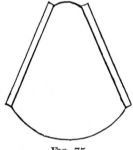

When monograms, coats of arms, or other devices are put on the end panels, the foundation should be made heavier than when left plain. Figs. 77, 78, 79, 80 and 81 represent different styles of hammer cloths, and figs. 82, 83 and 84, three styles of corners.

FIG. 75.

The colors of cloth fringe tassels, lace, etc, should be such as best harmonize with the colors used elsewhere. With Americans dark colors are the only ones used,

excepting when the interior is trimmed with light-colored satins ; then blue, or some contrasting, harmonizing color is used ; in all cases, however, the trimmings are of the same color, but of lighter shade than the cloth ; in some cases the panels are of velvet. In Europe velvet is sometimes used instead of

FIG. 76.

cloth, and the fringes, tassels, etc., enriched by being mixed with silver or gold cords.

CHAPTER XI.

WHIP SOCKETS.

SOCKETS OF LEATHER, METAL AND WOOD—MAKING LEATHER
SOCKETS—PECULIARITIES OF CONSTRUCTION—NOTCHED-TOP
RUBBERS—SOFT RUBBER LININGS—FASTENERS.

The whip socket, though one of the minor trimmings, is a necessary adjunct to the carriage. It, like almost every other article used in connection with the fittings of carriages, has undergone changes in manufacture, style, etc. Formerly whip sockets were made of a tin tube, painted, or covered with leather, or of heavy harness leather, shaped over a round stick, the edges of the leather butting together; near each edge a channel was cut to receive the stitches which held them together; the stitches were hid by an adhesive gum being put into the channels and the leather rubbed down smooth. The bottom was made of leather or wood, stitched in or secured by nails; the top was bound with thin leather. In making up, the leather is made quite wet, and, when sufficiently dry to crease, it is rubbed hard, and creased in ornamental devices. Leather sockets are yet used to a limited extent, but they have been nearly superseded by those of metal or wood.

Metal sockets are made of tin tubing, with struck up or cast top and bottom ; they are japanned throughout, or with japanned bodies, and tinned or plated tops and bottoms. Malleable iron is also used. It is japanned or plated.

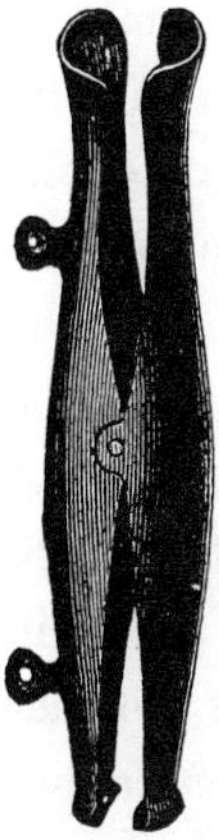

Tin tube sockets are made with metal springs, placed in a horizontal position inside, for holding the whip in position, and also with a notched rubber ring secured in a trench near the top, which answers the same purpose as the metal springs, but is more desirable, as it holds the whip without marring it.

FIG. 85.

Another metal socket is known as the "lever whip socket," fig. 85. This is made of two half circle pieces of iron hinged together a little below the middle, the parts being so shaped that as the end of the whip handle presses against the parts below the hinge they expand, and the top closes, thus grasping the whip firmly, and holding it in an upright position. These represent the low-grade sockets; they are finished in japan, silver or nickel plate.

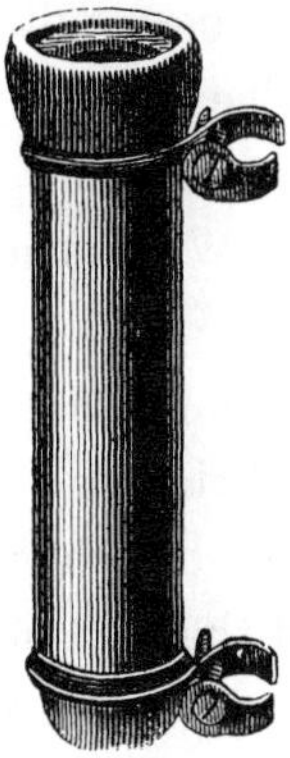

The wood socket, though claimed to be the oldest kind, has been so improved that the best qualitities are undoubtedly the most perfect in use. They are turned out of basswood, the tube being bored full size nearly down to the bottom, from

FIG. 86.

which point it narrows, until it pierces the lower end, when it is about one-fourth of an inch in diameter; this cone shape adapts the socket to any whip handle without clasping it, at the same time keeping the handle in the center; the top is bell-shaped, as shown by fig. 86, strengthened by wire, or bound with the metal to prevent splitting; a recess is turned in on the inside, near the top, for receiving a perforated or

FIG. 87.

notched piece of rubber, fig. 87, which holds the whip firmly in the socket in an upright position. Some of the finer qualities of sockets have a soft rubber lining, which fits the bore in the wood; in these the whip comes into contact with nothing harder than soft rubber when in the socket.

The improvements in socket fasteners have been quite as marked as in the sockets themselves. The fasteners are easily adjusted, and are so devised that they clasp the dash iron without defacing the leather. With some the leather is cut only on the inside.

As many vehicles are made without dash rails or other convenient appendages to which sockets can be attached, various devices are made which hold them in an upright position by clasping them at the bottom only, so that trimmers can always find the necessary attachments for securing sockets in any desirable position.

CHAPTER XII.

COACH AND CARRIAGE LAMPS.

PRIVATE CARRIAGE LAMPS—CANDLES—OIL—MATERIALS—NUM-
BERS— SIZES—MEASUREMENTS—TECHNICAL NAMES—PRICES
—STYLES.

The use of lamps on carriages is so general that a
work on carriage trimming would be incomplete without reference to them, notwithstanding the trimmer
has nothing whatever to do with their construction.
Originally a necessity for night driving, they became
so ornamental in character that, long after their value
as a means for light was passed, they were recognized
as one of the ornamental fixtures that could not be
dispensed with without positive injury to the appearance of the vehicle ; the light obtained from them is
now a secondary consideration, and, were it not for the
laws compelling the carrying of lights at night, the
arrangements for burning candles or oils could be
omitted, but law makes lights a necessity, and fashion
strengthens the decrees.

For all private carriages, the wax candle is the
cleanest and most desirable lighting material; the can-

dle is encased in the stem of the lamp, with the lower
end resting upon a spiral wire spring and covered at
the top with a cap, the hole through the upper end
of which is smaller than the candle, and as the candle
burns away the spring keeps the top end close up
against the top of the cap. Common oil is used, but
the smoke given off while burning, and the grease
which, working over the wick as well as from evapora-
tion, smears and dims the reflectors and inside of the
glasses, makes oil unfit for use. The only oil that can be
used to an advantage is a light volatile oil, best known
as "Lucene ;" this is used in hack lamps in most cities
when the laws compel lamps to be lighted. A light
that is sufficiently strong to enable a passer-by to distinguish the number on the hack lamp is all that is
necessary. Receptacles for this oil are made tight
and filled with cotton, thoroughly saturated with the
oil ; the tube, which is about one-eighth of an inch
in diameter, is filled with wick, and the heat from
this vaporizes the oil and causes it to burn as long
as there is any in the cotton; this is a very clean light.
The oil or other material used for light has nothing to
do with the construction of the lamp, excepting in the
parts holding the same.

Materials used are tin for all the outside metal parts
of the frame ; rolled plate (silver or copper) for reflectors and inside portions, and glass for the front and
sides. The qualities of these articles have much to do
with regulating the cost of the lamp. Plate glass is
used for all medium and fine lamps, the thickness and

purity of which, together with the grinding or ornamenting, are all graded according to quality. Common window glass is used in cheap lamps; there is also a great difference in the quality of the lining and reflector metals, as well as the tin for the body.

Lamp manufacturers sell lamps by numbers, but as each grade them differently, these numbers are of no use excepting in connection with each individual price list. The sizes used, however, are about as follows, the measurement being that of the glass :

Buggies and pony phaetons, about 3 inches; phaetons, two and four passenger, $3\frac{1}{2}$ to 4 inches; victorias, mail phaetons and T carts, round body, English mail lamps, about 5 inches; rockaways, four and six passenger, $5\frac{1}{2}$ to 6 inches; broughams and coupes, $5\frac{1}{2}$ to 6 inches; landaus, and Berlins, 6 to 7 inches; hearse, large, 6 to $7\frac{1}{2}$ inches; hearse, child's, 5 to $5\frac{1}{2}$ inches.

The glasses in most square lamps are of like width and length, but in hearse lamps the length is a little greater than the width. Lamps are commonly attached by a holder at the center of the back; the socket holder, a band which encircles the stem, close up to the body of the lamp, is no longer used, except in special cases.

Reading lamps for the inside of carriages are used to a limited extent; they are made oblong or oval, the long side being front; there is no glass on the outside. When used, the doors, which are double and hinged to the sides, are opened; these being lined with looking glass, are very convenient as toilet glasses.

The technical terms, describing the different parts of a lamp, are as follows : Body, the frame which supports the glass ; stem, the long tube forming the bottom ; collar, the ornamented projection at the top of the stem ; tip, the bottom ornament of the stem ; panel, the raised part on the top, to which the head is attached ; bottom and top heads, the respective parts of the head ; neck, the part which joins the head to the panel ; reflector, the highly polished concaved metal in the back and door ; candle cap, the cap which covers the top of the tube in the stem ; spring, the coiled wire in the stem which supports the candle.

A person ordering lamps can convey to the lamp maker the kind and proportions of lamp required, by using these terms, without a drawing. The prices of lamps vary from $1 50 to $50 a pair. A good pair of buggy lamps will cost about $6, and an equally good pair of coupe lamps about $25.

At the present time square bodies are the most fashionable for all but " mail lamps," which have round bodies, and " bull's eye " fronts, all made very plain. The reflectors are generally of silver, but gold is used, as is also gold and silver combined.

CHAPTER XIII.

TRIMMERS' TOOLS.

Trimmers' tools, owing to the material to be worked,
should be of fine quality and in variety sufficient to
enable the workman to perform his labor with ease
and dispatch. It is no uncommon thing to see a trimmer carry his kit in his coat pocket, but such men cannot do good work or do it quickly. In purchasing
the trimmer is governed by the price and general appearance of the tools, owing to his ignorance of metals
and woods. There is scarcely a tool in use by trimmers that is not made of malleable iron and finished
up in a manner that is well calculated to deceive any
but an expert in metals ; even the round knife is made
of this iron instead of steel. Then, too, there are steel
tools that are but a little better than those of malleable
iron ; these are made of steel rolled to the shape and
thickness desired, and all that is done to them is to
cut out to required form, grind and polish ; they are
steel, but yet they are comparatively worthless. The
best tools are forged of fine steel, the continuous work-

ing of which, to get the tool to required shape and size, toughens the steel and makes it more dense than it is when not forged. Cheap tools are also handled with soft kinds of wood stained in imitation of ebony, rosewood, etc. It is important, therefore, that the trimmer, when selecting his tools, secures those bearing the stamp of a reliable manufacturer.

There are two classes of tools—one the trimmer's kit, the other the shop tools. The latter consist of a stitching horse, a leather splitter, an iron vise, a loop press, a set of thumb screws, an iron square, a sewing machine, bench, anvils, and paste pot. On page 304 is illustrated a journeyman's kit, with the exception of needles, bench hooks, stuffing and loop sticks, screw driver, and a wrench, the names and retail prices of which are given herewith.

Few trimmers provide themselves with a good tool box, being content with anything that will hold the tools when going from one shop to another. A box, if properly made, should be constructed in such a manner that it can be on the bench at all times, and into which the tools can be placed when not in use. To do this the box should be provided with pockets on the inside of the back and ends, for holding all such tools as knives (excepting the round knife), channelers, edge trimmers, etc. On the inside of the front there should be sockets for prick wheels, scalloping irons, punches, etc. ; hammers, splitting gauges, etc., should be fitted into a rack in the center. The lid should contain a pocket for the round knife, needle pockets, and pin and needle cushions. Another style of box has a number of trays with recesses cut in the shape of the tool. These trays are covered with cloth, the under side of all but the bottom one being provided with a thin cushion, which presses upon and keeps the tools in their places when the trays are in position. Another style is one in which the ends and sides are hinged to the bottom, the top being hinged in the usual way. When opened, all parts fall flat, and are hooked together, making one large rack, which can be hung up if desired.

Highly polished tools are liable to rust, particularly in warm weather; the rust in all cases injures the appearance of tools, and in some impairs their value. Creasers, etc., require a smooth edge; if this edge is made rough by rust, a good crease cannot be made by it. To prevent injury from this source dip the tool into quicklime for a few moments, and put away in the rack without wiping.

The various articles composing a complete outfit for a journeyman, with the exception of the tool box, together with the lowest and highest retail prices, are as follows. See illustrations, next page.

SHOP TOOLS.

	Lowest	Highest.
Stitching horse	$4 50	$5 25
Leather splitter	5 00	8 00
Iron vise	5 00	15 00
Set of thumb screws (12)	8 50	18 00
Iron square	1 00	1 50
Anvils, 10 pound	60	80
Sewing machine	75 00	75 00
Total	$99 60	$123 55

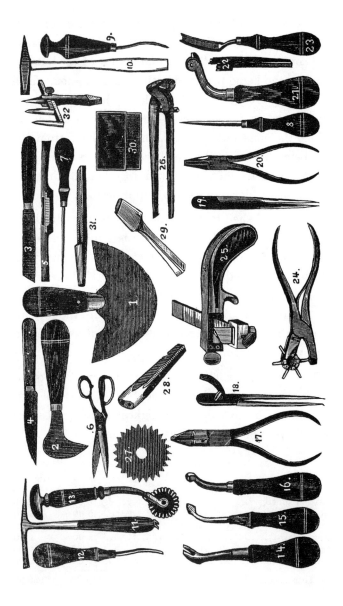

JOURNEYMAN'S KIT.

	Lowest.	Highest.
No. 1. Round knife	$1 38	$2 50
No. 2. Head knife	41	63
No. 3. Square-point knife	25	50
No. 4. Sharp-point knife	25	50
No. 5. Spoke shave	75	1 59
No. 6. Shears, 9-inch	1 17	1 25
No. 7. Seat awl	23	34
No. 8. Square awl	27	35
No. 9. Lacing awl	34	45
No. 10. Riveting hammer	50	84
No. 11. Trimmer's hammer, claw on handle	1 50	2 50
No. 12. Patent leather tool	35	50
No. 13. Scalloping carriage	1 17	2 00
No. 14. Claw	27	67
No. 15. Single tickler	24	50
No. 16. Single edge creaser	40	67
No. 17. Side cutting plyers	1 65	2 10
No. 18. Patent leather compass	1 00	1 25
No. 19. Common compass	34	50
No. 20. Pincer plyers	84	1 00
No. 21. Pricking carriage	55	1 00
No. 22. Round pinking iron	38	42
No. 23. Edge tool	50	1 00
No. 24. Revolving punch	2 00	2 50
No. 25. Draw gauge	1 17	2 34
No. 26. Cutting nippers	2 50	5 00
No. 27. Prick wheel	34	38
No. 28. Rivet set	42	1 00
No. 29. Oval punch	92	1 25
No. 30. Glass slicker	32	80
No. 31. Round punch	42	70
No. 32. Washer cutter	1 00	2 00
Three-foot rule	45	2 75
Screw driver	25	50
Wrench	10	50
Stuffing sticks, each	10	50
Loop sticks, each	10	10
Needles, per paper	5	5
Tufting needles, each	17	19
Total	$24 05	$43 62

CHAPTER XV.

REPAIRING CARRIAGES.

In no branch of the business is there so great a
diversity in prices as in repairing ; one man will charge
$5 50 for a cloth cushion, stuffed with moss and topped
with hair, while another will charge $8 for one of the
same kind ; the first has no advantage over the other
in buying materials or in the wages paid, and yet there
is a difference in price of $2 50.   It is evident, there-
fore, that one man loses money, or the other asks more
than the work is worth ; the probabilities are that the
low-priced man loses money, and that the difference in
price is due to lumping the job on the one hand and
carefully estimating cost on the other.   One man will furnish a shaft strap for 15 cents, while another charges
65 cents, a difference of 50 cents.   No man can af-
ford to furnish a strap fifteen inches long and seven-
eighths of an inch wide, with buckle and loops, together with making up and putting on, for 15 cents.

The points to be considered are cost of material, time consumed in doing the new work, and time required to remove the old trimmings, and get the part to be repaired in the condition that it would be if the job were a new one. The first two can be estimated accurately, but the last is the unknown quantity, and, unless a liberal allowance is made, all the contemplated profits will be swamped at the outset.

Manufacturers who have made a study of repairing find it necessary to employ the most skillful and rapid workmen; cheap labor will not answer. It is impossible to give any fixed rules of procedure, but one rule is absolutely necessary, viz.: that stock for repairs should be kept separate from the regular stock, otherwise losses will occur from cutting odd sized pieces and regular sizes from the same stock.

With the view to aid in establishing a uniformity in prices for repairs, a large number of tables have been obtained from different parts of the country, and from them the following have been compiled : The Eastern and Middle States' tables are for medium and fine work, and are safe guides for trimmers in other parts of the country who have but little of that class of repairing to do. The Western States' table is for low and m dium grades. The Southern States' table is for medium and fine, the lowest Western prices being about the same as the lowest Southern. A careful study of these tables will materially assist manufacturers and journeymen when estimating for repairs in the trimming shop.

Tariff of Repairs.--Eastern and Middle States.

Cushion, cloth or leather	$10 00	$12 00
Cushion, skins	16 00	— —
Cushion-top, cloth or leather	4 00	7 00
Cushion, enameled cloth	6 00	7 00
Re-covering cushion and back (buggy)	20 00	22 00
Re-covering cushion and back (coach or coupe)	25 00	28 00
Seat, high back, without cushion	12 00	15 00
Seat, low, with lazy back	7 00	9 00
Leather top buggy, old bows	50 00	55 00
Leather top buggy, new bows	90	1 00
Leather top, extension, new bows	135 00	150 00
Covering roof, leather, one seat	12 00	15 00
Covering roof, extension top, leather	15 00	18 00
Head lining, buggy, curtains	30 00	35 00
Head lining, extension top, curtains	40 00	50 00
Side curtains, leather and lining, each	9 00	12 00
Back curtain, leather	9 50	10 50
Curtain straps, each	35	75
Hood, leather	4 00	7 00
Re-covering bows, each	1 50	2 50
Re-covering bows, per set	6 00	10 00
Re-trimming shafts, per pair	4 75	5 00
Pole squabs	2 25	3 50
Re-covering dash of box wagon, double	8 00	10 00
Re-covering dash, low-front wagon, double	8 00	12 00
Re-covering dash coupe	10 00	12 00
Perch straps, buggy, each	75	1 00
Shaft straps, each	75	1 00
Re-covering glass frames, small, each	2 50	4 00
Re-covering glass frames, large, each	3 00	4 50
Curtain, light	65	75
Apron, leather	10 00	17 00
Apron, enameled cloth	5 00	6 50
Whip socket	1 00	1 50
Cushion straps, each	75	1 00
Top props, each	75	1 00
Slat irons, per set	1 00	1 75
Top-prop nuts, each	50	75
Club handles, per pair	3 00	4 50
Drop handles, per pair	3 00	7 00
Inside handles, per pair	2 00	6 00
Knobs in rail or curtain, each	15	25
Rug, best quality	5 00	7 50
Cleaning and dressing top	2 50	5 00

Tariff of Repairs.--Western States.

Cushion, cloth or leather, fall attached	$3 75	$6 00
Cushion-top, cloth or leather, and stuffing	1 75	3 50
Cushion, enameled cloth, fall attached	2 00	2 50
Re-covering cushion and back (buggy)	6 50	7 00
Seat, high back, without cushion	4 00	7 00
Seat, low, with lazy back	4 00	7 00
Leather top buggy, drop back	55 00	65 00
Leather top extension	75 00	80 00
Enameled cloth top, buggy	25 00	35 00
Enameled cloth top, extension	45 00	55 00
Rubber top, 28 ounces	35 00	45 00
Covering roof, leather, one seat	20 00	30 00
Covering roof, enameled cloth, two seats	20 00	30 00
Covering roof, extension top, leather	40 00	50 00
Covering roof, buggy, enameled cloth	12 00	15 00
Covering roof, rubber	15 00	18 00
Head lining, buggy	6 00	10 00
Head lining, buggy, and lining curtains	12 00	15 00
Head lining, extension top	20 00	22 00
Side curtains, leather, each	6 00	6 50
Side curtains, enameled cloth, each	2 50	3 00
Side curtains, black rubber	3 50	4 00
Back curtain, leather, lined	6 00	7 00
Back curtain, enameled cloth	3 50	4 00
Curtain straps, each	15	35
Hood, leather	5 00	5 25
Hood, rubber	2 50	3 00
Re-covering bows, each	1 25	1 50
Re-covering bows, one side, each	50	75
Re-trimming shafts, per pair	2 00	2 25
Pole squabs	3 00	3 50
Re-covering dash of box wagon, double	2 25	3 50
Re-covering dash, low-front wagon, double	2 50	3 00
Perch straps, buggy, each	20	25
Shaft straps, each	15	20
Curtain, light	25	50
Apron, leather, with dash pocket	6 00	6 50
Apron, enameled cloth, with dash pocket	1 25	1 75
Apron, rubber, 20 ounces	2 00	2 50
Whip socket	25	50
Top props, each	25	75
Slat irons, per set	2 00	2 25
Top-prop nuts, each	15	20
Knobs in rail or curtain, each	5	10
Toe fenders, per pair	1 50	2 00
Shaft rubbers, per pair, and putting in	25	35
Shaft springs, per pair, and putting in	40	75
Cleaning and dressing top and painting irons	1 50	2 00
Buggy washers, per set	25	40
Inside joints and putting in, per pair	75	1 00
Tubular bow socket	1 25	1 50
Front valance	1 25	1 50

Tariff of Repairs.--Southern States.

Cushion, cloth or leather	$ 7 00	$12 50
Cushion-top, cloth or leather	4 25	5 00
Cushion, enameled cloth	3 50	7 50
Re-covering cushion and back (buggy)	12 00	15 00
Re-covering cushion and back (coach or coupe)	20 00	24 00
Seat, high back, without cushion	12 00	14 00
Seat low, with lazy back	7 50	9 50
Leather top, buggy	65 00	68 00
Leather top, extension	95 00	100 00
Enameled cloth top, buggy	42 00	50 00
Enameled cloth top, extension	60 00	75 00
Covering roof, leather, one seat	12 00	16 00
Covering roof, enameled cloth, two seats	12 00	15 00
Covering roof, extension top, leather	20 00	22 00
Covering roof, buggy, enameled cloth	7 00	10 00
Head lining, buggy	17 00	24 00
Head lining, extension top	22 00	31 00
Side curtains, leather, each	10 00	15 00
Side curtains, enameled cloth, each	3 50	4 25
Back curtain, leather	8 00	12 75
Back curtain, enameled cloth	7 00	9 00
Curtain straps, each	35	75
Hood	3 75	5 50
Re-covering bows, each	1 25	5 00
Re-covering bows, full set	6 00	10 00
Re-trimming shafts, per pair	5 00	5 00
Pole squabs	2 00	3 50
Re-covering dash of box wagon, double	4 00	6 00
Re-covering dash, low-front wagon, double	5 00	6 50
Re-covering dash coupe	7 00	8 00
Perch straps, buggy, each	65	85
Shaft straps, each	50	65
Re-covering glass frames, small, each	2 25	2 75
Re-covering glass frames, large, each	2 75	3 50
Curtain, light	50	85
Apron, leather	11 00	12 50
Apron, enameled cloth	1 50	4 50
Whip socket	1 00	1 50
Tail-board strap	1 75	2 50
Cushion straps, each	60	1 00
Top props, each	50	75
Slat irons, per set	1 00	1 50
Top-prop nuts, each	20	25
Club handle	1 25	2 50
Drop handle	2 00	4 00
Inside handles, pair	3 50	4 50
Knobs in rail or curtain, each	10	15
Leather boot for buggy	4 00	7 00
Covering rockers, leather	2 50	3 00
Patent leather fall	1 50	2 00
Covering fenders	6 00	7 00
Rubber storm cover	8 00	9 00
Oil cloth	1 00	1 50
Brussels rug	1 50	2 00

CHAPTER XVI.

RECIPES.

The following collection of recipes, etc., are reliable, and can be made up by any person. Some were originally published in the "Harness Makers' Manual," and all have been thoroughly tested.

CLEANING TOPS.

Enameled leather tops that have been soiled by dust and rain should be washed with soft water and Castile or crown soap. Apply the water with a sponge and then scrub with a moderately stiff brush ; cleanse with clean water and dry with a "shammy." Never apply any kind of oil or top dressing without first cleaning the leather.

TO REVIVE FADED BLACK LEATHER.

Carriage tops that have faded and become gray can be restored by washing with a solution composed of four ounces of nut galls, one ounce each of logwood, copperas, clean iron filings and sumac berries ; put all but the iron filings and copperas in a quart of the best white wine vinegar, and heat nearly to the boiling point, then add the copperas and iron filings, let them stand for twenty-four hours, and strain off the liquid; apply with a sponge. This is equally good for restoring black cloths.

PATENT LEATHER BLACK.

Mix together $\frac{1}{2}$ pound each of ivory black, purified lampblack and pulverized indigo, 3 ounces of dissolved gum arabic, 4 ounces of brown sugar, and $\frac{1}{4}$ ounce of glue, dissolved in 1 pint of water; heat the whole to a boil over a slow fire, then remove and stir until cool, and roll into balls.

VINEGAR BLACK.

This is the most simple and useful coloring liquid for the trimming shop for blacking leather straps. To make the simplest, and, without doubt, the best, procure shavings from an iron turner, and cover them with pure cider vinegar; heat up and set aside for a week or two, then heat again and set in a cool place for two weeks; pour off the vinegar, allow it to stand for a few days, drain off, and cork up in bottles; this will keep a long time, and, while producing a deep black on leather, it will not stain the hands.

BALL BLACK.

For harness leather straps this is made of $\frac{1}{4}$ of an ounce of isinglass, $\frac{1}{4}$ ounce of indigo, 4 ounces of logwood, 2 ounces of soft soap, 4 ounces of glue, softened, and 1 pint of vinegar; the whole is mixed, warmed, strained and allowed to cool, when it is ready for use.

HATTERS' BLACK.

This black is unequaled for finishing. It is made by dissolving 1 pound of extract of logwood, ½ ounce of bichromate of potash, and 1 ounce of copperas in 1 gallon of water.

BLACK SHELLAC VARNISH FOR OLD TOPS.

Dissolve asphaltum in turpentine, using no more of the latter than is absolutely necessary; add a small quantity of bone black and enough shellac varnish to reduce it so that it can be applied with a brush.

A WASHING LIQUID FOR SILK.

Silk curtains, when soiled, may be made to look as good as new by washing them in a liquid composed of ½ pint of gin, 4 ounces of soft soap, 2 ounces of strained honey, well mixed; spread the silk out on a table and apply the mixture with a sponge, rubbing thoroughly; then wash in soft water, into which there should be put two tablespoonfuls of ox gall to 3 gallons of water; rinse the silk, but do not wring it; hang it out smooth to dry and iron when damp.

TO SEPARATE SIDES OF PATENT LEATHER.

Patent and enameled leather will, if the glazed sides are placed in contact in warm weather, become stuck together, and, unless carefully separated, the leather will be spoiled. The simplest and best way to separate sides is to place them in a drying or other hot room ; when hot they can be taken apart without injury to the glazed or enameled surface. If a drying room is not accessible, lay the sides on a tin roof on a hot day, and they will soon become hot enough to be separated without injury. Any attempt to separate without heating to a high degree will prove a failure.

POLISH FOR PATENT LEATHER.

Mix together the whites of two eggs, one teaspoonful of spirit of wine, one ounce of sugar and as much finely pulverized ivory black as may be required to produce the necessary shade of black. Apply with a sponge and polish with a piece of silk.

RUSSET STAIN.

Boil a given amount of saffron in water until the color is extracted ; cut a quantity of anatto in urine and mix the two together ; the proportions determine the shade ; the more anotta used the darker the shade.

YELLOW STAIN.

Picric acid water, in proportions of 1 to 10, heated to a blood heat, makes a good yellow. A bright orange stain is made by mixing yellow aniline with alum water.

RED STAIN.

Dissolve 1 ounce of cochineal in ½ pint of hot water

and add 1 gill of hartshorn. Alum or tin salts and a decoction of cochineal make a bright crimson stain.

TEST FOR BLUE DYES.

To distinguish Berlin blue from indigo and aniline blue in fabrics apply a few drops of the solution of the fluoride of potassium in water, apply a jet of steam to the spot ; if the blue is Berlin it will vanish ; if indigo or aniline, no effect will be noticeable.

CLEANING GLASS.

To clean glass in frames, when the latter are covered or otherwise so finished that water cannot be used, moisten tripoli with brandy, rub it on the glass while moist, and when dry rub off with a silk rag ; to prevent the mixture injuring the cloth on the frame use strips of tin bent to an angle ; set these on the frame with one edge on the glass ; when the frames are of a character that will not be injured by water, rub the glass with water containing a little liquid ammonia, and polish with moist paper.

TO CLEAN MOLDY LEATHER.

Remove the surface mold with a dry cloth, and with another cloth apply pyroligneous acid.

LIQUID FOR CLEANING CLOTH.

Cloth trimmings often become soiled, and unless cleaned the appearance is impaired. Benzine and naphtha are used with success for this purpose upon grease spots, but when there is no grease these materials fail, and are likely to produce bad results, owing to the oil that is contained in them. To remove the oil place a quantity of benzine in a bottle and drop into it a little oxalic acid; this will carry with it to the bottom of the glass all the oil remaining in the benzine, leaving the greater part perfectly pure. After standing for an hour or two, carefully pour off the clear fluid on the top into another bottle, and it will be ready for use.

To Clean Brass.

Wash the brass with roche alum, boiled in a strong lye in the proportion of one ounce to a pint; polish with dry tripoli.

To Clean Gilt Mountings.

Gilt mountings, unless carefully cleaned, soon lose their luster. They should not be rubbed; if slightly tarnished wipe them off with a piece of canton flannel, or, what is better, remove them if possible, and wash in a solution of one-half ounce of borax dissolved in one pound of water, and dry them with a soft linen rag; their luster may be improved by heating them a little and rubbing with a piece of canton flannel.

Powders for Cleaning Silver.

Add by degrees 8 ounces of prepared chalk in fine powder to a mixture of 2 ounces of spirits turpentine, 1 ounce of alcohol, ½ ounce of spirits of camphor, and

2 drams of aqua ammonia; apply with a sponge, and allow it to dry before polishing.

Mix together 1 ounce of fine chalk, 2 ounces of cream tartar, 1 ounce of rotten stone, 1 ounce of red lead, and ¾ of an ounce of alum, and pulverize thoroughly in a mortar. Wet the mixture and rub it on the silver, and, when dry, rub off with a dry flannel, or clean with a small brush.

POWDER FOR CLEANING BRASS MOUNTINGS.

Make a paste of equal parts of sulphur and chalk, with sufficient vinegar to reduce it to the proper consistency. Apply it to the metal while moist; allow it to dry on, and rub with chamois skin. For ornaments or engraved work clean with a brush. Or, make a wash of alum boiled in a strong lye, in the proportion of 1 ounce of alum to 1 pint of the lye. Wash the brass with this mixture, and afterward rub with shammy and tripoli.

TO PREVENT POLISHED STEEL FROM RUST.

Polished steel may be preserved from rust by coating it with a mixture of lard and pulverized black lead, spread on with a brush while warm.

PREPARED CHALK.

Pulverize chalk thoroughly, and mix it with distilled water in the proportion of 2 pounds of chalk to 1 gallon of water; stir well, and allow it to stand about 2 minutes, during which time the gritty matter will have settled to the bottom; pour off the water and place the chalk in a warm oven to dry. This is an excellent powder for restoring silver.

CEMENTS.

A good cement for ivory is made of good glue soaked to a jelly, warm it and add a small quantity of pulverized slaked lime, clean the parts to be cemented, warm them, apply the cement, and tie the parts firmly together; it gets hard in a few days.

For fastening leather to metal, coat the metal with a solution of hot glue, and the leather with a hot extract of nut galls, bind the leather firmly to the iron, and do not disturb until thoroughly dry.

LETTERING OR ORNAMENTING GLASS.

A mixture of flour hydrate of ammonia and chlorhydric acid, thickened with gum acacia, forms an ink by which with a pen letters or ornaments may be traced on glass, where they will become permanent.

STAINS FOR IVORY.

White ivory fittings that have become soiled may be colored with but little trouble.

Black—Lay the article for several hours in a strong solution of nitrate of silver, remove it and expose it in a strong sunlight.

Blue—Immerse for some time in a diluted solution of sulphate of indigo, partly saturated with potash.

Red—Dip the articles first in the tin mordant used

in dyeing, and then plunge into a hot decoction of Brazil wood, half pound to a gallon of water, or cochineal.

Scarlet—Use lac dye instead of the preceding.

Green—Boil in a solution of verdigris in vinegar until the desired color is obtained.

To Bleach Ivory.

Ivory that has become yellow by exposure can be whitened by washing in a solution composed of one ounce of nitric acid and 10 ounces of soft water; apply with a rough brush; cleanse thoroughly in clean water; or, by rubbing the ivory with fine pumice stone and water, and while damp exposing it to the sun under a glass vessel.

Drilling Glass.

Holes can be drilled through glass with an ordinary twist drill by keeping the drill moist with turpentine.

Moth Powder.

Supsulin (flour of hops), 1 dram; Scotch snuff, 2 ounces; camphor gum, 1 ounce; black pepper, 1 ounce; cedar sawdust, 4 ounces; mix thoroughly and blow it into corners, etc., with a powder bellows.

Paste that will not Sour.

Dissolve four teaspoonfuls of alum in one gallon of water; when cold stir in as much flour as will give it the consistency of thick cream, beat smooth, add one teaspoonful of pulverized resin, and twenty drops of oil of cloves, pour the whole into two quarts of boiling water, stirring thoroughly until it is cooked ; pour into a glazed earthen vessel, and when cold cover the top with oiled silk, and put it in a cool place ; when needed for use take out a portion and soften with warm water.   This will be found very convenient for summer use, at times when very little paste is required by the trimmer.

CROWN SOAP.

This soap, so much used by stablemen for cleaning harness, is made of whale or cod oil, lye of potassa and a small quantity of tallow.   The oil gives to the soap a dark·brown color, the tallow forming white granulations.

BELGIUM BURNISHING POWDER.

Mix together 1 ounce of fine chalk, 3 ounces of pipe clay, 2 ounces of dry white lead, $\frac{3}{4}$ of an ounce of carbonate of magnesia, and $\frac{3}{4}$ of an ounce of rouge.

TO REMOVE PAINT OR PUTTY FROM GLASS.

Make a strong solution of saleratus and hot water, apply with a brush until the paint or putty is well saturated, allow it to remain until nearly dry, then rub off with a woolen cloth.

CHAPTER XVII.

CARE OF CARRIAGES.

While the carriage trimmer is interested mainly in
his special branch, he should know how to care for the
complete carriage, for whatever injures any one part of
it injures another, and no one portion is more easily
soiled than the trimming. Fine cloths, laces, silks,
leather and mountings, all require care and attention
to preserve them in such a manner as will insure their
durability and beauty. Faded cloth, spotted silk, tarnished mountings and soiled leather detract from the
appearance of a carriage, and if such mishaps occur
before the vehicle is sold the manufacturer is the loser.
A good repository is the first essential requisite, without which it is impossible to protect the carriage from
injury.

The room should be finished in natural woods.
Varnished decorations of all kinds form receptacles for
dust and dirt, beside detracting from the plainness so

essential to a room where the color and form of articles like carriages are to be studied. It should be
lighted from the north, as colors show their true tints
and shades much better when subjected to a north
light than they do to light from any other direction.
The windows should be provided with blue curtains,
which can be raised or lowered easily, separately or
together, so that in showing a carriage the light may
be thrown upon one vehicle at a time. A repository
arranged in this manner, if well ventilated, saves much
labor in the care of the carriages. Dust is an enemy
to cloth and paint, and if allowed to remain on either
a short time it leaves its mark; but even that is less destructive than a close, muggy atmosphere. The air in
a repository that is not well ventilated will become
very foul, damp and impure during a night; the moisture which accumulates permeates the trimming materials, and causes a slimy sweat to settle on the paint
and leather, which will require several hours of sun-
shine and clear air to remove. This can be prevented
by having the repository ventilated near the ceiling,
in such a manner as to exclude the dust and allow the
escape of the foul air.

Next to proper ventilation is the dusting and washing of carriages. The dusting should be done each day
two or three times; if there is much loose dust in the
air use a fine, soft feather duster and dust lightly;
after dusting wash the paint, using clear cold water
and a large soft, clean sponge; fill the sponge with as
much water as it will carry without dripping, and pass

it lightly over the surface ; dry with a " shammy ;" one point to be observed in washing is not to wet too much surface at one time, for if any portion of it becomes dry before it is wiped with the " shammy," it will leave a streak. Washing is looked upon as a necessity by all first-class carriage manufacturers, their experience being that the varnish on a carriage that has been well washed while new wears much longer than it does when the washing has been omitted.

Slip-linings for covering the cloth or silk cushions and squabs in the wareroom cost a little, but they reduce the labor of caring for a carriage to such an extent as to pay for themselves in a short time. They can be held in place by means of slender pins ; covering dashes and wings with paper sacks prevents them from injury.

The importance of properly caring for the carriage is such as to warrant every manufacturer furnishing the buyer with rules to govern him. The following will be found complete and concise :

1. The coach room should be large, dry and well ventilated ; the walls and ceiling lined and finished in oil or varnish ; the windows large, but curtained with blue curtains, so as to admit a moderate amount of light ; the floors and ceilings should be kept free from dust or dirt ; if the floor is wet when sweeping the carriage should not be put in until it is dry.

2. If the stable is of brick or stone, the walls should be lined with a close board partition at least three inches from the wall, with openings at the top and

bottom to allow a circulation of air between the wall and partition. Never allow a carriage to stand near a brick or stone wall, or any other that is damp, as the dampness affects the paint and trimmings.

3. Ammonia destroys varnish and affects colors. Care should be taken, therefore, to locate the carriage room in such a manner that it will not be exposed to the fumes of the stable or manure heap.

4. A carriage should never be allowed to stand in the carriage room without being protected from dust by a cotton or linen cover; but this cover should not be put on when the carriage is wet or dusty. Dust, if allowed to remain on, eats into varnish; the cover should be so arranged as not to touch the carriage.

5. Carriages should be washed frequently, even when not in use. They should also be dusted every two or three days, and be exposed to the air in a shady place. In washing, use cold water and a sponge. Soften the mud by squeezing the water from the sponge on the panel or other part, and do not pass the sponge over the paint until the mud is soaked off. After sponging dry with a "shammy," but do not use the sponge and "shammy" in the same pail of water. Be careful to dry thoroughly, and protect the trimming from injury by water. Do not allow any part of the carriage that is washed to dry before wiping with the "shammy," as it will stain the paint. Hot, or even warm water or soap should not be used. Never allow mud to dry upon the carriage, as it will produce spots or stains. Always wash in a shady place.

6. Enameled leather while new does not need much washing; it should be well dusted, and may be wiped with a moist "shammy;" if it becomes dimmed make a suds of soft water and Castile or crown soap. Apply it with a sponge and dry with a "shammy" moistened in clean water; if the leather shows spots, rub them with cotton waste and linseed oil; if the leather becomes hard, wash it clean and oil with neatsfoot oil; when the oil has permeated the leather wash the surface oil off with crown soap suds. Dash and other smooth leather should be treated in the same manner as the paint.

7. The trimmings require a great deal of attention. All roll-up curtains, aprons, etc., should be unrolled and stretched out smooth. The joints should be "struck" so as to slack the leather, but not enough to allow the top to fall. Cloths, cushions and other removable portions must be well beaten and brushed, and all immovable parts be well brushed; this, while preventing injury from dirt, is also a protection from moths. Moroccos can be cleaned by rubbing them with a moist "shammy."

8. Mountings should be kept clean by repeated rubbing; all acids or powders injure the paint, leather, or cloth, and it is impossible to clean metals with them without coming in contact with the trimmings. If the metal is tarnished use a small piece of "shammy," that has been prepared by having rotten stone, or other fine polishing powder, rubbed into it, and afterward whipped and brushed to remove all surplus powder;

then rub with a dry rag. To clean lamps mix whiting
with spirits of wine; apply to the reflector and other
inside plating; when dry rub off with a rag, clean the
glass with water and polish with paper.

9. Oil the axles frequently, but use but little oil at
one time. Support the axle by a jack, having a leather
padded top; take off the nuts, and if much soiled, remove the grease with spirits of turpentine; remove the
wheel and clean the axle arm and hub box thoroughly,
then apply a few drops of castor oil, replace the washers, wheel and nuts, seeing that each has a thin coating
of oil. The fifth wheel and king bolt should also be
oiled enough to prevent the metal surfaces grinding.

10. A carriage should be inspected carefully to see
that there are no moths in the trimming, carpets, etc.;
if discovered they can be expelled by beating and
brushing; moth preventives are valueless as against
the moth grub, but they will prevent the fly depositing its eggs. Musk and other strong perfumes will
keep the flies from depositing their eggs in the trimmings.

11. If repairs are needed it is best to send to the
carriage shop; but the paint will become worn off of
step pads and tires, which can be restored by a little
black japan, which should be laid on thin.

12. Carriages should be revarnished as often as once
a year, but if the paint cracks badly varnishing increases the deformity, and there is but one way to correct it: to burn off the paint and repaint from the
wood. Repairing is as much of an art as building,

therefore do not send a carriage for repairs to any but skillful mechanics.

13. If a carriage is not in regular use it should be run out of the coach house once or twice a week, and thoroughly ventilated, by removing cushions, carpets, etc., and opening the doors and windows. After being well aired it should be thoroughly dusted and washed before it is returned to the house.

14. The person having charge of the carriage should examine it closely each day after it has been used, to see that there are no loose or broken nuts, bolts, tires, etc. If proper attention is given to this matter the carriage will always be ready for use.

CHAPTER XVIII.

CARRIAGE TRIMMERS' TECHNICAL DICTIONARY.

MATERIALS DESCRIBED AND ILLUSTRATED—TECHNICAL AND OTHER TERMS.

In compiling the Dictionary of Trimmers' Technical Terms, and names of materials, care has been taken to give such only as properly belong to the Trimming department. This necessitated adding some that do not belong to the trimming shop, but which are really parts of the interior and exterior decorations. Cant terms or shop phrases have not been introduced, as these are of no value as reference, and differ in application.

The illustrations are grouped together, forming the last pages of the Dictionary.

A

AFGHAN.—A lap robe of wool or cotton, knit or woven in ornamental devices, generally in bright colors.

APRON.—A piece of leather, enameled cloth or rubber cloth, attached to the dash or front of a carriage, used as a lap cover, a protector from rain or snow.

The leather or cloth cover to a baggage rack on a stage. In some localities the seat fall.

APRON HOOK.—A small metallic hook, attached to a strap for holding the apron in place when folded. (Illustrated.)

APRON RING. — A metallic ring, used in connection with the apron hook. (Illustrated.)

APRON FALL.—A piece of leather, attached to the top of the dash. A cover to the apron when folded.

APRON STRAP.—A narrow strip of leather, used to hold an apron in place when folded.

AWL.—A pointed metallic instrument, used for piercing leather preparatory to stitching.

AXLE WASHER.—A ring of leather, metal or other material, placed upon either end of an axle arm, to prevent the axle box wearing against the nut or collar. (Illustrated.)

B

BACK CROSS STRAP.—An ornamental strap, placed crosswise of the back end of a carriage body, the upper ends secured to the body at points near the back ends of the arm rails, and the lower ends to the pump handles near the scrolls.

BACK CROSS STRAP CENTER.—A metallic ornament, attached to the cross straps at the central point, where they cross each other, made in a great variety of styles and patterns. (Illustrated.)

BACK CROSS STRAP BUCKLE.—A buckle, having a screw

or other device attached to the bottom bar, whereby it is secured to the body. Used for attaching the cross-strap to the body. (Illustrated.)

BACK CROSS STRAP LOOP.—A metallic loop, to which the lower end of the cross-strap is attached. Sometimes used in place of a buckle. (Illustrated.)

BACK LIGHT.—The small window in the back panel or back curtain of a carriage. (Illustrated.)

BACK STAY.—A web or metallic strip, one end of which is attached to the back bow, the other to the seat or rail, to hold the back bow in position and prevent the top being thrown forward.

BACK QUARTER.—A strip of leather at the back corner of a top, two of which, together with the curtain, form the back of a carriage top.

BACK CURTAIN.—A curtain used on the back end of a carriage top.

BELL PULL.—A handle attached to the cord of a gong or bell ; made of metal, wood, ivory or other material. (Illustrated.)

BLIND.—A movable frame, with or without slats ; a substitute for a carriage window. The solid blind is also known as a "stable shutter."

BODY LININGS.—Cloth, leather or other material used in trimming.

BODY CLOTH.—The cloth used as the outside covering for cushions, squabs, falls, etc.

Bow Socket.—A metallic socket, used as a substitute for the slat iron.

Bow.—A narrow strip of wood bent at two points, three or more of which form the frame or support of the top.

Bow Rest.—The portion of a seat rail which projects at the corners, acting as a point of attachment for the foot of the back prop and a support to the top when folded down.

Brace.—One of the heavy leather straps which support bodies hung upon C-springs or corner posts.

Buckle.—A metallic frame having a loose bolt or tongue. (Illustrated.)

Buckram.—Coarse linen cloth ; used as a lining for parts of trimming.

Burlap.—Heavy, coarse linen cloth ; used as a foundation for squabs, etc.

Button Hanger.—An ornamental attachment to a footman's holder.

Bridling Springs.—Securing spiral springs by the use of wire so that they will maintain a level surface when in cushions, etc.

Button.—A small knob perforated or having an eye by which it can be attached to any part of the trimming ; japanned, or covered with cloth, silk or leather. These are sized by lines, one-fortieth part of an inch. The buttons shown are 18, 20 and 22 lines. (Illustrated.)

BREECHING HOOK.—A metallic hook attached to the upper side of a shaft, to which the breeching strap is attached. (Illustrated.)

BREECHING LOOP.—A metallic loop attached to the underside of a shaft; used as a substitute for the breeching hook   (Illustrated.)

C

CALASH TOP.—The general name given to a carriage top that is made of bows covered with leather or other material, and so constructed that it can be raised or lowered at will.

CAMBRIC.—A thin woven fabric of cotton or linen.

CAP.—A leather pocket used as a cover to the lower ends of bows at the point where they are attached to the seat.   A metallic covering to nuts or rivets. (Illustrated.)

CARD CASE.—A long, thin box open at one end; used as a receptacle for visiting cards.   They are made of hard rubber, ivory, or metal; the latter are generally covered with leather.   (Illustrated.)

CARPETING.—The covering to floors of carriages, whether carpet or oil cloth.

CARPET.—A heavy fabric, woven of wool or cotton.

CARPET LACE.—A coarse worsted fringe used for trimming the edges of pieces of carpet for carriage bottoms.

CALL BELL.—A gong or small bell placed inside the

vehicle by which the occupants of a carriage can attract the driver's attention.

CHECK STRAP.—A strap of leather extending from the bottom of a body to the perch.

CHECK LOOP.—A small metallic loop by which the check strap is attached to the body or other part of the vehicle. (Illustrated.)

CHECK STRING.—A cord extending from the inside of the carriage to the driver, whereby the occupant can attract the attention of the driver.

CORDUROY.—A thick cotton, woven fabric, corded or ribbed on the surface, used to a limited extent for cover to cushion, etc.

COTELINE.—The commercial name given to a figured silk fabric of French origin, much used for trimming.

CURLED HAIR.—The hair of animals, twisted into a rope and afterward picked out loose ; used for stuffing cushions, etc.

CURTAIN.—A leather or cloth piece, used to enclose carriages, that can be removed or rolled up.

CURTAIN FRAME.—A metallic frame, made in two sections, used to hold the glass in a curtain.

CURTAIN HOLDER.—An ornamental strap, attached to the top of a carriage, used as a support to curtains when rolled up.

CURTAIN LOOP.—A loop of leather or metal attached to

the curtain or quarter for receiving the end of the billet ; also known as case loop. (Illustrated.)

CANOPY.—An umbrella top, supported on a post attached to the back of the carriage body, used on light phaetons.

D

DAMASK.—A linen fabric, with raised figures ; an imita-of damask silk ; used for slip lining to carriages.

DAMASSE.—A fabric woven of mixed materials in imitation of damask, and used for the same purpose.

DASH.—The upright frame of iron, covered with leather or wood, at the front end of a carriage body, also called " dash board."

DASH FRAME.—An iron frame which forms the outlines of a dash. (Illustrated.)

DASH RAIL.—An extra rail placed outside of the covered rails of a dash. (Illustrated.)

DASH MOLDING.—A small metallic molding placed upon the top edge of a dash, used in place of the dash rail.

DOESKIN.—Enameled cloth finished to imitate dash leather, the back resembling leather in color.

DOOR HANDLE.—A metallic device with a bar or loop placed at right angles with the shaft, used for turning the catches to door locks. (Illustrated.)

DOOR STOP.—A band of lace or metal used to prevent the carriage door opening beyond a certain point.

DOOR CAM.—A device for holding the window in a carriage door at any hight, and to prevent rattling. (Illustrated.)

DRIVING CUSHION.—A cushion having a high back and low front, used on certain styles of vehicles when the driver is compelled to sit with his legs nearly in the same position as when standing.

DROP HANDLE.—A door handle, the bar of which is loose on the shaft, and falls down when not in use. (Illustrated.)

DROP LIGHT.—The window of a coach that can be dropped out of sight between the outer and inner frame of a body.

DRUGGET.—A coarse woven or felt fabric, printed in colors on one side, used as a lining for lap robes, etc.

E

EAR CUSHION.—A small cushion hung in the back corner of a coach, used as a head rest.

ELBOW REST. — A metallic arm-piece covered with leather, and provided with a pad or cushion top, used in open, standing-top carriages.

ENAMELED CLOTH.—Cotton cloth, one side of which is painted and grained to imitate enameled leather.

ENAMELED LEATHER.—Leather having one side colored and varnished, the surface of which is "grained"· by being "boarded," giving it a rough finish. Used for covering carriage tops.

EXCELSIOR.—The trade name of a preparation of wood, cut into fine fibers by machinery, curled and dried. Used for stuffing cushions, etc.

EYELET.—A metallic ring, with broad edges affixed, which, in place of being clinched on the two sections, are screwed together.   (Illustrated.)

F

FALL.—An apron attached to the front edge of the seat or cushion, suspended between the point of attachment and the bottom of the carriage body. (Illustrated.)

FALSE LINING.—An adjustable lining, made of linen or other thin fabric ; covering cushions, squabs, etc., of finer material ; also called "slip lining."

FELT.—A coarse cloth, made of untwisted fibers, fulled or wrought into a compact substance by pressure, with size.

FOOT BOARD.—Originally a platform for the footman, afterward used as a rack for the support of baggage, and so constructed as to be closed up when not in use, presenting a carved or finished face ; also called poll guard; also the dash or foot rest of a coach or other carriage, where no upright dash is used.   A "toe board."

FOOTMAN HOLDER.—An ornamental pendant, attached to the back end of a coach body at the corners, originally designed as a holder whereby a footman could support himself. Now but little used, and in this country only as an ornament.

FOOT MUFF.—A muff for the feet, made of furs, used as a protection from the cold while riding.

FRINGE.—An ornamental border, having a narrow heading, with loose or twisted thread pendants. The technical names of carriage fringe are bullion, festoon and carpet. (Illustrated.)

FROG.—An ornament of silk or worsted, woven to match the lace used. (Illustrated.)

G

GLASS FRAME.—A wooden frame for the support of glass in the movable windows of a carriage.

GLASS FRAME LIFTER.—A strip of lace, the lower end of which is attached to the lower bar of a glass frame, by which it is lifted out of the bed in the door or body.

GIMP.—A woven ornamental braid of silver, gold and silk or worsted thread.

GUARD STRING.—Silk cord, used for holding up lace and tassels, attached to doors or windows.

GRAIN DASH.—The trade name given to plain glazed patent leather, the hair side of which is unfinished, the japan being put upon the flesh side.

GIPSY TOP.—A buggy top, the back quarter of which is partially closed by a triangular curtain, knobbed or otherwise secured to the back bows and back quarter. (Illustrated.)

GIMP COVERED NAIL.—A trimming nail, having the head covered with gimp.

H

HANDLE.—The general name given to that part of the attachment of a carriage by which the doors are opened; also an iron frame attached at different points, as supports for the rider on getting in or out of a carriage. (Illustrated.)   A, ivory pull handle; B, lace handle; C, D, E and F, inside handles ; G and H, French lock handles.

HAMMER CLOTH.—An ornamental valance to the front, or driver's seat, made of cloth lined with buckram or leather, laid in ornamental folds, and embellished with fringe, lace, tassels, etc.   (Illustrated.)

HEAD LINING.—The lining to the under side of a carriage top.

HOLDER.—A loop of broad lace or cloth, padded on the inside, attached to the inside of the door pillars ; also called " arm rest."

HOOD.—An extra projection attached to the top of the front bow or bar of a carriage top, projecting forward as an additional protection from rain ; also known as " storm hood."

I

INSIDE HANDLE.—See handle.

IVORY TRIMMINGS.—All classes of inside trimmings made wholly or partially of ivory, white or colored.

K

KNEE BOOT.—A frame or apron used to protect the occupant of the "Hansom" cab.

KNOB.—An ornamental button of ivory or metal, for securing curtains. A, riveting; B, curtain; D, screw riveting; E, nail. (Illustrated.)

KNOB PATCH.—A circular piece of leather, attached to a curtain as additional security to the knob hole, or under the knob.

L

LACE.—A woven close web, with a loop surface, plain or of ornamental figures, used for trimming carriages, the technical names are : A, broad lace ; B, seaming lace ; and D, pasting lace. (Illustrated.

LACE PLATE.—A perforated metallic or ivory plate, used for securing the end of lace in position. (Illustrated.)

LAMP.—A carriage lantern, attached to the seat, boot or dash.

LAMP SPRING.—A coiled wire spring, encased in muslin and placed inside of the barrel of the lamp, for the purpose of keeping the candle up to the top of the cylinder until consumed.

LINING.—The general term for the inside trimmings of carriages.

LOOP —See curtain loop.

M

MAIN BRACE.—Long straps of heavy leather, stitched together, used as hanging-off straps for old-style gigs and all vehicles where C-springs are used.

MAT.—A thick pad, used as an extra covering for the floor or foot-board of a carriage.

MOCK JOINT.—An ornamented metallic form, used on panel-quarter coaches, in imitation of the top joint on falling-top carriages.

MOSS.—A dried vegetable fiber, used for stuffing carriage cushions, squabs, etc.

MOLE SKIN.—The technical name of varnished cloth, finished to imitate dash leather, the under side of which is colored to imitate plain leather.

MOLDING.—A metallic bead, beveled or half round, filled with soft metal, which supports tacks whereby the molding is secured to the body. Used as an ornamental border around leather tops. (Illustrated.)

MOLDING FINISHER.—A piece of metal used to finish the ends of metallic moldings, made similar to the molding, but of an ornamental form. (Illustrated.)

N

NAIL.—A slender piece of metal, having a head of metal or other material, used both as an ornament and a fastener. A, cloth-covered; B, japanned and silver tufting; C, ivory head. (Illustrated.)

NAME PLATE.—A metallic plate, upon which the name of the builder of the carriage is stamped or engraved.

NETTING.—The crossing of cords in the head lining of a carriage, as an ornament, formerly as a support for light packages.

O

OILCLOTH.—Heavy cloth, covered with numerous coats of paint, presenting an ornamental surface ; also called "oil carpet."

OIL SKIN.—Fine linen saturated with linseed oil, formerly much used as a covering to protect the paint of carriages from the weather.

P

PASTE.—A mixture of flour and water, forming an adhesive substance used for uniting cloth, etc., when trimming.

PASTING LACE.—A narrow lace, having two selvage edges, used for pasting over edges, instead of being stitched to the cloth.

PATENT LEATHER.—Leather having a smooth, polished surface, produced by being covered with paint, and baked.

PLUSH.—A thick fabric, having a long velvet nap on one side.

POLE PAD.—A cushion of leather, stuffed with hair or

other material, attached to each side of a carriage pole, to prevent injury to the horses.

POLE STRAP.—A leather strap, by which the horse is harnessed to the end of the pole, extending from the crab or yoke on the pole to the collar of the horse.

PILLOW SPRING.—A coiled wire spring, used for upholstering backs and cushions of heavy carriages. (Illustrated.)

PULL-TO HANDLE.—See handle.   (Illustrated.)

PLUME.—A feather ornament used on hearses.

Q

QUARTER LIGHT.—The window in a panel quarter of a carriage.

QUARTER.—The technical name given to that portion of the back of a carriage top on either side of the curtain ; also the side piece of a close leather top.

QUARTER SQUAB.—The quilted trimming which forms the lining to the quarters of a body above the top rail.

R

RAILING LEATHER.—Thin patent leather, used for covering seat rails, etc.

REP.—A silk and cotton fabric, having a corded surface.

ROLLERS.—Small wheels in a metal frame, attached to the under side of sliding glass frames.

RUG.—A coarse mat, made of woolen cloth, having a

long nap ; also of sheepskins with the wool on, colored ; fancy wool rugs are made of small pieces sewed together.

RUBBER CLOTH.—Cloth having one side covered with india rubber, used in place of leather for aprons and tops, and curtains of cheap carriages ; the heaviest kind is known as "rubber duck."

S

SATIN.—A glossy silk cloth, of a thick, close texture and overshot woof, used to a limited extent for trimming close carriages.

SASH LIFTER.—An ornamental knob, attached to a window sash as a handle for lifting.   (Illustrated.)

SEAMING LACE.—Narrow lace, having but one selvage ; used for covering cords and joining seams. See Lace.

SEAMING CORD.—A heavy cord, used as the body of a welt for seaming up cushions, etc.

SEAT ROLL.—Cord covered with lace or leather, attached to the front edge of the seat frame, to prevent the cushion slipping off the seat bottom.

SEAT FALL.—See Fall.

SHAFT RUBBER.—A block of vulcanized rubber, used to prevent shafts rattling at the coupling. (Illustrated.)

SEAT STRAP.—A strip of leather attached to the seat frame and passing over the cushion, to prevent it slipping off the seat ; also called a cushion strap.

SHAFT TIP.—A metallic thimble, used on the ends of shafts. (Illustrated.)

SHIFTING RAIL.—An iron rail, running around the top of a carriage seat, to which the top is attached, so constructed that it can be removed from the seat without detaching the top. (Illustrated.)

SHIFTING QUARTER.—A squab, shaped to fit the upper quarter of open standing-top carriage, the outside of which is covered with leather, to which straps are attached for holding it in position.

SLAT IRONS.—Thin plates of iron, connected in a group at one end, to which the wooden bows of a top are attached, connecting them to the seat or body. (Illustrated.)

SOCKETS.—A general name for the thimbles used on the ends of poles, shafts, whiffletrees, etc.

SPEAKING TUBE.—A rubber tube, covered with silk, passing from the inside of the coach to the driver's seat, by which passengers may communicate with the driver, the ends being furnished with wooden mouthpieces, the one on the inside being covered in imitation of a tassel.

SPRING BARREL. –A tin tube, containing spiral spring, around which the curtains of doors and quarter lights are rolled, operated by means of a cord attached to the lever of a ratchet wheel ; also called spring curtain rollers.

SQUAB.—Originally an extra cushion for a head rest; all quilted or stuffed linings for backs and quarters.

STAY WEB.—A twilled web which will not stretch.

SHAFT STRAP.—A harness-leather strap attached to the under side of the shaft, near the cross-bar and at shaft coupling.

SHAFT LOOP.—A metallic loop through which the shaft strap passes. (Illustrated.)

SLIDE.—An ornament of ivory or other material attached to the top of the inside guard, over which the window lifter passes. (Illustrated.)

T

TACK.—A small, sharp-pointed cut nail, generally having large flat heads; the kind known as gimp tacks, B, have small, round heads. They are put up in papers supposed to contain a certain specified number, and designated by ounces, the different weights being due to the sizes of the tacks. (Illustrated.)

TASSEL.—An ornamental pendant, having a close top and loose-twisted pendants, the kind known as coach tassel having a flat, braided head. A shows a curtain tassel, B an acorn or spring roller tassel.

THOROUGHBRACE.—A leather strap, made of several strips of leather, answering the double purpose of spring and body loop.

TIPS.—A general name given to sockets, such as shaft tips, whiffletree tips, etc.

TOP.—All that portion of a carriage above the quarter belt or seat rail.

TOP PROP.—A metallic bolt, having a long, flat base, by which it is secured to the bows of a top, used as a support and connecting bolt for the top joints. (Illustrated.)

TOP-PROP NUT.—A metallic nut, threaded and capped, used on the end of the bolt of the top prop. (Illustrated.)

TOP-PROP RIVET.—A rivet having a broad head, used to connect the hinge of a top joint. (Illustrated.)

TOP JOINT.—The metallic hinged brace or support to a carriage top.

TRIMMING.—The upholstering of a carriage with leather cloth or other material.

TUFT.—A knob of silk or worsted, used in trimming, to prevent the tie cord from drawing through the cloth ; also as an ornament. (Illustrated.)

TUFTING BUTTON.—A button used in place of the fiber button. See Button.

TUFTING CORD.—Fine, strong cord, used to secure the tufts and bind cushions and squabs.

TUFTING NAIL.—A class of nails having large heads, covered with cloth or other materials used in place of tufts, where the latter cannot be used. See Nail.

U

UMBRELLA TOP.—An adjustable top, constructed like an umbrella.

UMBRELLA HOLDER.—An iron support, jointed, for attaching an umbrella top.

UNDER TOP.—That portion of a cushion that forms the under side of a squabbed top.

V

VALANCE. —The strip of leather placed against the front edge of the front bow and the covered strip on the back edge of the back bow. The loose fall attached to the inside of a dash ; in some localities a "seat fall."

VELVETEEN.—A kind of cotton cloth finished to imitate velvet.

VENETIAN BLINDS.—Blinds made of thin slats, set into a frame, the edges overlapping each other, so as to exclude the sun's rays without preventing a free circulation of air.

W

WADDING.—Prepared sheets of raw cotton.

WEB LACE.—See Stay Web.

WELT.—A cord or flat strip, covered with cloth or other material, used as an ornament and for strengthening seams.

WHIP SOCKET.—A short tube, used as a holder for the whip.

348   THE CARRIAGE TRIMMER'S MANUAL.

WHIP-SOCKET FASTENER.—A device for securing the whip socket to the dash or front part of a body.

WING.—An iron frame covered with patent leather or other material, placed in a position to protect the occupant of a carriage from mud or dust thrown from the wheels when the carriage is in motion.

WINDOW FASTENINGS.—Metallic devices for securing the window frames in any desired position. (Illustrated.)

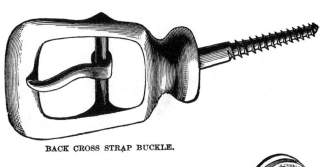

BACK CROSS STRAP BUCKLE.

APRON HOOK AND RING.

BACK CROSS STRAP
CENTER.

BUCKLE.

BACK CROSS STRAP LOOP.

BELL PULL.

BUTTONS.

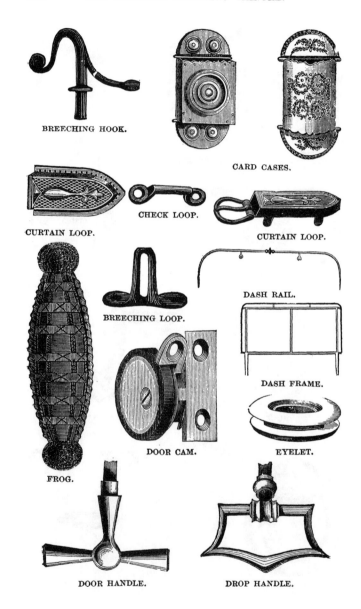

BREECHING HOOK.

CARD CASES.

CURTAIN LOOP.

CHECK LOOP.

CURTAIN LOOP.

BREECHING LOOP.

DASH RAIL.

DASH FRAME.

DOOR CAM.

EYELET.

FROG.

DOOR HANDLE.

DROP HANDLE.

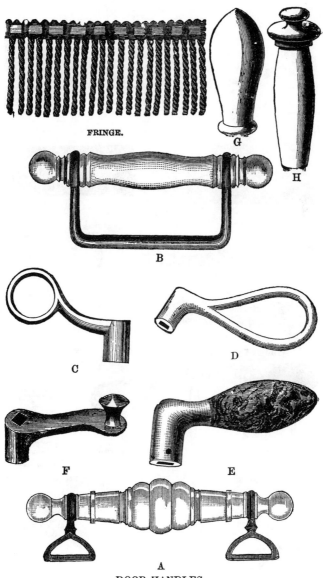

FRINGE.

DOOR HANDLES.

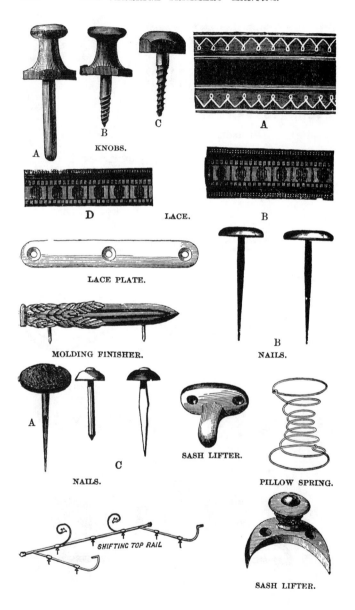

A   B   C

KNOBS.

A

D   LACE.   B

LACE PLATE.

MOLDING FINISHER.

B

NAILS.

A

C

NAILS.

SASH LIFTER.

PILLOW SPRING.

SHIFTING TOP RAIL

SASH LIFTER.

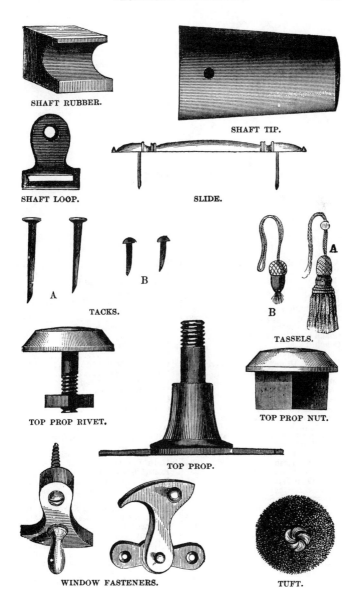

SHAFT RUBBER.

SHAFT TIP.

SHAFT LOOP.

SLIDE.

A

B

TACKS.

A

B

TASSELS.

TOP PROP RIVET.

TOP PROP NUT.

TOP PROP.

WINDOW FASTENERS.

TUFT.

INDEX.

SEARLS'

Bell Top and Cone Bottom

WHIP SOCKETS.

These Sockets are provided with a Metal Cap, which holds the Rubber and prevents the top from splitting.

All these Sockets have the Metal Cap and Rubber hooked in as shown by this cut: ☞

And are provided with the

Vise Fastener,

When lined with soft rubber they hold the Whip firmly, without marring it in the least.

They are finished in Bright Enamel; the bands are dull rubber finish, making them an ornament to any carriage.

ANSON SEARLS,

SOLE MANUFACTURER,

NEWARK, N. J.

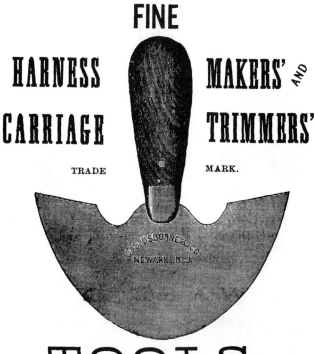